21st Century Individual

BIRTH OF THE NEW RENAISSANCE

Garrett Darling

21ST CENTURY INDIVIDUAL

Table of Contents

"For Jonathan Darling, XXXtentacion, Mac Miller and Virgil Abloh. Your spirits have kept me wanting to continue on, even when I felt ready to leave this Earth, to wake up another day, pull out more, and keep chipping away."

1

I.

Life on Earth

Chapter 1: An awakened conversation

This book was created to serve as a wake-up call to the individual. A personal conversation to be ignited within themselves. And 50 years from now, in the latter half of the 21st century, as multiple generations have had the chance to take the right path and grow beyond measure, that positive changes have rippled across the globe, and that mankind, along with the rest of the species on the planet, is thriving.

We can only hope that planet Earth and its inhabitants, are not too far gone out of reach of saving.

This book was created with the aim to be one of the contributions that give the 22nd-century individual a chance to look back on us with fondness and admiration. As the generation that turned the tide.

Let this book be a guiding tool for this generation's future geniuses and world-shifters.

For creators of all forms. The artists, writers, musicians, inventors, philosophers, architects, designers, engineers, scientists, developers, directors, actors and so many others.

And for individuals of services of all forms. The statesmen, activists, teachers, speakers, doctors, nurses, policemen, firefighters, business owners, farmers, psychologists, historians, and so many others.

...

Read these words slow.
Don't just read these words.
Read. these. words.

Don't continue reading until you allow these words to land. The same way you listen to a song and you feel the bass hit or the strings strum. The same way you hear beautiful notes and you get goosebumps all over your skin. The same way your feet soak into the beach's sands and the first wave touches your feet. The same way you sip that cold drink of water after being parched for so long.

Let each word soak into your mind.

You can read this book and learn logically.
You can read this book and be entertained.
But these are not the intentions of the creation of this book.
The intention is for you to UNDERSTAND and KNOW the power behind the words.
To grasp the wisdom that the words are pointing to.

OPEN YOUR MIND.
OPEN YOUR HEART.
OPEN YOUR SOUL.

Every word, every phrase, is written for a reason.
The purpose of this book is to open the door to a new world for you. A new you. This book is a gateway into a new reality.
Your old self will trail away and disintegrate with every page, and with every page, the new you, will begin to emerge. You will grow.
And the capacity to which you grow is parallel to how much you let go and allow the words to soak in your mind.
Read this book with the intention that it is exactly what you needed to hear.
It was written as such.

As time goes on, and you change, this book will change along with you.
Words will have deeper meaning. Less baggage, less ego, less rigidity, less distractions, less misinterpretation. More

resonance, more understanding, more truth. The words will soak deeper and you slowly will grasp the totality of the wisdom behind them.

As time goes on, and you become more powerful, and more wise, you will realize that you knew these truths all along.

And eventually, you will realize that I didn't write this book. You wrote it.

We all receive ideas, knowledge, and wisdom from the same place.

And as you read this now, some of you may think this sounds absolutely crazy. To you, I say hello. Please, continue reading.

To some, this may connect, and already make sense. Hello to you too.

And someday, for those that thought this sounded crazy, you will remember reading this section long ago and thinking how none of this made sense...but for some reason, as you return to this passage and read it NOW, it makes complete sense. To you, I say, welcome.

You are more powerful than you can possibly currently imagine.

And you are now realizing it.

We, are now realizing it.

This is the age of the conscious human being.

The conscious creator.

This is the age where we claim our power.

This is the age of the genius of the common individual.

You've been living in a world that you yourself created.
It's time to create something new.

Read these words slow.
Marinate in the sentences that make you feel something different.
Sit in the ideas.
Sit in the energy that sentences give you.

...

We are going into your life and smoking out all of the lies that you cling to. If you wish to continue to live the life you are living in the same way, do not read any further. Because once you do read it, you will no longer have a choice.

You will have no choice but to face your self.
You will have no choice but to answer your calling.
You will have no choice but to start moving forward.
You will have no choice but to shed who you once were and begin to undergo the transformation of you.
The evolution of you.
And it's not me who is transforming you.
It's you transforming you.
It's you and your direct connection to life itself. To the universe. To God.
THAT is what transforms you.

This is not a guidebook. This isn't a bible nor is it gospel. This isn't science, this isn't philosophy, this isn't a school.

This is just a book. A book filled with messages. Messages that have been created to illuminate your path.

The lights won't come on for everybody.

Maybe it's not time for you on your journey yet.

Maybe you don't have the focus and patience to sit down and read this in its entirety. Or maybe you do, but everything in it sounds foolish to you.

Maybe this isn't the catalyst that will turn on the lights. Maybe it's something else. Or maybe it is this book, but it's just the wrong time.

In any case, it's okay. You'll be ready when you are ready.

In writing and organizing the notes for this book, I already see its ignorance. I know that it lacks, and in the future, we will know more. This happens with all fields of knowledge. As mankind moves forward, the light shines brighter on darker areas that were previously hidden. But, for now, I see it's truths. I see the current truths. And for this, is why I share it.

To wait until I'm perfect, to publish the book, implies that I will be perfect at some point during my human experience. This simply will not be the case.

To wait until I'm better, is to continue working on this book forever. Life is ongoing. I can continue writing notes forever. Making adjustments to chapters. Adding new revelations. Discarding sentences that were worded less effectively, and replace them with sentences that are so much more wisely and creatively constructed, that they point to the truth more accurately.

It is time to depart from this work. I've created to the best of my abilities. I have spent many years writing. I've pushed my creative edges. I've exhausted my current potential. And I'm letting this piece of work go.

Like all pieces of work, I expect this book to see its fair share of criticism. Once a piece of work is released to the public, it now belongs to the people. They can do whatever they wish. Criticism is part of the game. I only hope that the same attention to detail the opinionated individual places on scrutinizing this work, or any work for that matter, is also placed on inspecting their own ideas, and on contributing something of their own merit.

I'm only human, as are the individuals that I have learned from. And so are you. This book is written by humans and for humans. Human beings on this earth that are trying. Nobody is perfect.

In order to change your world, you need to be able to ascend above it and see what has been created. See what has been created in your life so far. What has been happening, what's being created right now, and the trajectory of where you are currently heading.

The fundamental foundation for any real change, is meta-awareness. Detachment from the character you've been playing. Not getting completely wrapped up in this ground level of chaos but zooming out, going levels above, and getting a bird's eye view.

Build this space.
Cultivate this distance.
Be open.
Be honest.
Be humble.
And look at yourself.

2

Chapter 2: Mankind's shared history

We are living in a period of time that we are yet to understand its significance historically. We don't have a zoomed-out, honest, and introspective view of our generation's moments of the planet's history.

We're able to look back at the Middle Ages, the Renaissance era, the wars and famines of the 1700 and 1800s, and the world wars in the 1910s and 1940s. We can see thousands of years ago, albeit with limited accuracy, and we can see within the last 100 years with a decent amount of clarity. But we don't seem to understand how tightly knit everything is, how historical events are not that far apart, and how our modern day is living within the ripples of these past events. We don't understand how we are all living on the same floating rock, and we are just the latest inhabitants. We are all living within the ripples of the individuals that came before us.

We don't realize how close we are to past events, because the past to us is "the past". It's history. We boil down hundreds of years of great wars, social revolutions, fields of thought, structures of civilization, scientific findings and inventions, artistic creations and expressions, and minimize it to a simple word. "History". We live in our own day-to-day world, and forget about everything that happened in the past. To be forgotten. After all. It's in the past. And we are busy with what is happening today.

But we don't realize that we are still living within the large ripple effects of these events.

We're the descendants of powerful benefits and we stand on the shoulders of giants. Each generation providing another layer of wisdom, artworks, scientific understanding, philosophical conversations, and inventions to improve the quality of our lives. The abundance of water and food. Medicinal breakthroughs. Adding another layer to the expression of human consciousness. Pushing another inch toward freedom and prosperity for the people.

But we are also the descendants of struggles. There's still trauma in humans alive today from World War II, Korean War, and the Vietnam War. Lost fathers, mothers, brothers and sisters, and the subsequent reconfiguration of families, and more difficult life experience for the descendants that follow. There are still unexploded mines and bombs throughout Asia and Europe from past wars. Buried land mines from these wars still kill people every year. We still find dead soldiers from these wars and bring them home to be properly buried.

The common fear of marijuana as a drug that is bad for our health and destroys lives, but in reality, when used properly, is a powerful spiritual tool that has been scientifically proven time and time again to have health benefits. Thousands of country-men being thrown into rotting prisons because of having a little bit of this plant on their person. Looked at as criminals and imprisoned. It takes time to unravel and let go of the ignorance that has been placed into the minds of individuals and passed down generations as "truth". It takes time to change the ignorance within our minds and to change the crystalized ignorance within our laws and structures.

Modern-day Black Americans are still living within the ripples of being enslaved for hundreds of years and beaten down generation after generation following their freedom. Modern-day black individuals are the direct descendants of this experience. Black American children begin their life on Earth, inside a hole, passed to them by history. Misunderstood, others fearing them, having limited resources in their neighborhoods, and limited generational wealth. Photographs of slaves, our great great grandparents, exists in the homes of many Black families. The last Civil War soldier died in 1959. Around the same time, many of your parents and grandparents were born. We can have conversations with our elders, on how they could not buy certain homes, go to certain parts of town, and were denied certain jobs. This was not that long ago.

We are living in the ripples of history.

We are not disconnected from these events.

We are the descendants of these events.

Ripples in time we still are living in.

...

The world is constantly changing throughout history.

Constant wars and revolutions. Rebirths and restructuring of society. Scientific revolution, Industrial revolution, American Revolution, French Revolution, Spanish conquests, Roman conquests, World War 1, World War 2.

Constant pieces of powerful work birthed throughout time. Stream of consciousness entering and touching down on this Earth. Works of Michelangelo, Rembrandt, William Shakespeare, Ludwig van Beethoven, Nikola Tesla, Charlie Chaplin, W.E.B. Du Bois. Progressing mankind in their own niche and particular way. In art, architecture, philosophy, science, math. Expanding knowledge and wisdom. Sharing and spreading the arts. Progressing the elevation of consciousness.

So many changes.

But so much remains the same through time. So much remains standing over the years. The ancient structures of Egypt to the brick buildings of New York. The small streets of Spain to the gothic architecture of London. The languages we speak. The customs and traditions we live by. The meals we eat. The sports we play. The books we read. The knowledge we have.

All of this. We are children of all of this. Our ancestors created this. Our direct ancestors were a part of this. Our fathers, grandfathers, great grandfathers. Our mothers, grandmothers, and great grandmothers.

We are all children. We are all connected.

We are the descendants of the history we read about. And we are the ancestors that those that will read about us in the future.

We are connected. Genetically. Culturally. Traditionally. Even historically. We all share the same historical events. Immanuel Kant, Abraham Lincoln, and Mahatma Gandhi all lived in separate centuries, yet they all know of Leonardo da Vinci who came before them.

They were the children of their ancestors and of the history that came before them.

King Tut, Alexander the Great, Genghis Khan, Socrates, Galileo Galilei, Thomas Jefferson, Fredrick Douglas. Roman and Persian armies. Ancient Egyptians and ancient greeks. Aztec warriors and native tribes. They all occupied the same land, breathed the same air, and looked at the same moon, sun, and stars as you do right now.

They are our ancestors. And we are their children's children's children.

The oldest people alive today are but children. Everyone alive today on this planet are only the current inhabitants of this planet. Children of our ancestors. Everyone alive today stands on the shoulders of giants. We're living in the world that was created by our ancestors and their ancestors before them. And we who are currently living, both the young and the old, are the youngest of them. We are the children of history.

As you read this, you are alive. As you are alive, you are part of this generation. The present time in history. The present time is currently unfolding day by day. The experience of the present day, where you know about the past and history you've learned about, and currently living within its ripple effects, but the future remains unknown, and every day unfolds towards it.

This is the same feeling that everyone before you has experienced. That same feeling of living in the present moment, is the same feeling all of our ancestors experienced when they lived their lives. Knowing of the history before you. The great individuals before you. The accomplishments and the hardships before you. And unfolding day by day into the unknown future.

The unknown future. The unknown future that our descendants are so familiar with, but we are currently living through. We do not know the events we are walking into. We are unaware of the significance of the upcoming days, weeks, months, and years. It's a mystery to us, as we are currently living it. It's well-documented history for our future children.

The human experience is all the same.

Every generation lived in its own era in the timeline, but just dealt their own specific cards. Cards dealt from the previous generation. Different drawn-out lines in the sand, separating country from country. Different country relations. Different social climates. Different inventions most commonly used. Different standards of living for the average individual. Different problems that culture faces.

The Earth is one big playground, with a new set of players every century. We're just the modern-day inhabitants of this planet. The current human beings that are alive.

This is our turn.
And our time, like our ancestors' time, will also pass.

Nobody pays attention to the transient-like nature of human existence on this planet. Tens of thousands dying of old age every day, while hundreds of thousands are being birthed. Old members leaving the planet as new members are arriving and starting this human existence at 1 day old.

Humans are in and out of the planet, like revolving doors.
And now it is your turn here.

There may be a few generations ahead of you.
Eventually, only one generation will be ahead of you.
Then, you and your generation will be next up.
The last of a dying breed.

And then, it will be your turn. You will leave this Earth. You will die one day. You, and the body you inhabit, will experience death. The final curtain. It is unavoidable.

And, we too, become the ancestors that are read about. Our era, now complete. A memory for future present day inhabitants to reminisce about.

This is how life goes.

Look at the Earth in its entirety.
Floating in space.

Rich or poor.
Famous or common.
Black or white.
Born 10,000 years ago or 20 years ago.
We all end up in the same place.
We are all victims of being given life and having to eventually experience death.

We are all individuals on this planet, victims of the human condition.

Heartbreak, fear, loss, regret, guilt, existential dread.

Love, joy, togetherness, inspiration, wonder, and peace.

We are all human.
We are all connected.
We share similar joys.
We share similar pains.
We all cry.
We all dream.
We all love.
We all look into the stars and wonder.

We all come into this world.
And we will all soon exit.

3

Chapter 3: Current state

For the majority of time on this Earth for humans, life has been agonizing, traumatizing, and incredibly difficult. Existence itself was suffering. Constant wars, disease, and famine. Rape, murder, and pillaging. Intolerance and cruelty of religious, sexual, or creative expression. Unlawful trials and unjust punishments. Little understanding of medicine and science. Little to no regulations or safety measures. Little to no education. And poverty and untimely death everywhere.

Not too long ago, this was the average human experience.

Just look at your direct line of ancestors, go as far back as you can, and contemplate their own experience of life. Your parents born in the 1960s and their parents in the 1940s. Their parents in the 1910's, their parents in the 1880's, then 1850s, 1820s, and then the 1700's. War. disease. famine. poverty. Little to no high hopes or aspirations. Just survival and appreciation for what they had. Just suffering and trying to get by and do right for their next generation. In the modern day, this is still occurring in many areas on the planet. This is the human experience, not only of the past, but many of the present day.

But the overall quality of life for humans, as the years go by, has been increasing.

There has never been a better time to be alive for the average individual. Many individuals are able to have a constant source of food and running water. A place to live and sleep in relative comfort and peace. Access to many mediums of art and entertainment, and endless creations within them. Access to learning through schooling, or of their own volition through books and the internet. The ability, and luxury, to focus on higher aspirations and goals.

We have more equality than ever before. No matter your color, gender, race or religion, we have freedom. We can find work and and a means of income. We can move around freely. We have helpful structures within our society. Life expectancy is at its highest possibly ever for a human being in history. The strides in medicine and science has allowed us to combat so many ailments and diseases. Our understanding of nutrition and food. Less extreme poverty than ever before.

Individuals of the past have worked hard and died for us to live the life we have today.

Identifying poisonous plants and what is edible and inedible. Charting the territories and the lands of the planet. Developing towns. Building businesses. Giving value to one another. Learning to participate in life together. Building our infrastructures, skyscrapers, bridges, railroads, freeways, and river passageways. Facing their own creative work, and inventing new pieces of work in their own time period.

We must be grateful for what we currently have and where we currently are. It cannot be stated enough, just how lucky we are to have everything around us.

Even today, millions of individuals are playing their role, participating in the maintaining of civilization.

Sewage systems. Electricity. Garbage trucks. Mechanics. Technicians. Postal workers. Shop keepers.

But there's still work to be done.

The deterioration of our environment. Massive pollution and irresponsibly regulated business practices across the globe. Constant use of plastic. The melting of the ice caps. Forests being cleared. The overfishing of our waters. The irreversible destruction of habitats. The extinction of species.

A homelessness crisis in major cities all over the country. Cities like Los Angeles, in some parts, resembling that of a 3rd world country. Helicopters, metal bars on the windows of homes, trash everywhere, tents built over sidewalks, drugs, homeless wandering the streets, yelling, suffering. Labeled "homeless" and pushed away from one corner of society to the next, like a problem that nobody wants to solve. Seen as an inconvenience instead of humans that need help.

Many families in poverty, they themselves not too far above homelessness. Living in a state of servitude, constantly living on emotional and physical fumes. Working constantly, with very little to show for it. But surviving….hoping that maybe their children will have a better chance at life.

Many other families right above them, living check to check, they themselves not too far from poverty. With a little bit of extra cash, they are allowed more clothes, more eating out, a better car, and more sources of entertainment...but still living in a state of servitude, with an added dash of luxury. Miserable at their jobs. Exhausted. No time or energy for their families, for hobbies, or for a higher purpose. Just leaping from bed, to go to work, and come back to rest and do it again. Their human spirit beaten.

A broken medical system that takes advantage of its citizens. Charging individuals billions of dollars annually, bankrupting many. Overprescribing pharmaceutical drugs that often do more harm than good.

An unhealthy prison culture. Drug addicts being treated as criminals instead of humans in need of help. The mentally ill being treated as criminals instead of humans in need of help. The entering of individuals who don't deserve to be in prisons, the flourishing of prison life, and the improper and ineffective and negligent reintroduction of countrymen who served time, back into our communities.

An outdated education system that is lagging behind the modern century. The subtraction of courses that are desperately needed and the lack of potency in the courses that remain. Teaching the important courses that remain, the maths, the sciences, the literatures, inefficiently, with close-minded styles and environments. Lacking funding for tools, trips, and true immersion into their own studies. Curriculums trying to teach ideologies, instead of teaching how to think. Teachers not receiving real livable wages many deserve, to be able to have the mental ram to effectively focus on their students. The lack of healthy food sources. Little exercise. No meditation. Not developing real intelligence and capable individuals for our country. Just pushing them through the conveyer belt that is our current education system. The structure that every countryman as a young individual enters, is falling apart, and not receiving the attention necessary for its restructuring.

Poor leaders. The lack of philosophical leaders that lead with honor. Intelligent, principled, wise leaders with good in their hearts. That cannot be corrupted or swayed. That aim to have real plans, real solutions, and focus on meaningful changes through diplomacy, compromise, competency, and action. Leaders grounded in the timeless, selfless, courageous sense of duty to humanity and the people. The essence of all great leaders of past eras, and all future leaders that will ever touch this earth.

The deterioration of the modern individuals mental health. The average individual's unhealthy relationship with social media and the dismemberment it causes of any hope of a quality life. The deterioration of families, the decline of family values, and the widespread adoption of living a more selfish life in the face of an evolving dating culture and technological advances. The food being tainted with chemicals and pesticides, and being of low quality, creating unnecessary sicknesses and wide spread obesity. News and media that divides and outrage the individual for clicks, creating the need to proactively seek through the muck to find journalism with integrity, objective reporting and unbiased news. Corroding bridges, roads, pipes and subway systems. The lack of healthy borders, and healthy immigration. High costs of living. Crime. The diminishment of real discussions and open dialogue, and normalization of can-celling and repression. The division between men and women, liberal and conservative, races, ideologies, and the lack of respect and intelligent conversation amongst each other.

And the widespread running away from a higher purpose in the modern day individual's life, into alcohol, drugs, social media, clout, money, streaming services, video games, and a job of flatness and a life of monotone and continuous dreariness.

The giving up, and acceptance that life for ourselves, for our families, and for our communities, cannot get any better.

The depression, and acceptance of our depression.

The anxiety, and acceptance of our anxiety.

The hopelessness of the times we live in.

And these problems are not only our own. Many other countries share these problems, and many countries have more devastating problems than ours. Worse food insecurity. Dirty drinking water. Lack of civil rights and freedoms. Lack of education. Worse corruption. Worse pollution. Worse poverty.

We all have aspects of how we function that desperately need updating.

In the same way we look back 200 years and see the 1800s as an unfortunate time to live due to constant wars, inhumane work conditions, slavery of human beings, and diseases with no treatment, those that live in the 2200s will look back 200 years from then and see the same hardships, struggles and ignorance in us.

It is happening right now.
But it is OUR version of it.

We currently live in ways that our descendants will wonder how could we live in such a state.

To continue doing the same things without any renovation, at best, implies that the way we currently live on this Earth is the best way it can be done, and it doesn't need innovation. That we have it all figured out. But we are far from that. There's enough information, enough research, enough knowledge, and enough awareness, to realize that many of the ways we conduct ourselves is no longer the wisest approach.

We know something's wrong. We feel it.

We're depressed.

We're anxious.

We all try to find solutions.

We stay glued to social media.

We complain.

We argue.

We fall into the timeless ignorant conduct the human being is capable of. A space of existence that any human being, no matter the era of time, can live in. The anger. The division. The blame. The lack of seeing the bigger picture of life.

At a certain time in the past, with the information we had, doing what we did might have made sense. In some aspects, it may have even been an improvement from what it was prior. But we know we can do better. The knowledge is there. We KNOW there are wiser changes that can be made. And to accept how things are right now, to continue to participate in this without change, is beyond wrong. It's cowardice. It's the deterioration of our respective communities and countries, through passivity.

Hundreds of years from now, they will be watching us.

These times will look archaic in the future.

...

Many look at the bleakness of the world around them and will say that the powers at be keep a foot on our neck. That "they" suppress us. "They" don't want us to succeed.

But did the powers at be, force us to spend trillions on fast food?

Did "they" force the individual to spend billions on fancy clothes we didn't need?

Did the powers at be force us to spend trillions of dollars on prescription drugs that mask the problem, while we ourselves avoid our actual health of sleep, diet, exercise, and stress management that all have a higher chance of actually solving our issues?

Did the powers at be force us to work at a job we don't like, and stay working there year after year?

This is all our own doing and done on our own accord. We take our resources and our power, and this is what we do with it.

Believe what you choose to believe... Believe whatever conspiracy of who is in power and what their motives are and how cruel they are to its citizens. But somewhere along this whole process, their power stops, the conspiracy line stops, and with our own volition, the torch is passed to us, and we carry out our own undoing.

WE purchase unhealthy junk food.

WE purchase new clothes, even though we don't really need any, because we want to boost our own self-image.

WE spend countless hours on social media and the internet, entertaining ourselves instead of doing something better with our time.

Politicians we don't want in office, yet WE don't vote.

WE keep buying endless single use plastics, and keep our trash production through the roof and participate daily in the pollution and deterioration of our planet.

WE continue to destroy our minds and bodies with processed foods, pharmaceutical drugs, and endless social media and participate daily in the disassembling of our own creativity and power.

WE continue to distract ourselves, and leave our purpose abandoned.

WE settle down for a job we don't like and quit our dreams.

We are our own undoing. Through our laziness. Through our selfishness. Through our improper care of ourselves. Through our passive acceptance that this is the way life is.

It's not the "system" keeping us down. *We keep ourselves down.*

This is not to extinguish the responsibility of the corporations and politicians that keep things in place. This is to take ownership of the responsibility that is *rightfully ours.*

For us to move into the next step of the evolution of mankind, we must understand how we participate in keeping ourselves down.

All of our hands are dirty. No one is innocent.

...

The modern-day individual is the most self-centered creature this planet's history has ever seen.

All of our needs are met, for the most part: Food, water, shelter, safety, and education.

And instead of helping others up, we let them continue to fall as we focus on ourselves and seek the pleasures of our own existence. We have the opportunity to do so much more with the foundation we have, yet instead of using that to do something truly impactful in life, we use it for seeking a significant self-image through social media, chasing more material things, and filling our life with as much pleasure as possible.

We are spoiled. We have running water, heat, air, a roof over our heads, and food, and are relatively safe. And we complain. We lack perspective. We don't understand the reality of the state of the majority of individuals living on this planet. We don't comprehend the reality of how the majority of individuals have lived in the past. We are spoiled. Tunnel vision on our own wants and needs and the story of ourselves.

The average individual has the perfect foundation to really do good things.

To follow their purpose. To study their craft. To create. To innovate. To do something for their friends and family. To positively contribute to their community. To positively contribute to the country. To be something that the Earth appreciates having known.

But spend their time and energy on nonsense.

We seek pleasure by going to nightclubs and bars.

We eat constant processed food and throw the trash away with no care of where it ends up.

We buy excess clothing and gadgets that we don't really need, but we want so bad.

We scroll endlessly on social media, slouched over, our faces stuck to the screen, chuckling every so often at a funny meme we see, getting turned on by half-naked photos, like drones.

We watch show series after show series to keep us entertained from our boring lives.

Watching porn, eating junk food, drinking alcohol, and taking pills to temporarily feel better.

Obsessed with taking the best photos to post on social media with the best filter and best caption that best resembles the image we want people to see us as. Focused on ways for us to stand out and be relevant. Focused on ways to show everyone around us just how cool and famous we look. With our cool fashion sense and unique taste in music. Crafting the perfect aesthetic that represents us. Focused on the story of ourselves. Trying to establish the significance of our own existence.

Many of us just coast by.

Some of our lives are extremely comfortable and luxurious.

Some of our lives are comfortable enough.

But no real pressing issues to feel like any of our actions should change.

No real sense of urgency. No real purpose.

Our little world is comfortable.

A steady job.

A nice enough place to sleep.

Social media to scroll through.

Streaming services.

Leisure activities.

A cozy existence.

All of us are distracted.

None of us recognizing our own potential for something so much greater.

In a way, we're afraid.

Afraid to be so awake and aware of life on earth.

Holding onto comfort.

Afraid of change.

Resisting responsibility.

Resisting growth.

Our great-grandchildren, if they even have the opportunity to enjoy this human experience on Earth, will look at our time in history similar to the way we look at previous generations of history.

"The ignorance… they lived in archaic times".

…

The modern individual is spoiled.

We live in our own little world. Born in our little world, raised in our little world, and seeking to maintain our little world.

We live in carefully crafted worlds of distractions, constant pleasure-seeking, and constant pain-avoiding.

We have a superficial experience of life. We watch a mass shooting but it's just a thing we see on the news and move on from. It's an unpleasant sight that flies by our little world. We see something about our oceans being overfished or too much plastic, but it doesn't affect us too much, so we move on and go to our next source of "entertainment" for the night. Another unpleasant sight that flies by our little world. We walk down the street and see a homeless person suffering, but homeless people in our minds are "just a part of life" and we walk past them as if they are not real people, once with a home and family, suffering right in front of our eyes. Another unpleasant sight that flies by our little world. We see the stress of financial instability in our own family. Another unpleasant experience, that distracts us from our happiness. Another thing for us to avoid, as we concern ourselves of our own happiness.

The suffering of the world. And we leave the curtains down all around us, to ignore its ugliness.

We think we think deeply, but we do not. We think we feel deeply, but we do not. We think we truly understand the gravity of history, but we do not. We think we understand the preciousness of life, but we do not. We think we live deeply, but we do not.

We relish in our own little worlds.

Enjoying the liberties, freedoms, and inventions built by our ancestors.

Enjoying our spoiled lives of comforts and pleasures sustained by those that are currently on the planet with us, but in less fortunate countries.

Lifestyles of ultimate convenience and gratification.

Keeping the curtains down all around us.

Ignore everything. Ignore everybody.

Only until something hits close enough home, are the curtains lifted. Only until we experience real hardships OURSELVES, are the curtains lifted. When we ourselves experience a mass shooting, do we awaken to the mental health crisis of this generation. When we witness a loved one's drug addiction and unnecessary imprisonment, do we awaken to the broken nature of our prison system. When someone in our family needs surgery and you go bankrupt to get it done, do we awaken to the broken nature of our medical system. When we lose someone to gang violence, do we awaken to the grimness of our streets and what the youth are getting sucked into. When we lose a loved one in a war, do we awaken to the unnecessary violence countries wage against each other. When we lose a friend due to suicide and depression, do we realize how unhappy people are at their jobs.

For many individuals, only until you have an experience that carries with it so much power and relevancy, does your little world of distractions become interrupted, the curtains begin to lift, and you begin to notice the world around you.

Only when the consequences of society's problems come crashing into your little world, do you experience for yourself the REALITY of REALITY.

You begin to see how you have been living in a selfish trance. Concerned about yourself. Spoiled. Not caring about anything around you. Only concerned about yourself. Your social media. Getting your fast food. Watching your porn. Cycling from app to app, repeatedly. Playing your video games. Living life on repeat, in the comfort of your own bubble.

When something devastating hits close to home, people often say "it just doesn't seem real" or that it "feels so unreal". No. It is the exact opposite. THIS is reality. And the world you lived in was not real. Welcome to the world in which the majority of your ancestors have lived in since the dawn of time. Welcome to the world in which the majority of individuals living right now around the globe, have been living in.

Only until recent times could the average individual craft a world so distracting, safe, and spoiled, to the extent that any negative experience is "unreal". Like a modern day king or queen. Locked in their own castle. Scrolling on their phone. Watching the newest trending tv show. Caring about celebrity trends. Posting photos of themselves and tagging trending places. Eating whatever food they desire from plastic containers and throwing it over the castle walls.

No.
This is reality.
There are problems that need attention.

...

Well-rounded individuals are those that contain within their lives emotional, mental, spiritual, and physical wealth.

These are healthy human beings. Emotionally mature. Spiritually in-tune. Physically healthy. Mentally clear. Empathetic. Responsible. Open-minded. Compassionate. Understanding their moral responsibility to spend their money with businesses that have sustainable and harmonious business practices. Treating others with love and respect instead of getting caught in hate and fear. Being a leader of their own thought and disconnecting from echo chambers. Being open-minded, having humility, and having open dialogue with others with different perspectives than them.

Taking care of their physical and mental by eating healthy food, exercising, meditating, and cultivating a positive ecosystem around them. Well-rounded, healthy, effective individuals that lead the 21st century into a positive future.

And our lack of these well-rounded individuals reflects the broken nature of our systems.

If the state of the average individual is not an accurate enough tool of measurement of whether the systems in place are broken or not, just what exactly is?

But also, our broken systems reflect the commonplace nature of the impoverished individual. With the average individual lacking courage, discipline, a desire to learn, a desire to contribute, intelligence, wisdom, humility and the willingness to learn, a sense of duty, a sense of honor, love for their family, love for their community, love for their country, with no purpose, with the comfort of their distractions, *there is no output possible other than a broken system.*

With this type of individual being the most commonplace, we don't have the ability to create a system that is NOT broken.

We cannot complain about society. We ARE society.

The existence of our broken systems, shows why the average individual is so underdeveloped. But simultaneously, the underdeveloped individual, and how predominant they are on earth, shows why we have such broken systems.

And herein lies the great problem of the modern day individual.
We blame.

...

If we want anything to change, we must be the ones to begin it.

And if we are to begin change, we must begin with what we have the reach for.

We must begin with ourselves.
The onus is on us. The responsibility is on our shoulders.

We fix ourselves, we fix our society.

Although the responsibility is on us, this does not mean that many of the practices of the government and corporations have not been toxic and detrimental to humans and the planet. They have. What this means is, that to continue complaining about such corporations and such practices, while we do very little with the power we do have, with the reach we have as individuals within our families and our communities, is ignorance beyond comprehension.

It's the lack of recognizing your own power. It's the lack of recognizing the power of the individual. Union strike after union strike, it has been shown. Protest after protest, it has been shown. Revolution after revolution, it has been shown. Business after business expanded beyond imagination, it has been shown. Business after business, vanishing from the economy, it has been shown. It's the individual that holds the power. Our decisions, when multiplied across the country, across the planet, are the power. But it all starts with the individual. You. Recognize your power. Recognize the power of your attention. The power of your money. The power of your mind and spirit. The power of you being on your purpose. The power of you.

...

We often look back into history at the citizens of Nazi Germany and shake our heads. We like to think: "If WE were in that position, we wouldn't stand for it! We would be the German citizens that sheltered Jews and fought with the resistance. We wouldn't dare contribute to the tyranny that Hitler is leading. We would not be silent!"

But history shows us otherwise.

More than likely, we wouldn't do a thing.
We would... carry on.

We would… go with the flow of the current state of affairs.

And we know that because history tends to repeat itself. Humans often ignore the seemingly overwhelming problems of their current day and age. As long as our days go mostly undisturbed, we carry on like usual. As long as we have the status quo, we continue to maintain our narrow-minded self-interested goals.

And we don't do anything about it until US OURSELVES get directly affected by it so SEVERELY that we get pushed to the point of action.

It's when we have no choice BUT to take action, do we take action.

It's when things get so abysmally bad, do we decide to finally look up from our own lives and look around.

But we do not have this luxury. We must act. Now. In the future, if we do not change, our descendants will perceive us right now in the 2020's the way we see the German citizens that stood by in the 1930's.

"How could they just stand there and do nothing while all of that was going on? All the damage to the oceans? The forests? Their entire ecosystem? All their food being tainted? The police being unnecessarily brutal in their practices and no real reform push to upgrade on screening and improve training? The abusive handling of prescription drugs? Their terrible education system? The rampant crime, drugs, and homelessness? And nobody did anything? They kept focused on their own interests and made no changes in their own lives? They kept pointing to the government and businesses to change things? Why did they not do anything themselves?".

"Where were the inventors? The scientists?

They all tried to be famous on social media?"

We are messing up.

But the world is awakening. It's up to the individual to empower themselves and do the best they can to do their part. Nobody is coming to save us. Not a president, not a political party, not a messiah, not a guru, not an organization. It's up to the individual to empower themselves and be the inspiring positive force in their own environment.

It's on YOU to be hopeful! It's on YOU to bring this positive energy into the world! And through your own environment will you influence others.

Through your own positive actions and behaviors.
Through your knowledge and wisdom.
Through your humility and willingness to learn.
Through your kindness and love.

Through your purpose.
Through what you create.
Through the resources you acquire.

Through the opportunities you can share.

And like a wildfire, culture will start to change.

The way we consume will start to change. The way we think will start to change. The way we act will start to change. Collective consciousness will change. THE CHANGE ISN'T COMING. Nobody is coming here to save us, save our communities and save the planet. YOU are the change.

We cannot wait. We must mature. We must become competent. We must become wise. We must positively contribute to the Earth and to Mankind.

The more of us living on our purpose, the better our country is.
The better our planet is.

No matter what political side you stand on, no matter your background, your color, your creed, your religion, your gender.

Our respective countries are a better place when you are on your purpose. The world is a better place when you are on your purpose.

You becoming something that contributes to society. You becoming a thinking, intelligent, open minded human being that has open minded discussion. You becoming aware of how you use your money. You becoming aware of your own energy and how you affect others.

It all begins with you setting foot, and moving towards your purpose.
The thing that inspires you.

…

The 21st century is the age in which the individual will awaken. We will realize just how powerful each of us are.

The average individual.
The average human on this planet.

Our words matter. Our actions matter. Our lives matter. What we create. What we share. We can positively affect each other. More than we can possibly imagine.

And through *this*, through *this energy*, will the world change.

But it all starts in your mind and liberating yourself first.
Be the small light in your specific pocket of society.
This will change the world.

It begins with you.

4

—

Chapter 4: Direction of the Earth

Although there is great suffering in the world, and great suffering within the individual, this is the most positive time to be alive in history. It's been hell at every other point in history. And in our modern day, this is the least hellish it has been for the average individual.

But there is still much work to be done.

We are awakening to the world. And this awakening awareness can sometimes be painful and overwhelming. Especially now that we see the problems of the world. And at other times, it can be exciting and inspiring. Especially when we now see the beauty of cultures, of earth, and the love we have for one another.

Mankind, for the first time, is able to see itself for what it really is. With the internet, comes the beginning of worldwide introspection. Worldwide communication and dialogue. For the first time, we're able to see what other countries are doing in great detail. We're living during a time of great meshing. Many different races and generations listening to all kinds of genres of music. Different cultures practicing other different cultures' practices. Meditation and spirituality. Science and literature. Films and photography. Interracial families with children. Gay couples walking in love, holding hands. Religions befriending religions and cultures befriending cultures.

We all see the world now. This is no longer an ability that belongs only to the wealthy or the adventurous who could sail the seas in the past. This is no longer an ability that belongs only to the wealthy that had access to literature, and the ability to read. The average individual is able to travel to other parts of the world and their cultures and watch, listen and learn. Not just in person, but connecting to other parts of the world through the internet. Through the internet, the average individual is able to peek into other cultures and watch, listen, and learn. The average individual is able to look back into history, and watch, listen, and learn. Able to look into any field of knowledge and watch, listen, and learn. Able to have access to the wisest conversations and knowledge and watch, listen, and learn. We are entering a new renaissance. The individual is fundamentally changing. Society is fundamentally changing. Evolution.

The internet providing videos with long-form discussions with powerful creators and successful individuals, showing an aspect of these creative and free humans never before seen in history. Long-form discussions with different experts in different fields. Open discussions with groups of opposing viewpoints. Videos showing ex-addicts what drugs actually do and truly educating. Videos that interview homeless people, humanizing them, and shedding light on the reality of the lowest parts of our society. Spiritual teachers in closed room dialogues, now free for anyone to discover and listen as if they are in the room themselves. Forums for mass global discussion that serves as a big auditorium for the world to communicate in. The internet, in many ways, as one user described it, is serving as a "shared journal of humanity".

We're able to see the best of humans. We're able to see the worst of humans. We're able to see the cultures. We're able to hold a mirror and look at ourselves.

And we're able to see the mysteries and wonder. We're able to see the richness of the whole planet. The biodiversity, the ecosystems, the animals. The planets we haven't been to. We still have no idea how our ancestors built the pyramids. We're unaware of ancient civilizations that existed. Lost technologies, sunken ships, and buried cities. Herbal medicines and psychedelics experiences. Much of the ocean still remains undiscovered. There are still species in forests that remain undiscovered. We have no idea how dreams work and we are just barely learning about how consciousness works. We are seeing the effects that humans have on this planet. We are creating technology and learning how to use it simultaneously. We are becoming more aware of the average human's life experience.

What's going on today we can not fathom. We take many things for granted, not realizing just how significant our time on the planet is right now and how unique so many experiences are right now..

There is so much going on on Earth. This is a pivotal era of history. Nothing like it. There are so many beautiful mysteries to explore and make innovative discoveries. There are so many problems to solve. There are so many ways to contribute. There are so many crafts to study. There is so much to learn. There is so much to do. There is so much to create.

But instead of engaging with life, and truly engaging with our time here on earth, we keep our heads down, focused on our job, our bills, our own selfish wants, and desires, what we are going to do this weekend, the parties and clubs we want to go to, the shows we want to watch, the restaurants we want to eat at, the video games we want to play, the clothes and make up we want to have and the funny memes we want to see on our feed.

We need to look up.

The power lies within the individual. The power to shift everything is within the individual. We cannot move forward in mankind and still have the average individual unaware of their power and influence on this planet. On how they spend their time, how they spend their money, how they communicate, what they eat, and the following or dismissal of their purpose.

The individual must awaken.

...

People become great regurgitates of geniuses of the past, instead of looking forward into our current landscape, and our emerging future landscape, and seeing how we can navigate modern times.

With 21st century problems, comes with it the demand for 21st century solutions. New minds, in a new time, charting new territory. We need new ideas. We need new creations.

The modern-day individual tends to look to past inventors, writers, artists, leaders, and statesmen for answers. We look to inventors like Nikola Tesla, Marie Curie, and the Wright Brothers. We look to philosophers like Seneca, Marcus Aurelius, and Ayn Rand. We look to civil rights leaders like Martin Luther King Jr. and Malcolm X and see the change they spearheaded in culture. We look to artists like Jean Michel Basquiat and writers like James Baldwin.

But one could make the argument that these individuals, given the opportunity to speak to modern man, would tell us to keep our eyes forward.

They had to combat their current times. In their lifetimes, they used past greats as ingredients to help mold their own findings in life and helped push their generation forward. We must do the same.

We cannot look to the past for modern-day solutions. We cannot deify past greats and find solace in them.

We must look to the past and see great individuals that navigated their current times, and are handing us the baton to continue to meet new current times with our own minds. We must sharpen our own selves, do our own research on modern-day problems, take courageous steps into our own mysteries on Earth, gather our own knowledge and wisdom, and exercise our own creativity and ingenuity, to meet the present day, face to face.

We must take courageous steps into our own mysteries on Earth.

We must do the emerging future's work.
Not be regurgitates of past greats.
Not be secondhand versions of past greats.
But our generation's own greats.

...

We are entranced by the past. And it makes sense. This is the first time humans can look back to the past with such clarity. The ability to see the past in such detail has occurred in our era.

With the invention of the camera, and now the emergence of the internet, we are the first generation with all of this information. Well-researched documentaries, detailed photographs, and a profound width and depth of literature. Movies crafted by geniuses in their own respective fields, that recreate and showcase events of the past.

We're even able to see for the first time, alive and breathing individuals that were part of recent past events, and watch them be interviewed and tell their first-hand experiences to the rest of the world. War veterans, monks, politicians, famous artists. Knowledge that before would only be received during a private discussion over coffee, is now shown to the world.

And the sharing of all of this is so fluid through the internet and social media, that it spreads like wildfire. The common individual is now, more than ever, so much more wise and aware of historical events, philosophies, music, arts, wars, movements, cultures, and lifestyles of the past, then at any time in history.

But the story continues. The world keeps going. The artists, writers, inventors, and leaders of the past have left this Earth.

The weight is on OUR shoulders now.

We cannot stare at history. We must make our own history.

...

You must go deep into your craft. Study it. Learn of the greats. And begin to take the torch and carry it through the modern day. Use the ingredients you've required over your lifetime, go within your own space, and carve a new trail that never existed before.

Once you recognize and accept the God in you, you are unstoppable. Standing with the common masses of individuals, you are a God amongst unrealized Gods. Standing with other artists, musicians, innovators, inventors, scientists, philosophers, writers, teachers, cultural activists, and other individuals doing their best in their own chosen craft, you are a God amongst Gods. On the edge to the future.

Not sitting on the ride to the future, but helping create it.

Conscious movers. Conscious designers of life. Creators.

Aware of being infinite beings in finite bodies. An expression of consciousness, in the midst of the human experience. Understanding the preciousness of this experience.

And with this knowledge, not sitting on their potential, but manifesting it. Placing it in their hands.

For centuries, each individual was born within a generation, added their own pieces in their lifetime, and passed. And all of the individuals in a generation added all of their pieces, thus creating another layer of culture, and moving society another step forward. Forward in a direction that, if something not from this Earth were to look at humans and look at the trajectory of history, might think we are trying to create some sort of utopia where there is peace on our planet, harmony amongst countries, freedom for all people, and the ability for the individual to live relatively comfortable, freely, with food, water, and shelter, and enjoy each other's creations of art, music, film, literature and other creative crafts. To be educated, to be mentally and emotionally healthy, and to be wise. To play sports, spend time with those we love, enjoy our passions, and use each other's inventions that improve our lives. And, more than anything, for each and every individual to have the ability and freedom to face ourselves, be great ourselves, and be the greatest we can possibly be. The adventure within ourselves. To become competent in our craft. To become an intelligent human being.

This has been going on for centuries.
And we are in the present day of it.
Another generation at bat.

Writers. philosophers. artists. architects. musicians. fashion designers. comedians. scientists. inventors. teachers. visionaries. Civil leaders. statesmen.

They are all, with their chosen craft, building our future society.

Creating the future that we will all step into.

Architects, painters, sculptors, and drawers introducing abstraction. You begin to think in perspectives that were not available before. Reintroducing old perspectives that have been forgotten. Introducing new perspectives that express something modern. New inspiration for a generation.

Inventors creating new tools that improve the quality of our time here.

Engineers solving technical problems with new design, infrastructure and everyday items.

Musicians inspiring life directly. Creating the sound for your life and give it context never before available.

Philosophers and writers introducing new questions, new answers, new thoughts. Thoughts, ideas, and ways of navigating reality that has yet to have been discovered. Introducing new understandings.

Teachers introducing new thoughts and building mental capabilities. Building your knowledge, your ability to think, and making sense of the dissonance between old thoughts and new thoughts.

Comedians bringing people into the present moment with laughter while expanding their minds with ways of viewing current events. Filling them up with joy and nourishing their soul, while often becoming more nuanced thinkers.

Civil leaders introducing awareness to common people and serving on the front line of society. Working as the tip of the spear for real positive change within our structures and systems of civilization.

Journalists diligently researching with their elbows in the mud. Sharing to the common people events of our times, and exposing to the world what would have been secrets.

Animators. Chefs. Business owners.
Actors. Directors. Cinematographers.
Entrepreneurs. Composers. Statesmen.
Civil engineers. Urban planners.

Science. Education. Technology.
Public health. Social services.
Media. Commerce and trade.
Energy. Geopolitics.
Artificial intelligence. Computers.
Space and the cosmos.
Craftsmanship.

Like a beautiful ecosystem in the rainforest or the oceans, we humans have our ecosystem of collective consciousness. Complex, intertwined, and feeding each other. Individuals, with integrity, with their own passion, trying to help in their own way. Each human has their purpose, their field of interest. Their own impact in their community. Their own pocket of light in the world. Their own contribution to society.

This, multiplied, by millions, covers all aspects of mankind.
Ensuring the continuation of our growth.
Ensuring the raising of our consciousness.
Adding to culture.
Improving lives.
Inspiring others.
Helping others.
A precious balance of passions.

Where would we be without even just a single one of these fields and the individuals within them that find great purpose in it?

With all of our individual focuses, we play our own role in the balance and progression of our species. We help our community. We help our country. We progress mankind.

The music that we create, inspires someone's writing. Their writing, inspires someone to work on their film. Their film, inspires someone to focus on their own greatness and become the greatest athlete they can be. Their athleticism and commitment to their own greatness, inspires someone to follow their own dreams.

We are all inspiring each other. With our own purpose.

We are all moving each other forward.

The best thing you can do is focus on what is true to YOU. What are YOU inspired by. What are YOUR gifts. What do YOU feel within to create. What do YOU envision in this world. This is your focus. This is how you play your role on this Earth. This is how you play your role in this pivotal era of history. This is the greatest you.

There's many different ways to add value to the world. You living your purpose, whatever it may be, is it.

There's many different ways to contribute.
There's many different ways to add value.
There's many different ways to inspire.
There's many different ways to improve our communities.
There's many different problems to solve.
There's many different arts to create in.

Our crafts. Our creativity. Our intelligence. Our passions. What we have the true desire to do on this earth.

This is how we do it.

...

This is all uncharted territory. We are at the cusp of life. We've never been here before. It's important to understand that. We've never been here before, with all of this technology, in this specific place in time and history. This is all new to everyone here. Everyone on this planet right now is experiencing the present day together. We are all experiencing history together. Experiencing the emerging future together.

Look a year from now. It has yet to happen. It hasn't been created yet. It is a known year to our descendants. It's a chapter in history.

But it is unknown to us. It has yet to happen.
It is up to US to create it.

WE NEED TO FOCUS.
Our generation needs to FOCUS.
Each individual creating in their craft.

This creates our generation.

Live by what you want to see.
Create what you want to create.
Be who you would want to meet.

Live the life YOU admire.
Live the life YOU envision.
Be the person YOU are proud to be.
Be something the universe itself would be proud to have created, and experienced.

5

Chapter 5: The Power lies within the Individual

We cannot continue to blindly enjoy the fruits of this existence. We all must focus and commit to changing. We have no other real choice.

We can no longer pretend that everything is alright. We can no longer continue to go out and party, while the world burns. We can no longer endlessly consume a bunch of things we don't need and continue to add to the endless waste. We can no longer operate on this planet as a cog in the wheel, while we have ideas inside us that await to be curated.

Many of us are miserable in our own lives. We can't continue living this way. We can't take it. And neither can the world.

We live in a period in time that is critical and time-sensitive. As monumental as any war. As pivotal as our countries' revolutions. More epic than any movement. In the mere grandiosity of this undertaking, all of your trials, tribulations, and day-to-day concerns are of abysmally low importance.

What will change the planet for the better is the individual, en masse, facing their current bullshit version of themselves, transcending their trivial concerns and placing their attention on something greater than themselves.

And this is something that occurs within YOU. The individual. Face your OWN current bullshit version of YOUR self. Transcend YOUR OWN trivial concerns. and place YOUR attention on something greater than YOUR self.

In the same sense that millions of young kids had dreams of doing whatever they wanted in life in the 1910s, 1930's and 1940's but had to mature faster, set aside their childish wants and needs, and answer the world's calling and serve in the past World Wars, we must do the same.

We must answer our country's calling, the world's calling, and mature. We must battle our own ignorance and selfish ways. We must make changes within our own lives. This is our world war. This is *our* generation's great battle.

The evolution of the individual, *is the highest priority for the individual.*

That is your duty to yourself.
And that is your duty to mankind.

For happiness and fulfillment in your life.
For true meaning in your life.
And for the betterment of the world.

...

We must understand the power of the relationship that the individual has with themselves. This is an intimate relationship that every human being on this planet has. This relationship, the relationship of the human being with themselves, has deteriorated.

Real change, change that we starve for, begins with improving the relationship you have with yourself.

Every human must improve the relationship they have with themselves. Including you. This is the relationship that matters the most. Because this unhealthy relationship is what is causing the destruction.

The individual doesn't take personal responsibility. The individual expects positive changes in the world to happen but does not do anything themselves to contribute. The individual doesn't see how their own actions negatively affect anything in the grand scheme of things. The individual doesn't see how what they say and what they do has any real positive effect.

The individual is closed minded and thinks they are right and others are wrong. The individual doesn't take care of themselves. The individual falls prey to vices. The individual is run by their addictions. The individual distracts themselves from their higher purpose. The individual is attached to their excuses. The individual is comfortable. The individual blames external factors for the state of the county and the state of the world. The individual is immature.

The individual falls into echo chambers. The individual looks at his neighbor in the streets, grocery stores, schools and workplaces, and judges the way they think and live their life without trying to understand their experience. The individual is sucked into social media and scrolls all day, every day, leaving no space for real life, real creativity and real change.

And this multiplied throughout the country, and throughout the globe, has brought us to where we are today.

...

Advancements in knowledge, wisdom, and consciousness in OUR current day are what will allow future generations to stand on the shoulders of giants and reach new heights. "OUR", meaning THIS generation. You and I and all the people we know of all ages. Every human on this planet currently alive today. This current stage in history. Our inability to make these advancements results in future generations standing in the same mud we stand in.

It's our duty to push culture forward and give our descendants, our children, the opportunity to look at us in admiration and nostalgia. If we don't make progress, they will not be able to stand on our shoulders...for the same veil of thick ignorance will have been passed down to them unchecked and unaltered. Our existence will have been for nothing. We just blindly enjoyed the fruits of our own existence. Contributing nothing.

Future generations need foundations of new information, improved structures, new structures, empowered people, morally aligned culture, intelligent schools, creative spaces, loving families, structured homes, and battles fought and won, to continue building and creating from. New ideas. New epiphanies. New breakthroughs. New art. New films. New books. New inventions.

21st century problems must be met with 21st century solutions.

...

To fix our state of society and culture, we all must elevate as human beings. We don't all need to try to be supermen to save the world. Rather, make the adjustments necessary to do our part.

We don't have all the answers.
We can't do everything. We can't solve everything.

We can't have every purpose.

We are only one human being. Each and every one of us is just one individual.

But we can be the best individuals we can be.

For the average individual of the 21st century to be a thinking and caring individual. To be conscious of their footprint in the world. To be conscious of the effect they have on other people. To be on their purpose.

Right now, the individual does not live in harmony with the planet. We, the individual, me, and you, and every single individual must claim responsibility for our sphere of influence so we can begin to dissolve culture's problems with our newfound power of our own conscious choices.

So many of us are playing no beneficial role. If anything, we are doing our part of blind passivity. Sucking as much fruit from the system, as it further deteriorates. Getting ours and only ours. Getting ours to the detriment of who and what surrounds us. Unconcerned about the effects of our actions. Unconcerned of the ripple effects that our behavior causes. Unconcerned about the message we unconsciously spread to those to the left and right of us.

We must correct the trajectory of our planet, by correcting the trajectory of ourselves. An evolution of our own conscious doing.

It's time for each and every individual to take a step into their greatness.

We may not have the influence we would like to have to affect society and the world from the top down. But we have all the power and influence to affect OURSELVES and begin to affect the world from the bottom up.

Starting with ourselves, first and foremost.

How we spend our time. What we focus on. How we treat ourselves. How we spend our money. How we communicate. What media we take in.

And then our household. Our family. How are our relationships with our elders and our young? Our friends, our coworkers, and who we are connected with on social media. How we treat them and communicate with them. Do we maintain our values or support nonsense? Do we help when we can? Do we share knowledge? Do we listen?

What does your life mean on this earth? What will you create? What will you contribute? What will you try to transform and improve?

...

It's very difficult for the current state of culture, to continue to be as destructive, if the cogs in its wheels aren't being good cogs in the wheel.

Revolution begins in the individual's mind.

Become increasingly aware of your own life.

Take back control over your time.
Take back control over your health.
Take back control over your energy.
Take back control over your attention.
Take back control over your economic power.
Take back control over your thoughts and emotions.
Take back control over why you are here on this Earth.

It's on you.

6

II.

Purpose

Chapter 6: Personal Responsibility

Take personal responsibility for your life.

Personal responsibility does NOT mean taking responsibility and blaming yourself for every single outcome in your life. Some events are simply out of your control and you are on the receiving end of what life brings you. This is part of the human experience.

What personal responsibility means is you always have the power to work with what you have. You have the power to create more favorable outcomes with your ability to make choices. You have the power of perspective to empower yourself and feel more positive. You have the power of gratitude, appreciation, patience, and understanding, if you exercise them and bring them out of atrophy. You have the power to be the physical embodiment of courage and move forward in life, no matter what is thrown your way. You have the power to be engaged with who you are. You have the power to follow your purpose. You have the power to sculpt the reality that you choose.

This ability, to claim personal responsibility, is always in your power.

Many people are not ready to wield this much power. It scares them. They want to continue in the little world that they have. They deny their power and hold onto what is easier.

Leaving their little world means leaving the comfortable consolation prizes that come with it. They lose all the small pieces of their current existence they were able to have that made life easier.

Being able to blame others.

Complaining.

Having any type of victim role.

Feeling sorry for themselves.

Excuses.

Rationalizations.

They would lose all of this.

People would rather hold onto their consolation prices and continue the lack of fulfillment of living a daily life that they don't like...than take personal responsibility, uproot themselves, face their fears, and move towards what they truly want in life.

They would rather remain in this same cycle than uproot themselves and risk losing what they have. Even if they don't really like it. They would rather defend a life they don't even like living, then change it.

And the suffering from being stuck in this cycle is so intolerable, that they must distract themselves so it's less painful. They must find ways to numb it. They look for altered states of mind that make life more tolerable. Alcohol, tobacco, drugs, prescription pills, processed junk food. They try to escape to artificial worlds with stories more engaging than their own. Movies, television series, porn, video games, professional sports, videos on the internet. In these worlds, they can forget about their own lives and experience something different. They do anything to distract themselves from their own lives. Sitting lazily in their couch, refreshing their social media feeds, living their moment to moment life, every day, as if they're in a waiting room at the doctors office. Unhealthy romantic relationships where they can stay preoccupied by arguments, frustration, sex and break-ups. Unhealthy friendships where they spend the whole time drinking, hanging out, talking about the problems of the world, talking about drama in the workplace, playing video games, smoking weed.

They may even go to college and take classes, or work another job, just so they can stay busy and tell themselves they are moving forward, but in reality, they are still distractions. Just more productive ones. Ones that are easier to rationalize and get away with staying in your smaller world. Still avoiding your purpose. Still avoiding your higher calling.

Anything works. As long as it is engaging enough to effectively distract them. Because what will effectively distract them, is what will effectively dispel any negative emotions. Constant distractions. And it may temporarily relieve this suffering, only for it to return in worse form. Over time they become more angry, more irritable, more depressed, more anxious, more empty. And instead of facing their own life with courage, they return to their distractions and increase the dosage.

And down the rabbit hole, they go. For years.

Some individuals go so far down this toxic rabbit hole, and have been in it for so long, that they are unable to make the connection between their refusal to take charge of their lives and why they have these addictions. They are trying to distract themselves from the suffering they themselves are creating!

They are unhappy.

They are sick and tired.

They're not ready to move forward. They refuse to. Like a child not yet ready to leave kindergarten and go to the bigger grade with bigger kids. They don't want to move.

But some people ARE ready to move forward. And what separates those that are ready and those that are not ready, is the amount of suffering they are willing to tolerate until they are sick and tired of being sick and tired.

How much suffering must you experience until you are ready to make real changes in your life?

Most people aren't done yet. And they will continue to suffer. It's a dirty high. It's comfortable in this world. As painful as it is, they know it well. There is comfort in this discomfort. It hurts to be here, but it's predictable and safe.

Many people suffer so much that they reach the point where they feel like bursting. They become frustrated. BEYOND frustrated. And all of this, is a blessing in disguise. This is a GOOD THING. This is a pivotal moment where real change is possible. This moment serves as the catalyst to finally move forward.

Instead, unfortunately, many of the people that experience this will continue on the path of suffering. They interpret this bursting feeling as a bad thing. They interpret this increasingly intolerable suffering feeling they have, as a sign that life is becoming harder and harder and worse and worse. And they go further down into addiction and distractions and numbing.

Instead, WAKE UP.
WAKE. UP.

To live in the same place you've been living in, that is no-where near what you envision for yourself, and know about the *possibility* of moving forward, and NOT DO ANYTHING, will only lead to suffering.

Quit listening to laziness, allowing it to dictate what you do for the day.

Quit listening to fear, allowing it to imprison and control you.
Quit making excuses that keep you immature.
Quit making rationalizations that keep you unaccountable.
Quit being weak. Strengthen yourself.
WAKE UP.

Look forward, keep your attention forward, and move forward.

Forward movement is life.

THAT is where your true peace is. THAT is where your real self resides.

...

We're in pain as a society because none of us are doing what we know we should be doing. We're all distracted. We're living lives that aren't meant for us.

The voluntary relinquishment of your purpose disturbs your life, and society, in more ways than you can currently fathom. You are important. And the problems of the modern day stem from our belief that we are not. You believing there is no importance to who you are and what you do, en masse, has created a culture of passivity.

The progress of society depends on the individual's realization of their avoidance of what deeply calls them, and correcting their course in life. To answer their calling.

The manager at the store that wants to be an architect but thinks it's too risky to make the switch. The lawyer that stays at his firm trying to make his parents proud, but when he's home reads Henry David Thoreau and John Muir and in reality, wants to be a modern day naturalist. The college student that has switched majors three times and is collecting debt, but deep down never wanted to go to school in the first place and wants to be an artist. The car salesman that stays selling cars because it makes decent money, but hates it and would love to spend their time with children and teach them instead.

We must get out of our ruts and wake up from our human battery-like lives. Awaken from our battery lives and go into the sectors and fields that we are called to move into. We must refuse to sell our souls for decent income, and move towards what we truly want, and excel in those fields. Uncovering our genius, nurturing our genius, and going to where our minds are attracted to.

Technology, healthcare, medicine, infrastructure, government, psychology, environmental, education, music, literature, space.

The manager that turns to an architect can end up creating amazing designs. The waiter can leave and finally pursue what he wants and innovate the field he focuses on.

And even if the manager tries the architect route and fails and the waiter pursues innovation and fails, or the student tries the painter route and fails, because they are following inspiration, IT'S STILL THE ROUTE IN WHICH THEIR TRUE CALLING WILL UNFOLD. Failure is part of the process.

You leaving your current occupation for the one that inspires you, although it's a very motivating and movie-like action, doesn't guarantee success like in a movie. And to think that every single person that makes this switch will succeed in the first thing they move into, is foolish. But immediate success isn't the goal in the first place. Leaving your current lifeless path, and entering a purposeful path, is the goal. You answering your calling, and living every day focusing and nurturing it. You breathing life into it, breathes life into you.

The manager may leave his job and become an architect and fail abysmally at it. But in this space, he meets someone that works for renewable energy, and this sparks his interest. He then moves into that field, standing on the lessons learned from his architectural practices, begins to design and create for renewable energies, and him putting his mind to this fulfills him but then also facilitates mankind's growth!

As a people, we have become hypocrites. We get angry at politicians for not doing what's best for society. We get angry at them for not doing their job. Yet we do nothing ourselves. We expect the public servants to serve the public, yet we ourselves don't do what's best for ourselves and we don't do what's best for society!

We're like members on a ship that make up 99% of its crew, and we point to our captain and ship leaders for the ship not moving forward. YET NONE OF US ARE PADDLING OR CONTRIBUTING TO ITS ADVANCEMENT IN ANY SHAPE OR FORM.

Each individual, when aligned with a positive direction in their own lives, can positively affect everyone in their life that they come across.

...

In no way shape or form is this belittling or shaming people in their current occupations. Everyone's job serves a purpose. Otherwise, you wouldn't have sought it out, applied, and show up day in and day out committed. Your job keeps you and your family stabilized with food, water, and a home. And many jobs are playing a crucial role in helping keep society stabilized. The teachers, the firefighters, the garbage collectors, the grocery workers, the plumbers, the construction builders. Your job plays a role in the serving of other countrymen around you.

Your job maintains civilization.

With this, you must also understand the significance that your role plays. You are connecting with people on a daily basis. This is massive influence. You have the ability to spread positivity or spread negativity with tens of people to thousands of people. And this can either make them more joyful and positive themselves and spread more love, or angry and spread hate. All the people you interact with will interact with other people. And those people, with more people. Rippling from your interactions with individuals, millions of conversations will take place on this Earth, with your energy and signature commingled into it. You have the power to change the world exactly where you are right now.

What your job also does, is give you a solid foundation to build the rest of your life. If you utilize it wisely. It gives you the necessary comfort, security, and space to create your new path in life. If you make the sacrifices, cut out what you don't need, and buy cheaper items, it gives you the money to purchase the resources needed for your new path in life. The free time you have from your job can be used for feeding your new path in life. Even your job itself, if you arrive daily to it consciously, can serve your new path in life. These are hours of your life. And they add up. Your job can be an active meditation. A spiritual practice. Time that you can use to build character. Time that you can practice important traits and virtues that you want part of your life, for the rest of your life. Patience, gratitude, discipline, integrity, humility. You can practice healthy communication, listening and understanding, leadership and creativity. You may not be where you want to be yet, but you can embody the person you want to be, *right now.* Don't waste precious time of your life. Look forward, towards what excites you, and let that be your daily driver for truly showing up in your life, today.

You may feel like you are ready to leave your job and give yourself completely to your new path. You may feel like you still need to be there because of the solid foundation it gives you, and you are not ready to leave yet. In any case, evaluate your life. Be honest with yourself. And take the right course of action. You must begin moving forward.

...

Most of us feel uncomfortable in the world that we are in and the job we're working at. Depression. Anxiety. Stress. Unhappiness. Boredom.

When you act in accordance with what you don't like, then you will continue to perpetuate negative emotions. You will continue down the path of creating what you don't like, but more importantly, WHO you don't like. You are simply someone you don't want to be. You love yourself less, you respect yourself less, you admire yourself less and you care for yourself less. You're not happy with yourself. You're not being someone you would even enjoy spending time with, let alone living inside of.

It's hard to be happy with life when the idea you have in your mind as the greatest version of you, remains only an idea in your mind. The true you, the you that is devoting their time to creating what they want to create and being who they truly want to be, remains an idea. Instead of focusing on making this a reality, you spend your time working a job you don't like, come home to go on social media, watch entertainment and occasionally drink with your friends.

Most of us feel uncomfortable in the world that we are in and the job we are working at because we're not meant to be there. It's not for us. None of it is. The job we're probably working at, a lot of the people we are hanging out with, a lot of the activities we do, the person we are being. None of it is meant for you. You don't want to be there, yet you participate in it every day.

This isn't your home. You're an individual with ideas and visions bigger than the world that you currently inhabit. You're emotionally, spiritually, and creatively constipated. You don't belong in this world.

There is a world, not yet created, where you truly belong. Living a life more true to you. Being who you want to be, doing what you want to do, creating what you want to create, and living your one life on this planet with the most depth, meaning, and appreciation as you can. This is where your focus should be.

And, paradoxically, the moment you orient your focus to the world that is meant for you but not yet created, the moment you begin to even think about it and think about embarking on that journey, you start to create it. And you are now in it. In its seedling form.

…

When you grab an activity that is meant to play a supportive role in your life, and you put that as your primary focus, you will suffer. This is not what gives you life.

When you spend your time distracting yourself from your purpose, you will suffer. When you spend your time pretending your purpose is not there, you will suffer. When you spend your time solely focusing on worldly obligations and responsibilities, although important to sustain your existence within society, you will suffer.

Nothing will make you feel the way your purpose makes you feel.

And you will continue receiving this experience of pain until you learn its lesson and choose to focus on becoming that which you are meant to be and doing that which you are meant to do.

Until you change who you are and what you focus on in your life, your circumstances will always be different permutations of the same thing. Because you haven't changed. You will continue to create the same day. Same month. Same year. And you won't notice this until you finally change your ways and look back and see how you repeatedly created the same reality. You kept bringing the same type of people into your life. You kept having the same thoughts. Kept feeling the same way. Kept spending your time in similar ways. You kept chasing dopamine and validation… just in different forms. You continued to distract yourself from what you truly wanted to do.

You'll continue to elevate the quality of distraction but it will be a distraction nonetheless. And you know it is a distraction. But you will rationalize your participation in it. And you may get away with it temporarily, but you will still be miserable at the core. You will grow dissatisfied and unfulfilled and unhappy. You will continue to grow fatigued and lose the lightness and excitement of life.

You will be unhappy. And it's not because you are "overworked". Taking time off and "enjoying yourself" won't fix it. Buying more things won't fix it. Increased social status won't fix it. Doing more fun activities won't fix it. Prescription pills, new diet, sex, drugs, food, parties, cars, clothes, travel, none of it. Even meditation won't fix it, although it may lead you to the realization of the problem.

None of these things will fix it because they weren't part of the problem to begin with.

No new person, place, thing, or activity can substitute for the day-to-day agreement of you trading your life for something that you know you truly do not want to do.

No new person, place, thing, or activity can substitute for the day-to-day agreement of you being someone you know you truly do not want to be.

You don't like your life.
And you are not on your purpose.

...

People are afraid to be their true selves. To do what they truly love to do, and be who they truly want to be. But this is where the magic is.

People are living in the space between their true selves and the selves they pretend to be for other people. Most people are actors. Most people are playing roles that they don't want to play. Working jobs they don't want to work at, going to school and studying something that they don't really want to study, and talking about things they don't really want to talk about but they do it because that's how their current social circle talks. Life staying in place. The date changing, but the day staying the same. Getting older, but you staying the same.

Being the, desperately in need of an update, versions of themselves.

Not knowing that their true self, although terrifying to begin to reclaim, is their liberation.

7

Chapter 7: Answering your purpose

Everyone has one go in life. One. And the aim is to live as close to your truth as possible. To live the truest life to you.

Why do people say "living your truth"? Because everything else is false. Everything else, FOR YOU, is false. They are false goals. They are false you's. They don't fulfill you.

They don't touch you deeply.

Because it's not meant for you.

They're all distractions.

...

Everyone is on the journey, whether they are aware of it or not.

Everyone is doing the best they can with the knowledge and experience they have. With their insecurities and limiting beliefs. With your internal makeup and current paradigms and belief systems. With your external environment and upbringing. With your hopes, passions, and ambitions.

They are exactly where they need to be. Where they should be. Because they are there. There is no skipping ahead. The evolution of you and your consciousness is unique. None like it.

You are exactly where you need to be. Don't judge it. Embrace it. Understand its significance.

And begin to move forward from here.

...

Follow what inspires you. Your purpose's aura is inspiration. What may inspire one individual, another individual may find boring. Inspiration is the feeling of this is what YOU are meant to do. It feels good. It feels rewarding. It feels fulfilling.

This doesn't mean inspiration is the easiest thing. What inspires you may often elicit feelings of excitement, along with fear and challenge. It may be terrifying. It may be difficult. It may feel daunting and overwhelming. But, more than anything, there's something about it that feels right. It feels like your life is moving in the right direction. It feels like you are engaging and contending with life the way you are meant to. Sometimes you may doubt yourself. Sometimes you may think you should do something else. Something easier. Something more stable and secure. Something more acceptable. But you feel CALLED.

When you feel like there is nothing you would rather do, then there really is no other choice. This calling is the underlying driving force that propels you forward.

The path made for you to follow is drenched in this feeling. In the feeling of calling.

You have a million choices. That all elicit different emotions.

Follow inspiration. Listen to your calling.

You can't really choose what you are fascinated with. Rather, you discover it. The greatest successes of the last 1000 years, were from individuals that found what they were obsessed with and fed it immediately. Attraction, and obsession, is the underlying driving force toward your purpose, and the underlying force behind the completion of creations within your purpose.

It doesn't have to make logical sense. It often doesn't. In hindsight, the story will make sense. Looking back at memories and the adventure you went on. The rollercoaster of events. The highs and lows in your life. It will all make sense. But looking forward, you have little idea what is about to happen. Your logical mind can't make sense of what is happening in this frequency of life. As soon as you let go, trust, and allow, things start to align and magical things happen. Focus on your obsession, and refine it, and refine it, until it elevates your being and elevates your world.

...

What did you find called to naturally when you were growing up? The exact interest may be your purpose. Or something related to it. Maybe there's an essence of some of the things you did when you were younger that will lead you to your purpose. The essence of what you truly love. Your upbringing can be revealing. There may be gems hiding in your childhood that will lead you to knowing yourself. But simultaneously, do not be limited to just what has occurred in your life thus far. There is much more to life. Go in the direction that excites you.

...

You may not know your purpose right now. But you probably do. You just don't know it is your purpose yet. In your years on this planet, you have had ideas pass your mind. Some you were interested in more than others. And these ideas took residency in your mind. And have seemed to have never left. What interests you so much? What have you thought of creating? What fields are you so curious about? What do you wish existed on this Earth?

And even now, as you read this today, aspects of your current life are shining through, telling you the truth about yourself. If you pay close enough attention and examine. What do you research a lot? What are the traits of the activities you find yourself doing often? What do you think about? What do you truly enjoy? Filter through the clutter and find the gems.

...

If you don't know what you want to do and you don't currently have a purpose, does not mean you should artificially create one. Do not look to social media and to all of your friends and family, and feel the pressure of what you perceive is them moving forward in their own life, and start to react in a way where you stop listening to your soul, and you start to grasp at what you think success is and grasp at what you think is movement forward.

Give yourself space. Patience.
Do not become obsessed with finding your purpose. The wrong person will be looking.
Find yourself first and your purpose will be revealed.
Find yourself by listening to inspiration.
Your purpose will then reveal itself.
Your purpose will find you.
It's called "your calling" for a reason. And you following your purpose, "answering your calling".

You didn't choose it. It chose you. You simply listened to its beckoning.

...

And if nothing at all inspires you, then just show up. Show up every day and listen. Don't wait idly by and wait to feel motivating emotions to take action in your own life. This is a form of procrastination and immaturity. If you are not careful, you may fall into a life filled with distractions and never hear what calls you because of all the noise around you.

Be proactive. Create the environment in which inspiration can thrive. And show up daily. Read more books, watch documentaries, watch films, listen to interviews, go on walks, go on runs, go to different events, different cities, and meet people. Expand yourself. Meditate for introspection. Eat healthy and exercise so you can think clearly. Work on different projects. Research different interests. Give yourself completely to a higher version of yourself.

Potential awaits every individual. Give yourself completely to your potential. You must allow yourself to be swallowed whole by higher power. If nothing yet inspires you, be inspired by life itself. Be inspired by your temporary time here and the human existence you get the opportunity to live. This always exists if you are open to it.

If you focus only on the obligations of your daily life, and on your off time you rest just so you can wake up and go back to those obligations, you leave no space for anything greater in your life. Be proactive. Carve out time and energy. Create that space. And in this space, your purpose awaits.

...

Whatever you are meant to do, do it. Create your work.

Designers, directors, writers, inventors, producers, actors, musicians, craftsmen, composers, creators, pioneers, visionaries, scientists, philosophers, and engineers.

Some purposes are not to create pieces of work, but instead to play a dynamic role on this planet in their field of devotion. Their purpose is the role they embody. This is their work. Their work is not completed pieces of work in the classic sense, but a constant ongoing service to the world.

Doctors, nurses, teachers, professors, psychologists, speakers, activists, firefighters, farmers, public servants, statesmen, organizers, and leaders.

And some individuals will do both. They may create pieces of work whilst offering themselves to the world as the roles they know best.

Your purpose may also change and what you feel called to do may change. You may feel inspiration towards something that, for a time being you were excited by, but you eventually lost interest. This was part of the path. This took you somewhere.

You may fulfill your purpose, only to find that that was a layer only to be peeled away and you now feel impelled to go deeper. As you get older, you will mature. As your life evolves, your purpose evolves. As your purpose evolves, your life evolves. Life and purpose move hand in hand.

You have no choice but to move forward in life if you listen to inspiration and make decisions based on it. This does not mean there won't be any more lows following your choice to listen to inspiration. There will be. There will be both highs and lows. But while you navigate the world with the focus of inspiration, you will be moving forward, and being who you are meant to be.

Whatever you do, your creative work is your response to life.

Your creative work is your acknowledgment of the greatness and finiteness of existence. Of our precious and limited time here.

Your creative work is the ultimate form of love for this planet and respect for mankind.

Your creative work is an ode to life itself.

8

Chapter 8: Evolving

You're not trying to be something you're not. Rather, you're evolving into the next form of what you're supposed to give the world. You're removing all of the noise and getting deeper within. You're getting closer to your true self. Not further away from it.

Your old self WAS you...But your old self was *not yours*. Do not be so attached to something that you didn't even create.

Your parents, your family, your upbringing, your friends, your school, and your church, created it.

You, as a child, with no bearing of how to navigate the world, with no conscious awareness of the conditioning you are undergoing, with your innocence and ignorance, were just along for the ride.

Little to no conscious power to understand what was going on around you and create what you truly wanted. Little to no conscious power to be who you wanted to be.

You were a sponge that soaked what surrounded you. Soaked ideas, thoughts, emotions, ways of being, ways of behaving, ways of acting, social constructs, certain paradigms, and limitations of what's possible.

But now, you are awake. And currently, you have what you have, you are who you are and you are at where you are at. These are the cards you have been dealt. Accept it.

From here, you begin your awakened life by setting aim. Aim to be the person you want to see in the world. Aim to create the work you want to see in the world.

...

You are moving from the fake you to the real you.

Many people think that if you change, you have become "fake". That you "changed up" on them. But in reality, we are almost all raised fake, and those that claim you have "changed", have themselves chosen to remain fake. They have not sought to go deeper within themselves and embody that which is most true to them.

They've remained on the surface. Remained the individual that was crafted in their childhood and never evolved much further from this. Remained the individual crafted by their surroundings and not crafting themselves with their own minds.

They stay stuck, never maturing their thought process, changing ideas, updating beliefs, venturing out of their hometown, focusing on bigger aspects of life, working on projects they're passionate about but scared of, meeting different types of people, or going to different types of places.

They've remained in their comfort zone, paralyzed by fear. Numbed with distractions. They've made a home of a life they don't really like, but won't admit it.

Don't listen to individuals that speak negatively about you "changing" when life is meant for change.

Exercise your own intuition and creativity. Navigate your life the way you want to. Develop space from the outer world. Divorce yourself from external influence. Parents, friends, family, school, work, media. Have your own vision and move towards it in the way you feel is right. Give yourself a chance to see what you are made of. To see what you can do on this planet.

This is your life. And it's not going to go on forever.
Start to come into your own power.
See who you can become.

By denying this process of change, you are assuming that you are ALREADY real. That your upbringing, your childhood, your friends, your family, your school, your work, and society molded you to already be the person that you happen to 100% naturally resonate with. The stars aligned for you, and you happen to be exactly who you want to be, do exactly what you want to do, and are living life exactly how you have always wanted to live it.

Unless you were brought up in a very enlightened home that instilled in you the most empowering traits and gave you the space for you to grow in the way YOU want to grow and move in the direction YOU want to move into, you are raised and conditioned to be far from who you truly are.

First step is self awareness.
Then you dive deep and become the REAL you.
You are moving from the fake you to the real you.

You won't be able to create your own world if you continue to listen to others and their own created world. You'll never create your own world if you are constantly divvying up your time and energy and giving it away. Evolve by feeding your time and energy into yourself.

...

Spend some time with yourself and envision. Envisioning is good. You want to envision how life can go well for you. You are seeing how life can be for you, and those around you if you aligned yourself with your potential.

You get to where you want to get to by creating that reality in your mind first. Envisioning is a critical component of creating. You are giving birth to a new reality in your mind. Every invention, every piece of artwork, every body of music, has begun within the mind. Every beautiful physical human-made creation you see on this planet was created first, within the mind.

...

Envisioning without any action, is fantasizing.

Fantasizing is an action that is an expression of an individual that is not yet ready. It plays a fundamental role in serving as the foundation for the rest of your new life. It gives you a breath of fresh air. It gives you vision. It gives you something to aim for. It's potential that is marinating within the individual. Something is being created within you. Your whole being is rearranging and orientating ideas, visions, opportunities, and lanes in your life.

This is what you are doing when you are in school, bored. When you're at work, not engaged. When you're walking home, and drift into imagination. When you're laying in your bed, thinking about where life could take you. When you're in the shower and have time alone, and begin to dream.

But you can't do this forever. This is an important phase. But a phase nonetheless. It's a temporary period. Not a permanent home. Some individuals begin moving toward their purpose, but then make this phase of fantasizing, a permanent home. Talking about what they are going to do, but not doing it. They think they are moving forward in life with all their ideas and talking about what they're "going to do". But they've made a new comfortable place to be stagnant in. They are sitting on stagnant energy. Still letting time pass them by. Not really going anywhere.

You have been creating within your mind. You have been creating this energy within you. But soon you must depart from this and begin to physically create the world that you have been envisioning. You must begin to take action. You must leave this life of fantasizing and keeping your current life and enter the life of envisioning and taking action towards your new one. This is the mark of maturity. You are leaving the stands of people watching and judging others live their lives, and you are entering the arena where individuals are working towards their greatness. This is the beginning of your departure into true wisdom.

Once you make this transition, your thoughts and emotions will elevate with your action. Doing the work and being on your purpose, will elevate you to the mentality and embodiment that you seek. You are becoming who you truly are meant to be.

...

The you that you envision, sits still, waiting on the other side of the difficult and uncomfortable decisions in your life. Like on the other side of a metaphysical wall.

Like a vessel, the you that you wish to become, lies on the other side of those decisions, still.
Like a character, not yet activated.
Awaiting for its embodiment by your soul.
Awaiting for you to take action.

You must make decisions. Only you know the path. Do what's right, right in front of you, right now. Only you know where you must go. If you listen.

Ending a comfortable but unhealthy relationship. Taking fewer hours at your job to focus more on what you truly want to do. Or quitting your job altogether. Finally moving out of your family home so you can develop yourself under the pressure. Or downgrading your expensive lifestyle and deciding to move back into it. Putting down social media, entertainment, drugs, or alcohol that keeps you distracted. Cutting off negative friends and influences. Meditating and facing yourself. Facing that blank canvas. Facing that blank word document. Facing that blank project. Facing your work and summoning your creation.

As soon as you decide to make decisions, you are advancing into a new world. Exciting. But scary. You are shedding layers. Closer to the true you.

You can either allow your life circumstances to keep you boxed in, or you face these difficult decisions, get through them, leave this old world, move into the new world, and have the qualities you have been searching for, instilled in you.

Move forward.

The life you want is on the other side of these experiences, in bits and pieces. The person you want to become is on the other side of these experiences, in bits and pieces. This one experience teaches you humility. This other one teaches you self-confidence. This other one cultivates more courage. This other experience teaches you to have more personal boundaries. This other one brings in new people and opportunities into your life.

You need to start moving forward. There is nothing nourishing from your past world.

Movement forward is the answer.

And when you start moving forward, you may not know what's best. You may not know what to do. And you may be scared. That's the challenge that the universe places in front of you. And the very act of you moving forward in the face of this ambiguity and unknown, is the very reason why the person you are becoming is so much stronger, wiser, and more experienced.

People are afraid to jump from the solid footing that they have created on this side of life, and jump over the chasm of uncertainty and unknown, to the other side. The other side is just an idea. They think they will jump and try to land and fall right through, as if it were a mirage.

People are afraid to be naked over this chasm.
Jumping from the world you've gotten so comfortable with, over to the world of the unknown.
But this chasm is what creates you.
This chasm burns away all the nonsense.
This chasm builds your strengths.
And when you land on the other side, life starts to get going.

...

Whatever you choose to work on, the beginning of it will not be glamorous. You will be ridiculed, judged, and there will be attempts to persuade you to do something different. You may try to tell people about it, and they will think you're foolish. You yourself when you work on it, you're so new and inexperienced, that you feel foolish. This is the barrier of entry into your chosen craft. Every individual in every craft must go through this process of humility, patience, diligence, focus, and self-trust. This is the trial by fire. This trial by fire is what separates those that will actually do things in life, and those that will continue a life of not doing.

It's a fundamental shift in the way you are living your life.

You go from dreaming, to the act of summoning the dream. You are now engaged with the physical manifestation of it. The doing. The creating. The becoming.

Aiming and firing. Re-aiming and re-firing. Trial and error. Action and adjustment and more action. Setting goals and accomplishing them. Waking up and getting to work. Treating your body with respect, love, and care as it is the vessel for your ideas. Eliminating stress and distractions that will knock your focus out of alignment. Harnessing your power. Perfecting your craft. Your whole being is oriented towards your purpose. Your whole life is in support of actualizing your vision.

Then you will begin to have these momentary realizations. Realizations that you are on the right path. It hits you in waves as time goes by. The deep peace and gratitude from it. The Happiness.

This is how you know you are moving forward. There is nothing like it.

Once you have aligned yourself to your purpose, you have aligned yourself to your higher freedom.

You now have your keys to the world.

You listen to your own genius and live more spontaneously and freely. You stop living based on outdated rules and norms. You don't dictate your life decisions based on others' opinions.

You live in love and excitement instead of fear and hate. You are moving forward.

You are connected to the Truth of life. You now have your keys to the world.

When you're in this space of truth, all the answers reveal themselves. What matters is evident. What doesn't matter is evident. What you should be working on, reveals itself and reverberates with a warm glowing power that is unmatched. And all other paths, expose themselves as being wastes of time.

Your keys to the world are what allows you to navigate through the direct environment that surrounds you, and open doors to bigger worlds. It's what leads individuals that were born in a state of poverty, to rise to mental, emotional, spiritual, and physical wealth. It's what leads individuals to quit their monotonous life and live an exciting life filled with passion. It's what leads individuals to create powerful pieces of work. It's what leads to a life of fulfillment.

Once you have your keys, you are set. Do not wait any longer. Do not waste your time. Direct your energy into this. Harness this. Surround your life with this. Be this. And see your life transform.

9

Chapter 9: Harness your power

On the path to the actualizing of your greatness, you will see glimpses of the new world you're heading into.

When you read an empowering book and receive a new perspective. When you watch an eye-opening interview and hear struggles similar to yours. When you listen to inspiring music and your vision feels so clear in that moment. When you watch an inspiring film. When you meet someone new. When you go to a new city. When you go on a run. When you meditate. When you work on your project. When you practice your craft.

On your path, you will start to see glimpses of the new world. You will see bits of the fruits of your labor. You will begin to see the payoffs of the positive direction of your attention.

You're starting to see glimpses of your new world.

New ways of thinking. New confidence and grace. New peace of mind. New happiness. You notice a tendency to not get caught up in gossip and complaining as much. You notice a tendency to not get caught in your own negative thinking. You notice a tendency to not engage with people's negativity. You have more clarity. You carry yourself...differently. Your purpose. You start to see it. To feel it. Your vision. You feel yourself moving towards it.

In these moments on your journey, something special has occurred.

Through your focus, self-belief, and action when you worked on your project or practiced your craft, you have temporarily grabbed the sides of the portal that leads into your new world, and pulled it open. You've peeked inside and felt what the future is like if you stay focused.

Through your focus in a positive direction, when you read that book, listened to that interview, when you meditated, when you have a good session of work, you have temporarily grabbed the sides of the portal that leads into your new world, and pulled it open. You've peeked inside and felt what the future is like if you stay focused.

But...it was only temporarily. The portal closes. And you continue to walk the path that you were on. You continue to live the life you've been living. You go about your day, go home, and go to sleep.

But you have fundamentally changed.

The ingredients that make up who you are, have changed.

New potential for your life has been introduced. New confidence and clarity. New opportunities and paths for your life. You saw your vision. You felt it. New power, that you now *know*, that you have now *seen*, that you have now *felt within you*, exists.

There's no going back. *It's in you now.*

…

Every morning, you wake up with new, more profound, power. You felt it before, when you worked on your project. You felt it before, when you did yoga or meditated. You felt it when you listened to your music and were inspired. You have FELT your potential. Every day you wake up, you have this emerging vision that sits so vividly in front of you. And you have your past. And the decision on how you live today, is yours to make. Will you hold onto old thoughts of the past? Old ways of starting your day? Old habits? Old ceilings of your potential? Old unwise ways of spending your time? Or will you advance and move forward into the new.

You are becoming more powerful.

Every day, meet the world with your new profound power. Wake up and meet the new day with your new profound power. Meet the new present moment, with your newly-introduced way of living your life.

Right now, this new way of living your life is a seedling. In its baby form. It's new to you. It's new to your life. Give it your attention. Water it. And allow it to become the dominant way of your existence.

And you do that by embodying it.

Upon your daily wake-up, awaken to your deepest calling. Wake up and remember why you are here on this planet and what purpose you serve. This will give you the deepest, most meaningful, context for your time here on Earth. This is what will guide you to make the wisest decisions and give you the wisest perspective. You are training your mind to become accustomed to harnessing your power.

Harness all the power within you. Harness your new clarity, new confidence, and new determination in your actions, and move with this energy. Meet the new day with the new understanding of your potential. Meet it with your new wisdom, maturity, and understanding of life.

HARNESS this power and move forward. Do not get caught up in your past. Leave your past behind. Live in the flow of your evolving consciousness, evolving wisdom, evolving gifts, evolving creative abilities, and evolving responsibility in the world. Live in your evolution.

It is a conscious decision you make every day.

This is consciously living. This is choosing to be truly awake as a human being on this planet.

Do not wake up and begin to re-mind yourself of what has held you back in the past. And the past could be 5-10 years ago. The past could be yesterday.

Do not wake up and begin to re-mind yourself of the fear that you've held in the past. Re-mind yourself of the potential you continue to see and what's possible if you keep going.

Do not re-mind yourself thoughts of "I'm not smart enough", "I'm not skilled enough", and "I'm not ____ enough".

Re-mind yourself of your new dedication to the journey and willingness to learn and slowly chisel your life into what you envision.

Do not re-mind yourself of the insecurities you held onto for so long that withheld your personality in from being seen.
Re-mind yourself of the peace of mind you experience when you express yourself authentically.

Do not wake up and start the day immediately in reaction. Reaction to the obligations and stresses of the day. Do not fall back into old habits, old mentalities, old perspectives, or old ways of spending your time. Do not go down that path for another day. And another day. And another day. Your life is passing you by. Do not lull yourself back into your old unconscious, repetitive cycles. Do not lull yourself back into being asleep, having dormant and stagnant energy, and living your life on autopilot. WAKE UP.

Re-mind yourself why you're moving forward. Re-mind yourself what you are working towards. Actualizing your ideas. Fulfilling your potential. Being the person you know you can be. Doing your part on this Earth.

Every morning, remember why you are here. From here, your gifts are birthed.

...

Much of the pain felt on this Earth comes from the incongruence of the potential in life the individual knows they have, the power they deep down know they have to move forward into their potential, and their current place in their lives. These three are incredibly misaligned.

They see glimpses of what's possible in their life. More and more, they have moments of them seeing into the portal. Yet they continue living the same life. More power. But not being used. More ideas. But not being executed upon. And they experience a growing frustration with their current day-to-day life... but no real action being taken to leave it. A lot of "potential". But no real attempt at its manifestation.

This incongruence causes suffering.

Anxiety. Depression. Frustration. Unhappiness.

You are lingering in a world that you have outgrown and it's causing you pain. And it's all self-inflicted. And immaturely, you blame others for where you are in life. You blame your spouse, your family, your job, your boss, another race, another sex, the government, an ideology. You blaming external circumstances is your voluntary relinquishing of a good future. You are rejecting self-awareness. And you will still suffer. Until YOU change.

You have power. Do not ignore this and distract yourself. And every day you wake up, you are a day closer to your inevitable death, whenever it may be. And this awareness of your closer and closer death, combined with your inaction while you are here alive, amplifies your suffering.

Things must change. You must change. Celebrate the life you have! Honor life. Honor your ancestors that came before you. Honor those that will come after you. Honor mankind. Live with courage. Fulfill your potential.

If you are reading this book, a book that primarily speaks of you changing your own life, you know there's something within you that you know must change. You have actions within your reach that can begin transforming your life, that you day in and day out choose not to go near. And you will suffer because of this.

Start doing what you know you must do.

Fully embody your power and move forward into your new world.

Many individuals on the planet right now are not embodying their own power, not due to a lack of power, but due to fear of embodying it.

It opens up a whole different world. A world where you may be seen as a weirdo for choosing something so far away from the path that is commonly taken. Seen as a loser when you make mistakes. Seen as a failure for not accomplishing what everyone else thinks is "success". Seen as a threat for creating what challenges the status quo and improves the lives of the people. Seen as a fraud for trying to do something great but it's still so unrefined and you are learning. You have doubts. This new world opens up new problems and new chaos. It's unfamiliar. It's unknown.

But as soon as there is a glimpse into this new world, as scary as it may seem, you must keep moving forward, as you CAN

NOT GO BACK TO YOUR OLD WORLD WITH A PEACE OF MIND.

You now know your potential. It's not a secret to yourself no longer. You must move forward.

The greats of our planet. The writers, the artists, the statesmen, the builders, the scientists, the inventors. Received the same energy that you are currently receiving. The same energy that is tapped into and used as fuel for their creations, innovations, and accomplishments, is the same energy that the common individual tries to repress and numb.

That energy, when repressed, instead of harnessed and focused on something of meaning to you, develops a certain toxicity to it and wreaks havoc on your inner being. Your heart, mind, soul, and actions are not aligned.

When you do not take action in your movement forward, you turn your flowing energy that could've been used to fuel the creation of your vision, into a stagnant pool of frustration, anxiety, depression, resentment, guilt, and fear. You are sitting on energy. You are filled with it. But it's stagnant. You do nothing with it. You distract yourself. You procrastinate. You are filled with undisciplined and unharnessed energy.

That same pool of energy, when combined with action, leads to moving forward. Progress. Happiness. Confidence and trust within oneself. Accomplishments and finished creations. Peace of mind.

Your conscious mind holds the power.
It's your decision to make.
Action or inaction.
Flowing energy or stagnation.

The same energy that has the power to create, has the power to destroy. The same energy that has the power to destroy, has the power to create. The deciding factor is whether you choose to move forward or stay put.

Discipline your mind.
Focus on your work.
Focus on the handful of activities that mean the most to you.
And focus on the present moment.

Your focused mind is your liberation.
Your focused mind is the key to your ability to be a powerful vessel and create what is in you to be created.

Personal responsibility, and claiming the greatness you've been given, is what will lead your conscious revolution.

You are an individual.
Lead your own conscious revolution.
The individual's conscious revolution, en masse, is what will bring the evolution of humanity.

...

Stop shying away. Stop being squeamish. Allow yourself to be afraid. Allow yourself to have doubts. Allow yourself to be imperfect. Move forward, in all of your humanness, and strive to reach the greatness that your human can summon.

Do not allow the fear of your greatness to paralyze you. Lean into it.

So many of us are afraid to speak powerfully. Think powerfully. Move powerfully. Act powerfully. Create powerfully.

Fear of our own power.

Start to tilt that fear of your own power, to claiming responsibility for your own power. Do not reduce your greatness, when the world needs it. When your friends and family need it. Harness the power and DO NOT SHY AWAY FROM ITS MAGNITUDE AND INTENSITY. The power in your eyes and words. The power in your creativity and ideas. The power in your work. The power in you showing up to this path in your life every day and trusting where it's taking you. The courage, confidence, and clarity that you claiming your power give you.

And it can be intense. Your life will begin to change. More attention and judgement. More challenges and unknown territory. More influence. More responsibility. Harness all of your power anyway and don't shy away from it. Do not dampen your own light for your own comfort. You must know how to embrace and embody all that power. Like being in a sauna and handling the heat. All of that heat. Like being in a hurricane and holding onto a beam. All of the wind force.

All of that energy.

You must ground yourself every day to withstand and harness your greatness. To handle all the social pressure and judgement. To handle the risk and possibility of failure. To handle the unknown. To handle all the creativity and influence you have deep inside. To handle your potential and take action upon it.

To harness all your power in its totality, is equally exciting and terrifying.

But soon, with the relentless dedication to being your greatest self, to being your true self, with the growing experience of the dance between you and the power you harness, your greatness will become your norm. It will not be something you chase and force, but something you now settle into and welcome. You now allow more power, in all of its forms, to enter your life. You accept your power. You accept your responsibility. You are grounded in this reality. It becomes the natural state of your existence. You have developed space between your world and the outer world. You wake up in silence. You are still. You are at peace. You breathe. You are awake. You understand what to do.

You understand your role. And from this powerful foundation, you move about the planet.

10

Chapter 10: Decisions

Decision means to "cut off" in Latin.

To "decide", doesn't necessarily mean that you're choosing something, even though you are. At a deeper level, it means you're cutting off all other options other than what you've chosen.

It's important to realize that when you make a decision, you are cutting off all other decisions and the realities that would have unfolded from them. You are cutting off different you's. Every time you make a good decision, you are cutting off realities that don't serve you. Other realities that involve you being someone you prefer not to be and where you prefer not to go.

Understand this. Live by this.

When you live an awakened life, a life in which you are pro-actively making the best decisions for yourself, you will begin to construct the version of you that is aligned with your values, principles, and goals. You will construct the world you truly want to wake up every day and live in.

The only thing that can steer you towards a more meaningful existence and a greater you, is by understanding what you truly want in this life, and deciding.

Make sure the things you're cutting off are what you truly, deep down, want cutting off. Make sure, with your current knowledge and wisdom, you're making the best decisions. When you decide to do something, do not just understand what you are choosing. Understand what you are losing in the process.

...

Life will place in front of you crossroads, in which you have to make a decision, and you have no other choice but to decide what actually matters to you. The truth will reveal itself.

Life wraps up your actualized dreams and your actualized true core self under layers and layers of difficult decisions. Many successful individuals refer to "having to make sacrifices" on the road to where they got to. This is what they mean. Difficult decisions. The difficult cutting off of who they were, to be who they want to be. The difficult cutting off of old ways of living, to live more aligned with what they envision. Cutting off what they found comfort and security in, but now is the very thing that keeps them from getting to what they truly want in life. Cutting off what they found purpose or passion in, but now is the very thing that keeps them from getting to a deeper, more true, core self. Ending relationships with certain people, ending relationships with vices, moving cities, quitting a job, quitting school. Releasing the old and moving into the new. New relationships. New people in your life. New ways of spending your time. New habits. And you, facing your work, and summoning your creation. A new you, but simultaneously, a deeper, real you.

...

The path that those around you want you to follow, and the path to realizing your purpose and listening to your soul, often do not overlap. They are often separate paths, and you will be challenged to make decisions that choose one or the other.

You can listen to what your parents, your friends, and social media tells you... or listen to your soul. You can follow the laid out and accepted path or listen to your soul and carve your own path. If YOU don't follow what YOU are passionate for, YOUR life will be passion-less.

...

And when you make the decision forward and cut off what was holding you back from going deeper into your core...when you step deeper into your purpose... as the days go by and you go further along the timeline of your life...you will slowly start to see that old period of your life with more clarity. As the distance grows...like looking in a rearview mirror... you will see where you once were in its totality. You will begin to see the bigger picture of your life.

And you will feel the power of the path you are on. You will see with more clarity what exactly you are leaving, and where you are heading. You will truly enter a new chapter in your life.

And you now have contrast. You will feel, for yourself, how dull the colors and textures were of the life you were holding onto, because you now have the bright, vibrant, beautiful colors and textures to now compare it to.

This is growing wisdom.
You are becoming more of who you are meant to be.

But if you decide to stay, and you don't move towards your purpose, you will never see what you could have been in your existence on this Earth. You will stay in a place where you know deep down, you should have left. What was supposed to be a learning experience and a stepping stone for the rest of your journey in life, you have made your home. What was supposed to be a temporary experience, you have grabbed and made permanent. What was supposed to be a moment in time, you have put on a repeated cycle. Because you are scared to make the next step. In your fear, you have confused a chapter in your book, for the book itself. You become lost in a phase in your life and you prolong it indefinitely. Staying in your hometown longer than you know you should have. Staying a job longer than you know you should've. Staying in school longer than you know you should have. Staying with friends and in relationships longer than you know you should have. The list goes on of what people are meant to depart from, but don't.

You have made a chapter in your life, your entire life. And this is the state of most people's existence. They are stuck where they were supposed to leave a long time ago. And this is why escapism is the primary essence that is sought after by individuals and how they spend their time. They must cope with where they are at. They must relieve the depression, the anxiety, the stress, the misery, the self-hate, the boredom. Drugs, alcohol, porn, social media, streaming services, and junk food. Even productive activities like watching educational videos, listening to podcasts, or reading. If you are avoiding your purpose, no matter what you are doing, no matter how productive it may be, you are ignoring the most productive action you can take for your soul: Stepping in the direction towards your purpose. Making the hard decisions that you know deep down you must make.

Life is too big for you to get sucked into one tiny chapter of the journey and let it dominate your life.

...

Picture your future. Drive a stake into the future you have of your reality.

This gives everything context. This gives your present moment context, and all of your decisions context. Know what you want for your future, and that will help guide you to make the best decisions right now in the present. With the present moment now guided by the context of your vision, the present moments you will experience in the future will soon be that future you envision. You are connecting today to tomorrow.

You need a vision, but without smaller actions that you can take right in front of you and in your current reality, you will not reach that vision. You do not teleport to your higher vision, rather, you do what's in front of you to the best of your abilities, and that connects to the next step, to the next step, to the next step, until you reach that vision.

The present moment requires decisions. If you're not sure which decisions to make, choose the ones that have a little bit more of an essence of what you want in life compared to other options you have. It's okay to be afraid to take chances. Take the chances anyway. Try different things. Step out in the world and have that dance. Have that dialogue with your dreams.

Do not take things for granted. If you have an opportunity, take it. You are living life, but life is also moving at you. Follow what feels right, follow what excites you, and take opportunities. If you feel fear, this should not necessarily be a deterrent or a sign that "you should not do that". Fear and the unknown often go hand in hand. As you move into the unknown, you may experience fear. Accept it as part of the ride of life.

...

Your real power comes through your committed decisions and your intention. Regardless of external circumstances, your power is seated in intention and focus. This must be as clear as possible. You must decide and commit. This is the key that unlocks the door. This is what illuminates the path and carries you forward.

Your committed decision and focus allows your intention to collect with energy. It allows more focus to gather. This is your power as a human being with a mind and a heart and consciousness. This power brings your vision into reality. This power births your creations.

...

Who will you be?

The individual that actualizes their vision? The individual who is true to themselves?

Or the individual that lives their life with who they can truly be always a glimmer in the corner of their mind?

11

Chapter 11: Ecosystem

You are in an ecosystem right now. You're not an island. You are connected to people.

Best friends. Hometown friends. College friends. Work friends. Roommates. Coworkers. Dad. Mom. Brothers. Sisters. Boyfriend. Girlfriend. Husband. Wife.

People in your life are powerful.

People, and their presence, are powerful.

They may not understand just how influential they are on you. But that influence does not need their conscious understanding to exist. It exists. And your influence on them.

The connective energy that binds you and others into a relationship, whether casual or serious, is powerful. It serves as a hyperlink between you and them, where a reality is shared.

Who you are when you are around them and how you feel. What they tend to bring out of you and inspire. What they tend to judge about you and limit. Your perspectives about life. Their perspectives about life. The idea of what you think they are. The idea of what they think you are. The idea of what you think they are becoming. The idea of what they think you are becoming. Your perceived ceilings in life and what you think is possible. Their perceived ceilings in life and what they think is possible. Who you are becoming. Who they are becoming.

You are connected to many people. Each one different. Each one in a particular place on their own journey.

Some slowly and steadily making progress up. Some slowly and steadily decaying and getting worse. Some individuals are in the midst of awakening. Some are in the midst of a numbing phase of their life. Some are so deeply stuck in their own ways of thinking, that they've been in the same place for years. Some have been awake for years, and are living life with gratitude and purpose and continue to climb in their reach, influence, and gifts. In any case, every human individual you see, is battling within themselves, the great battle of mankind. The battle of consciousness within the individual.

Every single individual you know is somewhere in this great battle. Your dad. Your mom. Your friends. Your coworkers. Your teachers. Your girlfriend and boyfriend. Everyone.

You, right now, are currently in an ecosystem. And individuals within their own battle, are all around you.

Your ecosystem, and the individuals that are in it, can make you or break you.

Your ecosystem can fill you with incredible inspiration and power or can fill you with immobilizing fear and anxiety.

Your ecosystem can be your greatest source of love, happiness, and peace in your life, or it can be your greatest source of frustration, unhappiness, and stress.

Your ecosystem can make the higher version of yourself a comfortable place to be, or make it an uncomfortable place and lead you to sink to your lower self where you are more accepted.

Your ecosystem can aid your focus and give you the greatest support. Or it can keep your vision scattered and keep you stuck in the unhealthy cycles you are trying to abandon to improve your life.

...

When you begin to rise in your consciousness, and become more aligned with your purpose, you begin to awaken in the ecosystem that you are currently in. You are developing a growing awareness of yourself and your own behaviors, and with this growing awareness, one of the things you begin to notice is your current physical and energetic placement and orientation on this planet. You begin to see what's going on around you. Who's around you. How they spend their time. What the goals and aspirations are of your peers. Just how positive or negative those around you are. What's the general mood and spirit of the town you are currently in. What places you frequent that are destructive to your goals and general wellbeing, and what places are constructive and building a better life for you. Where is support coming from and where are distractions coming from. You will begin to realize just how positive or just how negative your ecosystem is. If you have good friends or not. If you live in a city that inspires you or not. If your ecosystem empowers you to grow and evolve and be your best self, or would rather you stay relatively the same as you've been all these years.

Most of us were not born into an empowering ecosystem. An ecosystem filled with support, kindness, and happy human beings with healthy communication.

An ecosystem that encourages us to follow what is true to ourselves.

Once you begin to awaken, you will notice the disempowering qualities of your current ecosystem. The distractions, limitations, and negativity surrounding you. Unhealthy ways of communicating, unhealed trauma, toxic relationships, addictions to vices, procrastination, excuse making, and a lack of personal responsibility. Many of those around us are distracting themselves from their purpose and settling into the comfort of the daily cycles they have created. Quietly suffering. Trying to escape their calling. Trying to avoid facing themselves. They aren't moving towards anything. Doing a million things, except what matters most. Distracting themselves with, ironically, what they deep down really don't care for doing...but are addicted to. Addicted to their cycles.

This is where they are at in life right now.

As you awaken, you will start to see the people around you and be aware of the crossfire you are often being caught in. You are getting caught in the crossfire of these individuals and their own distracting period in their lives. You are caught in it. They need to gossip or complain, and they start a conversation with you. They need to watch distracting television or music and it's loud, and you are in your room and can't focus. They need to drink and need a drinking partner, and they peer pressure you. You want to focus on your craft, and they want to go out to party. You want to read something knowledgeable and they want to make fun of you. You have a vision and they project their ceiling of life onto you and put doubt into you. These individuals that distract themselves are so common, judgemental, and toxic, these friends are so common, that we think the friendships we have with them are good simply because of past shared memories, a few shared hobbies, and similar senses of humor. You...get along. But in reality, we often think it's good because we have never experienced anything better to compare it to. We're just so accustomed to friends and family around us, being a certain way. And never thinking much of it.

As you awaken, you may begin to realize that many of the friendships you had were you and this other individual both attached to your comfort zones together. You were both kept intertwined as friends, because you both enjoyed stagnating in your lives together. Spending time, doing nothing, together. Judging each other's ideas and passions to do something bigger in life. Going to the same bars and events. Playing the same video games. Complaining about the world together. Smoking weed. Like crabs in a bucket, doing nothing but keeping each other down. Together.

...

There may be relationships that you maintain for years that are fruitful for both members. But this is able to occur due to both you and the other individual growing in your own ways. You are both facing yourselves and progressing in life, so you are somewhat on the same wavelength. You are engaged with life, not full of misery due to your avoiding it. You are aligned within yourself, not distracting yourself. And so you both are able to offer love, support, a good laugh, inspiration, knowledge, and guidance. Whether you see each other every day, or once a year, a relationship exists. You still connect.

But as you grow, you will begin to recognize many of the relationships you have, are not like this. Unfortunately, at least in today's age, many individuals are not growing. They stay where they are at. Staying relatively around the same place emotionally, mentally, consciously, and purposely. This is an uncomfortable truth. But a truth nonetheless.

They remain the same. And as you grow, and they remain the same, your relationship will change.

As you move forward, you outgrow old ceilings, old ways of thinking, old behaviors, old habits, old toxic ways of communicating, and old negativity. And as you outgrow all of this old, you outgrow the relationships you have with individuals that decided to stay confined within them. While you are maturing, they are not. While you face yourself, they are not. While you follow what is true to your soul, they distract themselves. While you focus on your vision, they make excuses. You are separating and living on different wavelengths.

When you are on your purpose, and your light shines, those around you become more aware of their own lack of movement towards their own purposes and the lack of their own light. You do not have to do or say anything. Your existence, and your commitment to your path, and this being in front of them, is enough. You focusing on your work more. You trying to learn. You eating healthier, exercising, and meditating. You wanting to complain and gossip less, and talk more positively about people or interesting subjects. You trying to live a better life. Your existence alone shines a light on their mediocrity and unrealized potential. By you growing, and you being you in front of them, their deep pain of them not truly being themselves and all they can be, will rise to the surface. They will be uncomfortable.

By you connecting with your true self and allowing yourself to be powerful, your very presence is a threat to others that fear their own power and fear connecting with their true selves. When you begin to realize your own power, this carries with it a truth that shines around you. A truth that scares most:

You were able to awaken. And they know they can too.

And them witnessing you do it, and them seeing someone they know move forward, they now become more face to face with themselves. And it's scary. It's a lot of pressure. A lot of responsibility. It takes humility and acknowledgment of how they've acted in the past. It takes courage to change their ways and to begin to be themselves around people that may judge them like they judged you. It takes focus, discipline, and diffi-cult decisions. They must face certain death of who they were and an unknown future for the new individual that they would become.

But many of those around you will experience this discom-fort, and are not ready. They do not want to grow. And as you grow, those that are unhappy with themselves and that do not want to move forward, will often try to drag you down. They will still want to gossip. To complain. To drink, do drugs, and party. To waste time.

And refusing to participate in someone's negative programs is refusing to relate with them. You not wanting to gossip and complain with them, is your refusal to build rapport with them and connect. You not wanting to drink, do drugs, party, or play video games with them is seen as you thinking you are better than them. They may begin to feel that you are "changing up" on them.

You will relate with them less and less. You yourself will become uncomfortable. These relationships carry so much heaviness and stress.

As you grow, you will often no longer feel welcome in this old world.

On your journey, you will become increasingly different. Who you are will be different. You may think that you are still the same. You may frequent familiar places as you did before. You may occasionally do the same activities with the same group of people as you did before. You probably still have the same inside jokes and personal style of communicating with your group of friends. But it's not the same. And you know it. Deep down you sense the incongruence. You sense that something is...different. It feels different.

Who you are and how you relate to people, is changing. And if you force yourself to be like how you were in the past for the sake of relating with people from the past, you are doing both parties a disservice. YOU are not truly happy and THEY are not getting the authentic YOU. They are getting a fake, put-on version of you.

These are people you got along with. Were once friends with. But now only have memories with, as you are moving forward. The memories and how things used to be, will blind you to the present-day state of your friendships. People allow sentimentality to distract them from seeing the reality behind some of their relationships and how detrimental they may be being.

When you want to communicate with friends that haven't progressed in their own lives, you have to go backwards to do it. Not because you are better than them, but because YOU are moving forward in YOUR life, and to hang out with old friends that harbor the same old ceilings, thinking, habits, gossip, and lack of development, would YOU be going backwards in YOUR life.

You are compromising yourself and distracting yourself from your own path. In this old ecosystem, you will tend to hijack your own self and turn the dial down on yourself, to ensure you can relate with them. When someone is talking about negative stuff, we nod our heads, smile in approval, and uncomfortably laugh with them. When someone gossips, we gossip with them so we can relate with them and have something to talk about. When those around us are having drinks, we will have drinks with them so to not be the odd one out.

You are engaging in energy that deep down you want no more part of.

Quit playing these pretend games.

Step into yourself fully and don't hold back any longer.

Do not lower your standards for yourself just to get people to like you. When you're this person, you don't like it anyway. And neither do they. You can both sense the bullshit.

Do not dampen the intensity of your own light for other people's comfort. Do not dampen the intensity of your light to fit into an ecosystem that is no longer for you. Move forward.

...

Begin to develop an awareness of those around you.

Be aware of those around you that make life more miserable.

Some people live chaotically and are full of stress and problems. To them, there are always problems and reasons to complain. Things that require you to use your time, energy, and peace of mind. If you love them and want to keep them close in your life, then this is your decision to make. But understand that a large part of your life will be managing chaos and trying to live day-to-day coping with it. Your mind, occupied with trivial matters, won't have any room for higher expansion.

Some choose to see life as a soap opera. They love dramatizing their life. Getting lost in a rollercoaster of emotions. Lacking a bigger sense of purpose that would incentivize the disciplining of their emotions. They are addicted to arguing and creating problems. Their reality is this. And if you are in this as well with them, don't expect to live anything other than. If someone is constantly arguing, do not get mixed into their energy. You think you can change their mind but what you don't understand is you are entering into a dark black hole. You will continue to engage in something that, unknowingly to you, is sucking all of your light. You will become more and more depleted and fall to their level. You cannot make anybody happy. They are where they are. Unhappiness is often an addiction, and those addicted, instead of opening themselves up to a transformation of themselves, will sabotage what is around them, including their relationships, to keep themselves unhappy. They will suck you into their drama. They will suck you into their negative way of viewing life.

Some of the people close to you, are the very people that, in modern days would be referred to as "hating on you". It may be easy for us to clearly identify the "enemies" that hate on us. These are people who we've never really gotten along with. It's easy for us to identify them and remove them from our personal lives and not take their opinions so seriously. We may even let their hating motivate us. But these are not the individuals that we should be concerned about. In your mind, their opinions and the power behind them, although perhaps annoying or frustrating, have been largely dismissed.

The individual of hate that does ACTUAL damage and holds us back, are the individuals that are closest to us. The people that are INSIDE our ecosystem. The ones with words we DO take seriously and with opinions we DO care about.

Most of this "hater" energy comes from our current "friends". But these friends are cloaked and not properly SEEN as a hater. And so we soak in this "hating" energy unknowingly. Whether due to our ignorance or naiveté, due to sentimentality and our love for them, or due to our loneliness, desperation, or low self-worth. We think some individuals are our friends, but they keep us down more than anyone else we know. You make any moves outside of your norm, and they judge you. You try to do something better for yourself, and they judge you. You try to live a healthier lifestyle, and they are there to bring you down and distract you. You try to pursue something, and they laugh at you and say it's not possible.

And it influences your mind. It changes your day-to-day productivity.

It influences what you believe your potential is. It influences how you see yourself.

It influences what you can create. Fear and limitations seep into your mind. Self-doubt clouds your decisions. You're not as productive. You stagnate. You settle into your comfort zone, even though deep down it makes you unhappy.

Be aware of how people around you make you feel.

Do not allow past good memories to blind you to the relationship you have with them in the present moment. Do not allow the sentimentality of your friendship to downplay the negative emotions underneath the surface that you are experiencing in the present moment. Do not let sentimentality blind you from the reality you experience daily. Do not allow your fear of loneliness to keep you attached to someone that isn't good for you.

Sacrifice relationships you're holding onto in the present moment, that belong in the past, and begin to fill up your life more with what you see in the future. This is how the future enters your life. There are higher levels to be lived.

Be wary of those that make you feel bad for no real productive reason. That doesn't support you or inspire you. That judge you and criticize you without any real supportive feedback. Those that add un-needed doubt, fear, and pessimism into your life. Those that don't want you to stop your bad habits. Those that may even encourage your bad habits. If this describes your "friend", then they are not your friend. Many of these friends aren't even aware of how negative they may be. In the same way that most drivers think they are above-average drivers even though this would be statistically impossible, there is a lack of self-awareness that blocks the individual from realizing just how harmful their behaviors are.

You may have been good friends once. Maybe you both were distracting yourselves from your purposes, and you woke up, and now you are aware of your unhealthy behaviors. Or maybe you were both growing together, but at some point, they began to stagnate. Maybe they were real friends at one point, but that true friend relationship and all of its great experiences came and passed. And now they are filled with bitterness, resentment, and unhappiness with their own lives. And that taints the friendships they have, including your own. Maybe they are scared to progress in their own lives, and so they want to keep you from progressing in yours, so as to not be alone.

In any case, it's heartbreaking and painful. They are hurt. Healthy and happy people don't hurt others. Hurt people hurt others.

...

As you move forward in your life, you must become conscious of your relationships and curate what surrounds you.
Some relationships need communication to improve.
Some relationships must be let go.

For some of those around you, they may truly desire change and your words are of service to them. Whether you visibly see it or not. They may currently be struggling, but deep within, they are open to a new direction in their life. Your words may offer new perspectives, that over time, begin to widen their wisdom and understanding. Your words may add ingredients to help synthesize ideas within their mind, spark their creativity, and inspire a new direction in their own life. Your words may be empowering for them and are precious, as they may have nobody in their lives that has faith in them to be more than what they currently are. They may have a path in their own life that they start to see and believe in and you being there empowers them. By you being there, you having conversations with them, you spending time together, and you guiding them or giving them resources, you help them reach new heights in their life. They WANT change.

You play a role in their life. You are connected to their ecosystem as well. In their ecosystem, they may constantly receive words that tear them down, and you are the glimmer of light in their life. In the same way wisdom and light entered your life through other individuals, and your evolution was able to happen because of their existence in your life, you may be the same thing to other individuals in their life. You are playing a powerful role in society by being a light amongst those that surround you. Be patient with your family and friends. Be understanding. Know where they are at and be kind. Have gratitude for having family and friends in your life. Listen to them. Support them and encourage them. Give them space to grow at their own pace. Be the space in their life that will not judge them, but encourage them. And help them if they ask and you are able to help them. The patience and love within you, is what keeps us all united.

But don't confuse patience and love, with long-term compliance with their stagnation, inaction, and continuation of unhealthy behaviors. With certain people in your life, speaking to them, those that don't want to change, is like yelling into a void. Don't suffocate your light in an attempt to help those around you, when they do not want it.

Some people are so far gone in the realm of ignorance, that there is no retrieving them. Beliefs stacked on beliefs stacked on beliefs, and their sense of self is intimately intertwined with every layer. They do not want to change their beliefs, or change their sense of self, for losing one means losing the other. Aside from a life-changing experience to wake them up, aside from hitting rock bottom and being forced to relinquish what they currently hold onto, aside from a near-death experience or a psychedelic trip to completely shake up this fortified ignorance, there is little hope of changing this in the near future.

You can try to speak to the core of their souls and have a heartfelt conversation. Light and truth might come into their life through you. And you can try. But aside from this, if this does not work, there are no words you can currently tell them that can move them. There are no words that would inspire them to think outside of the cage they created themselves and to move forward in their life.

They must reach that moment in their life on their own.

Sometimes, the best thing you can do to help someone you care about, is to move forward without them. After exhausting your options, your absence may be a better teacher than your presence.

...

A person that has the intention of bettering their life is doing so because they actually believe it is somewhat possible. A vision of a different reality has opened up in their mind. Things have shifted and they are in a place where they can receive information in an empowering way, begin to interpret life in a positive way, and begin to make changes in their life. They want to evolve, they want to look within themselves, and they want to truly change the way they live. Some people are not ready yet. They are not interested and their minds reject any new ideas of moving upward. They wish to stay where they are at.

Don't get entangled in their lives. Let them be.

Many people don't want to be uprooted from their comfortable level of life. And you will only waste your time trying to move them. Whether it's by managing them, helping them get their lives together, constantly arguing with them, trying to get them to do basic things for themselves, trying to get them to take opportunities, or making sure they are putting in the effort. You are having these high expectations for people that they don't even have for themselves. You are squandering away your own time and energy.

The atmosphere at higher levels of life is fundamentally different. More focus, harder work, discipline, uncomfortable decisions, and being outside your comfort zone more often. Facing your insecurities, fears, traumas, and toxic ways of behaving and communicating. Facing the limitations you've listened to, comfort zones you stay in, responsibility you've rejected, maturing you've denied, and your purpose you've played games with. More attention, more pressure, more healing necessary, more focus necessary.

Many people don't want to go to these higher levels.

This is a personal project within every individual and their own life. Do not project the relationship you have with your life, unto others.

Not everyone wants to go to these higher levels. Do not try to drag those that do not want this, with you. People will find a way to return to the level that they feel they deserve and what they are most comfortable in. And if you are disrupting their attempt of returning, you will soon be the recipient of their frustration and resentment.

Ultimately you are engaged with individuals who are distracting themselves from their purpose, and are now distracting you from yours. And you are foolishly naive to continue your attempts to move them upward with you. Your care and empathy, will soon be revealed as good-hearted, but foolish and naive. You must understand that you must take care of yourself.

Always be kind. But don't sacrifice yourself in the process. Do not be a martyr unnecessarily and sacrifice yourself to help them. You can not only be more of a help somewhere else, but be happier and nourished doing so. Take care of yourself.

Keep your mind, emotions, and being at bay. Be a lighthouse. Lead by example. Lend a hand if they truly need it, but be emotionally aware of their effect on you. Like a lifeguard attempting to save someone from drowning, through their emotional immaturity, lack of self-awareness, and addiction to cycles and repeating them, you run the risk of drowning yourself. They will continue on their own destructive path, and only distract you from your constructive one. The more you engage with this energy, the more your energy becomes affected in the process.

In the future, maybe you can join worlds. But right now, no. Give them space. They may finally learn what they must learn, from you moving on.

Love from a distance. Support from a distance.

...

Everyone is on their own journey. Just because your lives intertwined for a period of time, doesn't mean it was meant to stay that tightly intertwined forever. Just because you were close with someone in your past, doesn't mean you should be as close with them in your future. Do not allow guilt to keep you from growing and doing something different in your life. Do not allow sentimentality to stop you from doing what's most nurturing for your own mind and your own soul. Do not allow the fear of breaking habits and routines to keep you from moving into what you truly want. Do not continue to engage with the old when you want something new. Venture out into the next phase of your life.

If your world starts losing parts of it, do not be scared. In order for your world to transform, and to rise, you must eventually lose the old. Be courageous. Trust the process. And continue to move forth.

...

So many ecosystems disallow individuals to follow their dreams. To be a novice in their craft. To be new at something. To try to create something. To be an inexperienced student of the pursuit of their dream. To make mistakes.

People judging you for trying to be inspired. Thinking you're corny because you're trying to chase your dreams. You are made embarrassed. You are shamed. Judged. Ridiculed. Looked at funny. Judgemental tone of voice. Doubtful words. Discouraged. You are unable to be yourself without repercussions. Your potential and possibilities are limited. Your creative abilities and expression, are capped. There is little to no room for expansion.

These people make living a greater life for yourself more uncomfortable.

And when an ecosystem makes it so painful to be a novice in your craft, it will be difficult to actually move forward towards your vision. Being a novice in your craft is the first step to mastering it. To be new at something, and be a bit nervous, scared, intimidated, embarrassed and overwhelmed, and move forth into it anyway. To be working on a craft for so long, and to release what you have created. When surrounded by people that discourage you, in your most vulnerable of moments, that is enough for many to stop trying. When individuals are discouraged by those around them, that is unfortunately the final nail in the coffin. This is enough for them to quit pursuing what they want to pursue and settle for something that will receive less criticism and is generally more accepted.

For far too many individuals on this planet, they are working a job they don't like, and being versions of themselves they don't like, because people in their ecosystem are holding them down from doing something greater. Too often are individuals with incredible potential, buried under the judgements of those around them. Getting caught in the crossfire of projected limitations. A negative and discouraging environment, is the norm for most individuals.

As you awaken, as you try to move forward and change, your past follows you. And this is what stops people from realizing their true self. They try to maintain who they traditionally have been, even if it's not the real them. They try to maintain these relationships. They cannot help it. They are deep in this ecosystem. It's how you live day to day. It's how you communicate and relate with others. Those around us have great influence on us, and us unto them.

While those that surround you are stuck in the past, you will be stuck in the past. Past thought patterns, habits, behaviors, ways of communicating and ways of living. Stuck in the past and only able to see life through this lens.

This is why it's key to changing our ecosystem when we are trying to REALLY change ourselves and our own world. We can have a new self trying to emerge, but if we are constantly surrounded by old friends and family and places, which are eliciting the same thought patterns, interactions, and cycles of behavior, it makes it so much harder to make that shift.

Old mental programs attempting to resurface.
Old emotional programs attempting to revive.

It's hard to be who you truly are, when you are surrounded by people that see you as someone that you are not. They see you as your old self. The self that was created by your teachers, your parents, your school, your media, your church, your neighborhood. Created by everyone but you.

It's hard to be who you truly are, and begin to be comfortable with who that is, when you are surrounded by people that constantly reignite the old you.

Old ecosystems contain with it old habits, environments, people, triggers, and influences. Instigating and reemphasizing patterns. Increasing rigidity. Disallowing change.

You need fluidity to change.

A new ecosystem, allows fluidity. Allows change.

A new ecosystem allows no triggers. Blank slate. Freedom.

When you put yourself in an ecosystem that allows you to be whoever you want to be, the process of becoming who you want to be, becomes easier. An uphill battle becomes a downhill battle.

...

Many of the people around you are generators of negativity in different forms. Insecurities, fears, doubts, limitations, judgement, animosity, pessimism, hate. And of course, you yourself are not perfect, nor never will be. But to surround yourself with those that are disproportionally more negative, have little awareness of their own self and where they are at in life, and lack the care enough to change it, will only make your own life unnecessarily more difficult. You absorb others' opinions, thoughts, and uncared-for emotions, and allow it to enter into your mind. And this makes your own thoughts, emotions, and life, heavier. They paint your life in colors that you don't want.

You must learn to ground yourself, evolve, and begin to allow this heavier material to come in and go out with little effect. But also you are not perfectly impenetrable. The most peaceful individual in a sea of hate can only last so long. You must detach from the environments in which these individuals are predominately in.

Could be family members, high school friends, college friends, current social circle, coworkers, roommates, or some of those you follow on social media. Find the sources of what brings you stress in your life.

Allowing anyone and everyone into your life is the surest way to dilute your potency on this earth. Your mind will become oversaturated with that which serves no purpose other than to keep you in a state of doubt, and keep you in the same monotonous cycle that they are caught in.

Keep your mind focused.

Many of the greatest creators on Earth may or may not be consciously aware of this, but instinctually they are. This is why many go through the process of curating who and what surrounds them, as they chase their dreams and create what is true to them. If they could, in any which way, they would. But to access the highest connection possible and achieve their greatest work, they must put themselves in the most potent position possible.

This is why the highest level creators in the world have the highest standards for their ecosystem. Anything lesser than the highest, will bring their connection lower. And when their connection is lowered, their focus and clarity is lowered. The purity of their work is lowered. What they create is lowered. They feel the lack of true fulfillment. They know there's more. They feel it. And they are falling short.

And so their tolerance for nonsense is nonexistent. They do not allow anyone and everyone in their lives. They are instinctually well-aware of this relationship between themselves and their genius, and they do their best to cultivate it, tend to it, enrich it, and respect it. And keep what depletes it, away.

And this consciously-curated ecosystem and personal boundaries, are not only for their work, but for the quality of their lives in general. Not only for their best work, but for their happiness, for their peace of mind, and for them to get the most of their human experience on this planet.

...

We are individuals that are awakening. And there's a hint of guilt involved, similar to 'survivor's guilt', because intuitively we know there are uncomfortable truths that need facing. In order for us to continue to grow, in order for us to create what we must create, in order for us to truly help others around us, we must face these uncomfortable truths.

Not all friends will be with you to the end.
Not all relationships.
Not all the places you go.
Not all the creators and the content you loved.
Not all the activities you do for fun.
A lot must be let go.

If you are to continue evolving, your ecosystem must evolve with you.

Not everyone and everything is going to come with you.

Things must be dropped on your way forward. To make room for the new.

Do not feel guilty for your own growth.

You are becoming a different person.

Embrace that.

Do you see your future self being with these kind of individuals? Do you see your future self going to places like this? Do you see your future self spending their time like this?

Your current world and the world you envision;

you bridge that gap by adding, subtracting, communication and love.

Adding new.

Subtracting the old.

Communicating with what is already there in your world and will remain.

Loving what has been in your life that has loved you.

Focus on creating your new world. New city, new environment, new friends, new relationships with current friends, new areas you frequent, new media you subscribe to, new ways of spending your time. In this new world, you are welcome like never before. Your true self can flourish.

But first, we must identify what currently surrounds us. We must identify those around us that truly love us, and love them more than ever before. We must identify those around us that keep us down, and question our relationship with them. We must communicate with those around us where the relationship is less black and white, and more gray and complicated... Individuals that we love, but are struggling within and hurt us in the process. Individuals that we care for, but drain our energy. We must understand our current ecosystem.

...

You must understand that you are not the end all be all ultimate genius creator and source of your work. You are a vessel. You are a messenger. It's up to you, operating your human body and navigating through this physical world, to make this happen. Whatever resources needed, get them. Whatever environment you need for your work to be its purest and potent form, create it. If you have a desired effect in mind, then it is your duty to dedicate the time and focus necessary to create it. Paint the picture that is in your mind as vividly as you can.

...

It is important to understand that there is YOU as the artist and there is the YOU as the one that looks out for him or her.

And it is up to you to put yourself in a position where you are able to create as effortlessly as possible. Put yourself in a position where you are powerful, at peace, and inspired. Put yourself in a position where you can access the greatest connection to your Truth. Where connecting to your gifts is the path of least resistance. You must become your own manager, sift through the worldly distractions, and create an ecosystem that is the most positively potent for you. Create that, for yourself, as it is solely your job and nobody else's.

To achieve great heights, you must release what is below.

...

When you reevaluate your life, you'll begin to realize that everything that you were being, this less true version of yourself, you'll realize that your entire external life is a direct reflection of who you were being. Your entire ecosystem is the physical expression of what you were being within. You have created all of this.

You created the world you're in, and participated in its creation with every step. You participated in keeping this world intact. You interacted with all of the characters. You attended the events. You engaged in the activities. You continued to talk to the same people. You continued to maintain the same accepted behaviors. And you woke up everyday and decided to play this role again.

The individual that you were being, intertwines with the outside world. What you have created (your world and who you are) merge, entangle and take root into society. You are "Michael the wild, funny guy". "Emily the safe, predictable nerd". "William the guy going for a business degree". "Isabella the girl going for a liberal arts degree". People expect you to play a certain role. Ways of behaving that you are known for. Beliefs to maintain. Relationships to continue a certain dynamic in. A role you are expected to fit in. After all...you've been being that for so long. This is what they perceive as the "real you".

You can leave this world. But it will be challenging. When you created this world, you and this world you created were also participating in the society that we are ALL always participating in.

You face hard decisions no matter what you do.

If you stay, you will be miserable. The world is worse off for you not following your truth. Your family and community are worse off. You are worse off.

And in moving forward, you must mature. You must become brave and make difficult decisions. Speak more truthfully. Take responsibility. Put more effort into your dreams. But, with this path, you, your family, your community, and the world, are closer to living in a state of peace, passion, love, and happiness.

...

Begin by spending some time alone. Away from what distracts you from connecting with your true self. Away from expectations and people that influence you to be a certain way. You must take some time to be with your self.

Like a butterfly that cocoons, humans work very similarly. We are social creatures…and while we are surrounded by other social creatures, it's very difficult for us to focus our energy on not living up to certain expectations, engaging in behaviors that we are known for, maintaining "who we are", and engaging in the dynamics of the relationships that we have to continue their stability.

We must be alone and focus that energy on creating ourselves, recreating our world, and allowing us to express and bring that newly created world into society.

…

Your focus is one of the ingredients required to bring "you", into fruition.

To reach into the depths of the mind and summon your creation, you need to focus.

To bring out who you are meant to be, you need to focus.

Your environment alters your focus, and the level of depth you're able to reach.

Society, your family, your friends, in its many judgements and demands, pressures you, holds you, and locks you into a confined, limited set of expressions.

What is deemed ..."acceptable". "Normal". "Expected of you".

You must put your self in a place where you are, if only for a bit, freed from this prison.

Place yourself in an environment in which you will not be judged or reprimanded for the ritualistic expression required to bring your truth to life.

Do you need to dance, to bob your head and move your body, to hum and sing? Do you need to speak out loud? Speak to yourself quietly? Walk back and forth? Allow yourself room to formulate ideas and thoughts?

Need to listen to music that connects you deeper to your vision? Listen to the same sounds in a loop because they put you in a specific mental space where your vision is more clear and you make more connections? Songs and sounds that people around you would judge you for, but for you, it propels you forward?

Do, what others may think, is weird?
Place yourself in an environment where you will not be judged.

Where you can have a private intimate connection with your self.

Where you can believe in your self.

Where you are free.

Set your self free from society's hold.

Be bigger than society. Connect with the Universe itself.

This is your workshop.

This is where you will create you.

This is where you will create your work.

And in time, you will stretch this freedom. You will grow accustomed to its feeling. You will become more confident in it. You will enjoy its nourishment to your soul. You will love the life it breathes into you. And you will soon refuse to be anything BUT. You will soon no longer put a lid on your being-ness.

And you will then be able to serve society powerfully. In the way the Universe meant for you. You're not listening to society's pressure. To your friends and what they think is cool. To social media and what will lead to more status and riches. To family members with their own idea of what you should do. You're listening to a higher guidance.

This is your metamorphosis.

...

Give yourself SPACE.

You need space to THINK.

Space to think about what YOU want to think about.
Letting your imagination wander in directions that interest you.

Actively thinking about where you want to go in your life and what you want to do.

Actively thinking about what interests you and trying to deepen your understanding of them.

You need space to have amazing thoughts and creativity rise to the surface.

You need space for your visions to come through, and for you to know the path to walk.

...

And you also need space to see and understand your ecosystem. Zoom out and see yourself in your own life. See yourself in your relationships from afar. Does anything need communicating? Do you need to establish your personal boundaries more firm? Do you need to be more understanding, accepting, and forgiving? Do you need to end friendships? Do you need to create new ones? Do you need to be alone more often? Do you need to connect with more people? Do you need to move cities?

Be wise with your energy.

...

A lot of the pain from following your purpose comes from the pain of changing your ecosystem. And a lot of the pain from the changing of your ecosystem, comes from your own maturation process. From looking at your ecosystem, and realizing just how much you've contributed to where you are at in life. Realizing your own fear of speaking up and communicating, your own fear of ending unhealthy relationships, your own lack of honesty, your own fear of growing, your own fear of facing yourself and facing the truth of your life. It's easy to blame others for why you are at where you are at. It's easy to not accept the reality of who you are in life right now.

But the responsibility is on you. You are the one with the knowledge and the awareness. And you are the one being distracted away from what you truly want. It's on you to communicate. You're in an era of your life of great change, and the unhealthy relationships around you consume you, and don't give your true self that is trying to emerge, any room to breathe. As the individual that is awakening in your own crevice on Earth, in your own little ecosystem, around your family, around your friends, the onus is on you to have the uncomfortable but necessary conversations, if you want to see yourself grow. It's your responsibility to make the changes necessary.

It's difficult to communicate with people in your ecosystem. It takes loving and respecting yourself enough to stand up for yourself. It takes courage to speak to those around you and communicate your personal boundaries, knowing that your words will affect the relationship. It takes vulnerability as you don't know how they will respond back to you. It takes faith in knowing that if this is a true relationship, it will survive.

But as long as you maintain these relationships in the current state they are in, you are participating in negative repetitive cycles and if you don't say or do anything to change it, you are part of it. You are passively approving it. You have set the bar of your personal boundaries below what is true to you. You are lying to yourself. And you lie to them. Be true to yourself and give yourself the opportunity to expand in the ways you know is possible. Be true to them and give themselves the opportunity to know the truth of who you are, what your relationship is, and awareness of aspects of themselves, and yourself, that they may not see.

This is true love. This is a true relationship. This is how you move closer to what you are meant to be in life. This is how you grow. This is how your community grows. This is how mankind grows.

...

You communicating with those around you, destroys the current context of the relationship. The one that currently stands. It ruins it. You cannot go back to it. What has been said, has been said. You are bringing them awareness to something, and once an individual is aware, they cannot become un-aware. This is the power of awareness.

But you communicating, and it bringing the inevitable deconstructing of the relationship, is akin to a muscle being worked out, and having to be torn down, for it to be built back stronger. In your relationship, if there is a true friendship, true love, true openness and humility, something new, something better, will emerge. A less rigid, less constricting, more freeing, more authentic, relationship.

They understand you more now. And you will understand them. They know more of who you are. They know more of your direction in life. And you will know more of who they are and their direction in life.

Having these conversations and establishing this space, will clear your conscious and the weight on your mind and heart, but also you will be aligning closer and closer to who you know you should truly be in your life. You will get your time to focus, you will have more of a peace of mind, and you will be able to nourish yourself in ways you couldn't before. And when you do spend time with those that you love, you will be much more present and the experience itself will be richer than before. They are getting the true you.

When you are truly real in a relationship, your relationships are finally getting the real you. Your relationships are changing. You being real, makes the relationship more real.

Whatever happens after you being honest, happens. But what happens afterwards, is meant to happen.

You will know where you both stand, and if it feels right, you will connect deeper than ever before. If it does not, you will feel yourselves going in different directions.

Whatever happens, is meant to happen.

...

Honesty aligns you to the life you are meant to live. It levels you up.

You enter a transition phase in your life in which what is truly meant for you, remains in your life, and what is not, exits. Sad, but joyous. Equally chaotic and harmonious.

Be honest. Be real. This allows everything to start falling into place.

After this transition period of gain and of loss, you will be in the realest direction of life that you will have ever been on.

...

Living fake and inauthentically has become what most people are accustomed to. Making other people happy, but being fake to make that happen. It's become the norm to hide your emotions, hide your true thoughts, hide your true expression of self, hide your true thoughts about your relationships, hide your true passions and the direction you want to go in life.

In your fear of being honest and real, you stay stuck at your current level in life. Fear of being real, is being afraid to level up. So much effort going into maintaining an old reality, and the job unhealthy relationships in them, when there's a new life in front of you, where freedom is waiting for you. Where your purpose is waiting for you.

...

Let your ecosystem rearrange. You are changing. You're growing. Your ecosystem takes time. Subtract what you feel you must subtract. Unfollow. Unfriend. Block. Quit replying and engaging in toxic relationships. Stop hanging out with people that are not good for you. Stop frequenting locations that are not good for you. You cannot be in toxic relationships and not be unaffected. You can be distant. You can be emotionally mature and remain level headed. But you can not be unaffected. Their presence in your life changes the very essence of how you live.

You may need to endure being where you currently are and you are not in the position to subtract from your ecosystem.

Whether they are someone like a roommate that pays rent, a close family member that lives in your home, or close friends that you care about. If you're not in the position to subtract, then communicate. Do your best to create an empowering ecosystem, with what you currently have. Do not be silent and try to push on and move forward, struggling. You will only become more resentful and frustrated over time. And accomplish very little. And have relationships deteriorate. Open your mouth and communicate how you feel.

Personal boundaries and space are the way to protect your energy.

And they will not stumble into your life. You need to establish it. You need space from the outside world. Space from parents and their opinions and judgement. Space from social media and its constant noise. Space from friends and them trying to distract you.

Family and roommates walking into your room while you work, asking you to do things at random times. Friends calling your phone, texting you, wanting to hang out or gossip. You constantly looking over your shoulder because of others around you interrupting your peace of mind. Your focus being interrupted due to your inability to create personal boundaries. Without personal boundaries, you will never summon what is meant to be summoned from you.

Protect your energy.

Focus your energy.

...

Family and how you communicate with them, like most close relationships in an individual's life, is complicated. There's love and honor involved. Money, resources, and obligations involved. But there's also outdated thinking involved (especially amongst older generations). There's fear, doubt, judgement, and bitterness usually involved.

So it's tricky.

Don't expect your family to be disciplined. Don't blame them for not being as strong or not being as aware as you'd like. Help them with where they are at. Have patience and empathy, but ensure you are not getting drained. Let them be who they are and do what they want. Do not try to control.

Lead by example. Don't impose.

Let them know your OWN goals, or at least when you need space to focus, and communicate it.

Communicate with those you love to give them the opportunity to grow.

If you see the space for it and you feel it will be welcomed, or if it is asked for, talk about higher aspirations, ideas, and healthier ways of living with them. Talk with them to give them the opportunity to grow. Communicating with them is you being able to shed light onto their life. The conversation you have with them could be the very light they need to begin to align with their own light and get on the right path.

Give them the light, support and space that you would want if you were in that position. Give them space to listen, introspect, think, and evaluate their own life. Give them the space to start making changes in their life. Patience. It's not just about yourself and establishing personal boundaries to ensure that you are perfect and happy. If you are the individual waking up in your pocket of time and space, in your quiet home, in your own country, surrounded by other individuals close to you, it is on you for change to happen. You have responsibility on this earth. Do not abandon it.

The power of one small supportive conversation is untold.

Personal boundaries must not be placed just to defend yourself from experiencing uncomfortable and complicated emotions. This is disguised selfishness and immaturity. You are only wanting people that fit in your life the way you want them to, and dismiss them if they do not fit that, in the name of "personal boundaries". You must have personal boundaries, but they must be maturely placed. And for them to be maturely placed takes experience, maturity, compassion and spiritual growth. You will learn over time.

...

Staying in your ecosystem with your established personal boundaries, may not be enough. Your ecosystem may be so corrosive to your spirit, you may have to remove yourself from this space completely if you wish to have a fighting chance to survive, and the possibility to thrive. You may need to develop real distance and physical space from your family and friends, so you can truly develop your self. If you must leave those you love to truly focus, then do so. To give yourself and your loved ones a chance for a better life, put yourself in the position to where you can have a fighting chance to make it happen. Give yourself the chance to come back with more wisdom, opportunities, resources and ways for them to elevate their own lives.

...

Be honest with yourself.

If you begin to feel trapped in the town you live, you should feel trapped. Because that means you've awakened to your cage. You're becoming more conscious of the limits of your surroundings, and the lack of opportunity. And more aware of other cities that are more in tune with your vision. And your feeling of being trapped is the fire under you to get you going. It's your soul's way of ensuring the continuation of your evolution.

Let your hometown be just that. Your hometown. The place that holds your nostalgia and memories. And just that. You move on. You move forward. You go experience more of life. And in future days, you may return back to your hometown and recollect memories, reminisce on what created you and what was such a big part of your formation, and connect with loved ones.

But that and only that.

If you feel called to stay and serve your purpose in your hometown, then stay. There's honor in this. But most will feel called to go beyond. There's so much fruit in exploring more of the world, and your soul knows this. There may be nothing inherently toxic with where you come from. Your friends, your family, the people in the town. They may be happy and loving individuals. You may just simply, want more in your life. New experiences of life while you're here on this Earth. Different experiences that your hometown may not be able to provide. There's more to the world. And there's more to your own world, if you want there to be. Parts of you will awaken and light up when you travel, meet new people, and do new things. Parts of you that will never awaken otherwise. You may always come back to your hometown in the future. Or you may continue on with your life in new ways.

If you feel you must venture, you must venture.
Experience more. Expand more. Be who you are meant to be.

This is why many successful people of today and of history, the individuals that move forward and actualize their vision, often leave their hometowns and leave old social circles. They continue the process of discarding what is disempowering around them, and continue to climb higher and grab the empowering pieces. Whatever is around them in their current present-day reality, they move towards the wisest decisions they currently have the ability to know. Whatever surrounds them TODAY, they do their best to follow what feels right. They are active forces in their soul's evolution. They are putting in their part by listening.

And this often means leaving their hometown and moving into different cities. Ones that foster their creativity. That inspire them to explore. That make them want to go outside and connect with people. That move them to look into different niches and enclaves of creativity. To discover pockets of culture. To meet people who get them to think differently and feel differently. To meet individuals with unique personalities and lifestyles. To meet individuals with their own chosen crafts and ideas. To see great works of art that have been created over time. To see and feel the same streets that the creators before them walked. The dimly lit neighborhoods, the quiet parks, the cafes, the waters. To connect with the energy that inspired their work. Their humanity deepens. Their knowledge expands. They connect more with that which we are all connected to. Moving into this space and making it their new day-to-day ecosystem, begins to transform them. And it deepens the connection they have with their creative genius and with their chosen craft. It deepens their connection with life. They are getting closer to their true selves.

...

Few people on this planet are being themselves. And those that decide to truly be themselves, the highest version of themselves, the evolved version of themselves, are the ones that end up reaching levels where they receive the often natural byproducts of attention, admiration, resources and opportunities. We are in awe of these individuals. We are captivated. We are inspired. We see something magical in them. They are connected to something deeper than the average individual. And people can feel it. Famous artists, inventors, leaders, writers, directors, actors, and musicians. Because of their unwavering focus to connect to their deepest true selves, the natural outcome of their existence is astonishment by those that are not. They cannot help but capture the eyes, ears and minds of those around them. It's inspiring.

Albums, books, inventions, paintings, philosophies, movements, speeches, films, businesses, buildings, fashion pieces, sculptures. These individuals and what they do, MOVE us. Culture is not something that naturally exists on this earth. Individuals like this CREATE culture. They are the ENGINE that MOVE people.

Individuals like this, individuals that are connected to something deeper, have been creating culture before we were born, and individuals like this will be creating culture after we leave. Those around you that are alive today known for their created great works, and those today that are unknown and in the process of creating great works, are the present day focused curators of energy on this Earth. They are dialed in into their greatness.

This is their time on Earth. And they recognize this.

And the people that aren't connected to their true selves but are instead choosing to stay stuck at a job they don't like, being in a town they are miserable in, staying in relationships that drain them, being cool and fitting in, getting through the day and coping with distractions, or other lesser orientations of their energy, stay unhappy and a version of themselves that desperately wants to evolve. And they believe that people that reach these higher spaces are "special".

And they are special. But they aren't special in the sense of they are something you are not. This is not why they are special. There is no difference between them and you. They may be gifted, but you too, are gifted. They may be fulfilling their potential, but you too, have potential that can also be fulfilled. They are human. You are human too. You are both pieces of the universe. There is no difference between them and you.

They are special in the sense that they decided to listen to their soul's evolution despite all the societal pressure that tells them NOT to. They listen to their soul's evolution despite the self doubt, the fear, and the insecurities that tell them not to. They listen to the same voice you choose to ignore. They have decided to invest in the relationship that they believe truly matters the most. They decided to put their attention and focus on the reality that they know is their greatest truth. They are focused on uncovering the greatness they feel within themselves. They made the decision to not shy away from the intensity and magnitude of their power. Instead, they faced it, stepped into it, and harnessed it.

Listen to your soul's evolution. No matter the outcome, create what you are meant to create. No matter how big or small the impact, focus on what you are meant to focus on.

Be who you are meant to be.

…

Protect your energy. Keep your space sacred.
And begin to curate a positive ecosystem.

A healthy ecosystem has reciprocity with the individuals participating in it. Not by force or by status quo, but because you are both in a healthy mental and spiritual space where your cup runneth over. You have abundance in your life. You feel good, you are empathetic, and so you share the goodness that you have. And them onto you. Whether it be positive words, a good laugh, or just your friendly and loving presence. Could be good conversation, support, guidance, or actual physical resources. But in any case, you both give each other value and both of your lives are better off for it.

Surround yourself with people that love life itself. In the face of all the trials and tribulations of being a human on this earth, they have decided to love life, and to embrace it while they are here.

Surround yourself with people that love themselves. They take care of themselves, They are self aware, and they ensure that they stay focused on what matters in life. They have humility and listen to others when needed. They don't allow distractions to dilute their love for life and for what they want to accomplish. They love themselves, as if they were to love their own child. They are happy with their own lives, as they are focused on their own craft, taking care of their own selves, getting out of their own comfort zone, and living their own lives.

And surround yourself with people that love you. Not simply love you verbally and they tell you they love you. But they love you in the act of loving you and caring for you. They are happy in their own life, and secure within their own selves, and so only wish to see you happy and thrive. They inspire you as they want you to be fueled with confidence and passion for life. They compliment you and praise you as they want you to feel appreciated and aware of all the good that you do. They give you helpful critiques and tell you what you need to hear, even if it may hurt, so you do not veer away from your path. They help you when you need help, and don't make you feel guilty for you asking for help. They respect your boundaries if you wish to be left alone, and don't make you feel guilty for your need for solitude and quality time with yourself. They love you, they love your potential and they love your progress. They want you to have a good experience of life.

Surround yourself with people that are not necessarily in search of being "right", but are in search of the truth. Individuals that are not only open to changing beliefs and views, but are looking for it. They are honest and humble, as to keep their own mind enriched and open to learning and leveling up. They are searching for higher echelons. Higher paradigms. Higher levels of understanding. Higher levels of existence. Higher levels of vibrations. Higher levels of creativity. Higher levels of intelligence. They are malleable. They are on the path of life. Aging beautifully.

And because of this honesty, humility, and intelligence, they are applying in their own life, they have a respectable and trustworthy mind. You are able to have real dialogue and real conversations with them that will bear fruit that is difficult to find in life without these conversations. They review your thoughts, beliefs, behaviors and work, and see your life from a different perspective than you do. They give you feedback as to shed light on possible areas of ignorance. They are catalysts for your intellectual and spiritual expansion. They aid your progress in life.

Surround yourself with people who see your value. They appreciate your value. A genuinely cool person that is surrounded by "losers", may begin to think that he himself is the loser for his "lame" passions, hobbies and joys in life. A person full of love that hangs around people full of hate, may begin to think he is weird for being so caring and empathetic and begin to tone down his expression of love. A creative person that hangs around logical thinkers that don't appreciate creativity, may begin to think he himself is odd and tone down his own imaginative and expansive ways. A person that wants more out of life that hangs around people that want to continue doing the same thing, may begin to think his dreams are foolish and beyond his reach. If you hang around people that don't see your value, you will think you have no value. Be with people that don't disallow you to be yourself, but allow it. They allow you to be yourself without judgement. They allow you to enrich your own life by going deeper within your own truth. They appreciate who you are. And as you go deeper into your own truth and your own being, you inspire them to do the same.

Surround yourself with people that understand the process of mastery. Individuals that know that you must humble yourself, risk embarrassment, make mistakes, and learn, to succeed at whatever it is you want to succeed at. They support you, but more than anything, they are supportive of you connecting with your self, and allow you to go through the process of evolving and discovering yourself. They allow you to be like water. They understand your journey and allow you to try different things, adopt different behaviors, move into different fields, work on different projects, and BE different, without judging you.

If you are focused on becoming the greatest version of yourself, who you are now is not who you are going to be.

The beliefs and opinions you have will change.

How you behave right now will change.

The way you approach life will change.

How you spend your time will change.

It is important to have people around you that value this and understand this.

They allow you to be vulnerable and open minded. To change opinions, change beliefs and become something different. To grow. To evolve. Because when you inevitably grow and change, it can either have been a socially approved process that is encouraged, or a process where you are judged, reprimanded and discouraged.

Surround yourself with greatness. Being around those that are healed, shines a brighter light on areas within yourself that need healing. Being around those that are more focused and driven, shines a brighter light on ways you are using your time that are holding you back. In the face of what is significant, you are able to feel more of your own insignificance. Your flaws are revealed and broadcasted within your own mind. This is a powerful catalyst for self change. Who am I? What parts of me are keeping me down? What can I do to better myself to better reflect what I see in others that inspires me? Where am I trying to go? How must I evolve to continue moving forward?

Many individuals will see greatness and in response to that, feel a lack of enoughness within themselves. They use this energy they are seeing in someone else, to get down on themselves. Instead, use the greatness you see as inspiration for you to become your own greatness. A clear vision of the new level of thinking and being to exist in. Use the greatness you see as awareness of the place you want to go for yourself. Listen to the calling. Evolve. Being around higher caliber individuals on this planet unlock higher aspects of yourself that you have never seen before. Surrounding yourself with greatness, familiarizes yourself with greatness. You and greatness become intertwined. You become great. Thinking at this level, moving at this level, being this level, begins to become your new home.

But more than anything, surround yourself with good people. Kind. Humility. People that are trying. People that are giving. People that would do the right thing, even if nobody is there to see them. People that are present.

...

There's a you that's stuck living with negative family, negative friends, a hometown you've been wanting to leave, or working a job you don't like.

And there's a you that lives in the city that you love, with healthier relationships with loved ones, with higher individuals around you, and spending your time doing what you feel called to do. In a better environment. In inspiring gyms with focused people around you. In neighborhoods where people are focused on their own crafts, excited for life. In cafes and restaurants where people are happy and enjoying their life.

You have to start making an effort to put yourself around the people you want to be around. Proactively create your new ecosystem. Move to the city, frequent the neighborhoods, go to the places, be amongst the people, meet the people.

Curate for yourself the ecosystem that brings out your greatest self to the surface. This is what will bring you the most joy throughout your day, throughout your life, and keep you most focused on your purpose.

There's many different variations of an ecosystem that are possible. It's on you to experience more life, find what resonates with you, and move into those spaces.

...

If you're in a place where you have very little living people of inspiration around you, then surround yourself with those that have immortalized their genius into their works. Let films, literature, music and great pieces of work from the best creators in different times of history be your soul's companions. Fill your world with this.

If you cannot yet meet those that inspire you that are currently living, have them in your life, if not in person, through video, sound and printed words.

Read the wisdom and creative collection of words. See closely the greatness behind it.

Books, videos, crafted collections of sounds, podcasts, interviews, documentaries, biographies. Listening to conversations on the internet of more wise individuals than in your current direct physical ecosystem. Key for the modern day individual to expand their boundaries and their reality beyond what they can possibly imagine they can experience in life. Wisdom will still be in your life, and touch and transform your existence.

Go out into the world and get close to your inspirations. Go to events. See them in person. Go to Q&A's, interviews, openings and live shows. Go to the cities. Go to the neighborhoods and see the beauty of the architecture and design. Show yourself the possibilities of what can be done. Of where your mentality can be at. Of what can life be. Know that higher consciousness is possible. That less suffering, and more happiness, is possible. Introducing yourself to bigger and better things will get you thinking differently. Glimpses into where you want to go will give you the drive to leave the world you are currently in and enter the new one you envision.

A lot of your positive mental input serve as launch pads. They inspire you and push you forward. Get you thinking in that higher frequency. It gives you the juices. The motivation. It helps you understand that reality. It feeds your mind the ingredients to help create this for your own life. It is pushing unto you the new world. As you walk into the new world. It helps you focus and create it. The more you have in your focus of what you want, the more you will exit your old reality and thrust yourself into the new one forming.

...

You do not want to be searching for an ecosystem forever, and trying to curate the perfect ecosystem for you to face your work. Waiting for your ecosystem to be perfect before your pen touches paper, your fingers touch the keyboard, your voice touches the mic, you will never get your work done.

The most important thing you can do is carve out time and physical space for you to work right now, where you are currently at in life. You can create your own little world, in the very ecosystem you are currently in. Wherever you are currently at, learn to bear the discomfort of truly being yourself in the face of judgement, but simultaneously, and more importantly, create a private space for yourself, where being yourself, and working on your craft, is more effortless. Create a space where you feel safe and secure to think freely. Create a space where you can truly be yourself. Create a space where you can focus on what you want to focus on and let inspiration move you in a new direction in life. Move away into a silent space, whether your own home, or your own room in a home. Find a place to be with your work, and work. If you can't get away from noise, wear headphones or earplugs and make it work. Or leave and work somewhere else. Whether in a studio, or in a cafe where nobody knows you or will bother you. In your car, in your backyard, at a park, at a library, or at a supportive friend's house. Follow what feels right. Find where you are able to think at a higher level. This is your energetic home.

Everyone is different. Do what you can with what you have. Give yourself a chance to progress.

Do what you can with what you have, and work in the here and now, but simultaneously keep an eye on your future and create a path where further along in the timeline of your life, 6 months from now, a year from now, 2 years from now, you are in an even better ecosystem that's more aligned with your true self. Whether you must eventually leave your job, change cities, move away from home, or move back into it. Plan on your future and take the steps towards creating that ecosystem for yourself.

But right now, in your current ecosystem, in your private space, in your energetic home, it is you and your work. It is you facing yourself. You facing the universe. You are in the arena where greatness arises.

You may not be with the other individuals and creators you admire right now. But as you let go of what distracts you, you humble yourself and dedicate yourself to the path, and you truly focus on the depth of your work, you are with them energetically. You are all in the same place. Reaching in the same bag. In that deep deep place.

And eventually, you may even attract each other.

Surround yourself with your dreams, no matter where you are, and watch your life become what you dream of.

...

Level up who surrounds you.
Level up your relationships.
Level up your personal boundaries.
Level up the places you frequent.

Mental discipline, passion and focus is key. But a proactively created, higher level environment, is also key. Being inspired, positive and focused will no longer be an uphill battle. It'll be your natural state. Being your true self won't be this weird looked-at behavior that you only allow glimpses to the surface in your social environment because it's judged when it comes out. It'll be your norm.

You are a completely different person when you're in the right ecosystem for you.
You are more yourself.

Life is just...better.

It is naturally healing and regenerative.
It is naturally fueling and inspiring.

It is naturally aligning you to happiness and taking care of yourself.

It is naturally fueling your focus on your purpose.

With a positive ecosystem, you learn faster. Grow faster. Realize important lessons of life, sooner. And you are able to live the rest of your own life, with more richness of awareness, knowledge of navigation, and gratitude for the whole experience.

You live life in the energy you want to live in.

12

Chapter 12: Greatest weapon against the individual

We are too close to the experience of the modern day to see its abnormalities. When in the storm, it's hard to realize the severity of it, when it's all you've known. When you've been born into it and are currently living within it. Aspects of what is considered normal to us and to everyone around us, a hundred years from now, will be seen as abnormal. Our lifestyles are unique to our era, yet it feels so commonplace to us. Because everyone around us is living the same way.

But this way of living is so unique to our generation. So unique to the current inhabitants of the planet and rare for those before us and those that will come after us. And there are aspects of it that are harmful to our physical, emotional, and mental health, that must be left behind. Something is wrong. Depression and anxiety is unfortunately a common state. Many of us are unhappy and unfulfilled. Yet we don't seek to find its origins. And when we do seek, we look around while missing the obvious right under our nose. It is our generation's thinkers' and leaders' role to identify those abnormalities and help individuals to evolve from them. And we must get uncomfortable, face ourselves, and evolve from them. Mankind's future success is birthed from our current day's mistakes and learning from them.

We, the current inhabitants of this planet, are all massively distracted from the truth about mankind and don't see that we are all connected. We are all massively distracted from our crafts. We are distracted from the realization of our own power. We are distracted from our own peace. All of this is disrupted. Our obsession with our own self image and social media. Our succumbing to our soul sucking jobs and acceptance of that reality. Our stuck ways of communicating. Our underdeveloped traits of patience, discipline, and humility. Our addiction to numbing ourselves with drugs, alcohol, porn and entertainment, and avoiding what must be faced. We are distracted and led astray.

You are receiving the energy you are searching for daily, but you disperse it through your distractions. Energy is dropped into your hands daily, and you let it slip through your fingers.

It is time to let this all go. It is time to come back to your path.

...

Evolution is the natural path of the individual. To not progress in your life, you must be proactively resisting your own evolution. To not evolve, you must distract yourself.

The greatest weapon against us, as individuals, is distraction. Right now, most people spend their lives dancing around what truly matters to them instead of attacking it head on. Living in a world of...distractions.

Social media, porn, junk food, casual sex, drugs, video games, streaming services, materialism, self image, unhealthy friendships, and relationships.

The majority of your distractions exist purely through your voluntary participation in them, and would cease to exist the moment you decide it's time for them to cease. The remaining distractions, those that you don't proactively participate in but exist in your ecosystem, exist in your ecosystem through your daily passive approval and lack of personal boundaries, and would cease to exist, or at least influence you less, with the appearance of stronger personal boundaries and your ability to say "no".

In the modern day, the individual that is not aligned with their purpose will be torn into pieces by influences much greater than their purposeless self. Your purposeless self cannot defend itself from distractions by willpower alone. The pull of immediate pleasures is far too great. You must answer your purpose. You must rise. And in this rising, your distractions will drop in strength, and begin to fall by the wayside. Without a sense of purpose to keep you aligned, you will fall prey to that which your particular lower self desires the most.

You in your purposeless state makes the perfect consumer. You having no bigger purpose to focus on, makes you the perfect rag doll. You are ripe. You yearn for stimulation. You are in constant need. Constant want. Never satiated. Always wanting more. You want to feel good. And distractions will help make you "feel good". This is not the path for you.

You must carve out the world you want to live in, through your higher vision, humility, healing, proactivity, discipline, and courage, and move forward.

But first, you must begin to know yourself. You must identify your distractions. You must be honest with yourself. Begin to see how you have been living.

13

Chapter 13: Excuses and rationalizations

Excuses and rationalizations are the masters of all distractions, as they control which distractions enter your life and which ones don't. They will open the door to many distractions, and keep them in your life indefinitely. You must find what bad behaviors you are rationalizing to find what is corrupting your progress. In order to continue to grow, you must identify what is holding you back. And this will get very uncomfortable.

What is disarming you of your greatness?

Drugs? Alcohol? Gambling? Too much video games and social media taking your time and energy?

Or is it more insidious than that?

Are you pushing away your real work, due to a job or school? Pushing away your real work because you think you lack the tools necessary to start? Spending a lot of time studying what you want to do and spending little time actually doing it? Planning, planning, planning, but no doing? Envisioning and dreaming what you want to do, but taking little real action towards it? Or maybe you are putting in effort into that real action, but not nearly as much as you know you're capable of? Do you think you're actually focused, but you're really...not?

Are you staying in a toxic relationship that is keeping you distracted?...spending so much time in your life eating out to restaurants that you don't really want to go to...spending time arguing and constantly drowning in a sea of nonsense that keeps you from working on what really matters? Are you staying at a job that you know drains your time and energy and leaves you empty at the end of the day, but if you made lifestyle adjustments you can take less hours and spend more time on your purpose?

Wake up to your rationalizations. Wake up to your rationalizations, the hard way, as there is no other way. Look at your track record. Look at your own lack of results. Look at your own lack of fulfillment. Feel it. Sense that gap of who you are now and who you know you can be. If you look at your life closely, and you are honest with yourself, you may see that you are, more or less, in the same place as you were 6-18 months ago. Not much has changed. What has historically been stopping you from actually growing and moving forward in your life? What are the reasons you always tell yourself why you can't do what you've been wanting to do?

But do not stop here. Keep looking. Look at what has incapacitated not only you in your own past, but your family and in their past. Your parents and grandparents. What has your genetic lineage been predisposed to do? What unhealthy behaviors are they drawn to, cling to, and rationalize away, that stops them from living the life they truly want? Vanity? Alcoholism? Comfort with their lives? Stubbornness to receive wisdom from others and change their patterns? Lack of dedication to finish anything? Blaming their spouse or their job? What are their own insecurities, neuroses, bad habits, addictions, and toxic cycles? Why were they not able to be the maximum version of themselves? What side path were they steered towards and unknowingly went down?

What about your friends and your hometown? Does everyone get stuck in the mindset of "hustling" at a 9-to-5 job and never further educating themselves on the possibilities in life? Never challenging themselves and venturing out of their hometowns and seeing the world? Spending all of their money on clothes, alcohol, drugs, clubs, and parties on the weekend to keep themselves in a constant loop of having to go back to their jobs to make money again for the same stuff? Spending their free time sitting around in a circle in someone's backyard drinking beers, instead of working on something they are passionate about to get them out of their stuck, repeat-like, lives?

What about your culture? What incapacitates those that look like you, speak like you, and live where you live? Does your family's culture usually tell you to go to school and get a good job, and so those that look like you, end up following a path that's more true to their culture, and not to themselves? Do they have a tendency to blame another demographic of people for the reason why they themselves are not where they want to be at in life? Blaming another political party or another race? What keeps individuals in your culture from truly prospering?

What about the generation that you grew up with, with all of the historical events and technological advances that you share? Those around the same age as you? Are you all stuck in the trance of social media? Are you all envious of those that are famous, and put little attention into your own life and what YOU can possibly do? What has delayed the creation of the life you all wanted? Stuck doing what is immediately gratifying like porn, video games, and the internet, and never developing real patience and hard work? Stuck trying to look cool with your social media photos, fashion, and music taste? Are you focused on more glamorous occupations like being a rapper, model, influencer, or producer, but in reality you have no real passion for it, and so you are kept distracted from what you are truly meant for? What keeps those to your left and those to your right, stuck?

You need to be aware of your programming to break the cycle.

This is how you will grow.

You can break the cycle in your own life and become something great. Become who you are meant to become.

As the latest descendant of your genetic lineage. An individual from your own neighborhood. From your own generation. From your own culture...you can break the cycle. You can break the cycle, and teach and impart healthier cycles in your children's upbringing. You can teach those that come after you, to be introspective, critically thinking, open-minded individuals, that are true to themselves. And when you multiply this behavior across communities and countries, this is what will change the world.

Everything starts with the individual reflecting upon themselves.

Everything starts with YOU looking into your OWN life.

...

Most people are afraid to move into their true selves.

They have excuses for not moving forward and they rationalize the behaviors that keep them stuck.

Immature individuals will always find a reason for their lack of action towards their own greatness. They always find a new current excuse to hold onto.

They LIVE in the moment of holding onto a reason for why they cannot take action. Time may move forward and their reasons may change, but they always find a reason to hold onto as to why they cannot take action. They live in this purgatory space of holding onto some sort of reason as to why they cannot move forward. They make this place, a home.

They make a home of pushing action to a future date. When they have more time off from work is when they will take more action. When they get this degree. When they finally move out. When some sort of external event that they have been waiting for and depending on, finally happens. They push their real work off into "tomorrow" or "next week" or "next month". Not realizing that when they go to sleep, and wake up, it is not "tomorrow", but yet another today. The present moment is all there is. There will only ever be "todays". And if you cannot snap out of this trance, and realize that "today" is all that exists, and begin to take action TODAY, you will never move forward. Waiting and waiting for all of the stars to align, you will be waiting for a lifetime.

Give your true self, room to breathe. Start taking action, NOW. Action breathes life into your true self. You cannot wait for your current world to perfectly align for you to start creating the world you want. You must proactively carve out the world you want and move yourself into it. Aggressively and assertively move into the world you envision. Begin now and start to craft.

The stripping away of the excuses you've used, is painful. You've attached yourself to them. They made you comfortable. But now you are letting your excuses go. And so you are losing yourself. It's scary. But this is your old self. Your old self is dying. Old immaturities are burning away. And this makes room for anew. You are becoming more refined. Actual progress. True wisdom and maturity. True health and wealth. The true you.

A new world.

...

Rationalizations are sneaky and often actually make sense. That's why they're so effective in disabling. Because it doesn't LOOK like disabling. If it was so obvious, you would surely see it and be able to handle it. But what if your mind doesn't want to handle it? What if your mind wants to be lied to?

What is a lie so cunning, that you STILL get disabled AS IF it was an actual mess up, but carried NONE of the responsibility? How powerful a lie! How destructive it would be.

A blatant mess up disables progress....but it's so obvious! It carries TONS of responsibility! So you can see it, label it for the problem that it obviously is, and address it accordingly.

But...this cunning lie? It's EQUALLY as destructive...but carries NO responsibility. So it stays within the system to wreak havoc. Undetected. For weeks, months, years.

These are rationalizations.

It holds both the power of immobilization and the power of disguise.

It's like a traitorous friend. A spy amongst your ranks. A snake within your garden.

It provides the potency of actual setbacks but has zero paper trail leading back to it. Rationalizing the job you are staying at. Rationalizing you not starting yet on your work. Rationalizing your addictions and destructive behaviors. Rationalizing unhealthy friendships and relationships.

It's so important to drill this into your mind.

IF YOU ARE TO BE TAKEN DOWN, YOU WILL BE TAKEN DOWN BY YOUR RATIONALIZATIONS.

The actions you are taking, in order to even take them in the first place, you have constructed a mental framework that finds it okay to take those actions. You've rationalized them. So in your own mind, you think everything is alright. You must look within deeply and have UNCOMFORTABLE introspection. You must have an honest conversation with yourself on who you are being as a person and how you are spending your time.

Develop awareness. Ask close friends and family around you. Ask mentors and individuals you look up to. They may see in you ways you can't see yourself. And ultimately, you must look into your own life. Meditate. Go on walks. Open your mind. Expand your thinking. What sucks up your time? What sucks up your energy? What keeps you distracted from doing what's most important?

...

Throughout your journey, you must maintain the ability of waking up to your excuses and rationalizations, as they may creep through the back door from time to time.

Meditate. Spend time looking at your life. You must be able to have moments of introspection that serve as sobering smacks of reality. To be able to see how you have been allowing life to slip through your fingers. How you have been holding onto triviality. How you have been holding onto behaviors that keep you from moving forward. Allow these moments of realization to humiliate you. Humble you. Teach you.

Awaken to life's finiteness. You will not be here forever. Mature. Do not waste time.

14

Chapter 14: Self image and social media

It's important that when discussing the modern day individual and their weaknesses, that we discuss the distracting nature of the self image and what comes along with it. The desire for attention, validation, love, and admiration from others. And, at a more neurotic level, the desire for relevancy and for fame. Overall, it is a yearning for the acknowledgment that your existence is special. That, you, are special. The seeking of a significant self image.

And because of the commonplace nature of social media, it's important to include it in the discussion, as it plays a vital role in the individual's pursuit of a significant self-image. Social media has become readily available, widely accepted, and a staple of modern day culture. The invention of social media has allowed those that crave this significant self-image, the possibility to now create it. It has allowed those that want to be a somebody, an easy avenue to become a somebody. And those that may have never craved a more significant self image are now constantly shown the idea that a significant self image is what "success is"...and they now find themselves flowing with the current of culture, flowing with the current of everybody else around them, and attempting to do the same.

And now, with the domination of social media, the individual's self image is a far more relevant value than it has ever been in history. The self image now, unfortunately, plays a fundamental role in everyday affairs. It's as if if you go to an event, and it is not shared on social media, then attending the event was next to pointless. It's as if if you went to a beautiful place, and didn't take photos, that you can't help but feel a missed opportunity and a bit let down. It's as if when two people are having a conversation, the two real individuals are absent, and the two individuals speaking are the perceived self-images. It's as if if you are not receiving likes and comments, then who you are and what you do, are irrelevant.

It seems that today, life itself is not enough.

A more significant self image must be had to properly enjoy life.

...

The best way to describe the truly accomplished individual is that they are truly aligned. They did the work within themselves and developed courage, dedication, gratitude, and patience. They've done the work regarding their craft, spending their time and energy studying, learning, practicing, and deeply tapping into their gifts and expanding on them. And they've let go of pleasing other people and trying to impress them. They've let go of the rules society has placed on them. They are aligned. They are focused. They create real works.

And what you see of them now… the admiration they receive from others, their fame and riches, their quality of life, may have been desired by them. But it often wasn't their main aim. They came as byproducts of their successful alignment. It came as a byproduct of the space they now exist in.

Many individuals want this kind of life. They want the respect, love, and attention that truly aligned people receive. They want the quality of life, the lifestyle, and the aesthetic of the truly aligned. It's so attractive. Alluring. Exciting. And its attractiveness has become so intoxicating, that it has now become the main goal in life for many individuals. The goal of nothing other than the achieving of this lifestyle and this aesthetic.

Not refining their own particular craft.
Not honing in on their passion.
Not growing and maturing.
Not adventuring into their own lives and becoming something.
Not creating bodies of work they are proud of.

Just achieving the lifestyle and aesthetic. Period.

You crave the quality of life of someone that is going deep and aligning themselves, but you do not go deep and align your own self. You want to look like the image, and identify with it as closely as possible, but not actually do the work of the image. Wanting to look like a rapper, model, influencer, entrepreneur, or whatever alluring occupation you see, but not do the actual true work of them. Focusing on creating the perception of the life, and little to none of what actually got them there.

And social media is the medium of choice. Social media has become the lowest common denominator for creativity and recognition of uniqueness. Everyone can do it. The lowest form in which any individual who craves to be someone, can immediately begin shaping and curating their image to begin to be that someone. It provides the sense of being a "somebody", in the least effortful, and quickest return, way. It provides a sense of achieving your "dreams", and although superficial and empty in the long run, the feedback given is immediate and provides enough validation to feel as though it is real. The likes are real. The comments are real. The attention is real. But your evolution is not.

Social media has now created a public world stage where individuals now have the opportunity to craft an image of their dreams, present it to the world, and start to receive the attention of "being" that image. Create a celebrity image with none of the work of the celebrity. Go to hangout spots, have the outfits, have the aesthetic, have the styled photos, of a celebrity.

Everybody is a superstar in their own world. And because of our new 21st century ability to receive constant validation through our social media, unless you are open to criticism and growth, you will only become more deluded. Diva behavior has become normalized. Many individuals that use social media are not normal human beings anymore. They are celebrities. With their friends, with family, they behave like celebrities. In public, they carry themselves like celebrities. And even in their own mind, they are celebrities.

You become a professional social media poster. A master of aesthetic. Extremely skilled at portraying an image, but your actual life changing very little. Getting the right photo and right caption for the presentation of self, but ignoring your actual self. Aiming to have the best filters, the sexiest poses, and the perfect balance between the most accepted but still unique captions, that will elicit the most likes, but putting very little of the same effort into actually moving forward in your life. Like a gambler waiting for the jackpot on a slot machine, you post something new, and wait for the likes and comments to roll in.

To someone of true focus and accomplishment, the images crafted on social media have become predictable. They are transparent and easily identifiable. And yet the common individual is sucked into this world. You chase to create your own "unique" image, and receive your own validation, unknowingly wasting your life away. It is too alluring to drop. You're excited to post your new photo, and display to the world something even cooler or sexier about yourself. And you feel like you may be going somewhere in life. But in reality, you are no closer to ACTUALLY BEING who you truly want to be than you were 6 months ago.

You are the same person, with better fashion. Same person, different city.

Same person, more creativity with your captions. Same person, more high quality photos.

You're on a hamster wheel, feeling like your life is going somewhere with your public life, but no real movement forward in your private life.

Your focus is on the wrong thing.

Your addiction to the feel-good chemicals you receive from everything surrounding your self image, is what's stopping you from the very meaningful existence you truly crave. When you are focused on being perceived a certain way, focused on looking cool or sexy, focused on looking special or famous, you are stopping yourself from making any real meaningful progress in your life. This addiction is distracting you.

You are too self-interested to create meaningful work. Or to live a meaningful life. Like a leech, your addiction is sucking you of depth and real uncharted creativity. It's distracting you and keeping you in a loop of chasing ways to display to the world just how cool and sexy and fascinating you and your life is.

While the most accomplished creators and in-tune individuals in this world are creating beautiful pieces of work, living a life true to themselves, and occasionally sharing this to social media, you are the shell version of who they are being. While the individuals that are making real impacts on this planet are focused on learning and expanding and working, you stay on the surface, focused on your image. You may LOOK like you are doing something meaningful, and you may have achieved the APPEARANCE of doing meaningful things, but in reality, you are not. Deep down, you know this.

You don't spend time and energy focused on refining your craft. Studying your skillset. Studying the greats. Reading books. Watching interviews. Practicing. Expanding your comfort zone and trying different things. Practicing more. Refining your craft more. Creating pieces of work and releasing them to the world.

You spend your time and energy refining your image. Taking the perfect photo. Writing the perfect caption. Shopping and searching for the fashion that represents the perfect look. Studying famous people so know how to emulate their behaviors. Watching hours of make up tutorials and workout videos to help you have a more significant appearance. Finding the best filter that creates the celebrity look.

You don't go to the places that inspire you and give you ideas. The museums, studios, parks, stores, live talks, meet ups, performances, and architectural masterpieces.

You seek places that feed this image you are chasing. Parties. Clubs. Fashion stores. Superficial events and functions. Different parts of the city to show your outfit and appearance off. Different locations that would make you look like you have a fascinating life on social media.

You don't meet people and make genuine and exciting connections, where you share ideas, laughs, good times, and are both inspired.

You make connections that are soaking with self-interest. You cannot help but focus on how being seen with them may increase your own status, or how they can help you live a cooler lifestyle, or how they may help you connect with people who will.

Your self image being of priority to you, fundamentally alters the course of your life.

Moment to moment in your day, your behaviors move from doing any real meaningful work and living authentically, to now fulfilling your craving for attention and validation.

You have become a junkie.

This shapes the life you will live. The experiences you have. The people you meet. The relationships you have. What you create and how pure it is. Who you ultimately become.

This path will lead you to a version of yourself that is a shell of what your actual potential is. Your addiction to your image, is creating for you, a shallow existence.

You can feed your image or you can feed your purpose.

Both decisions will move you in different directions.

The people that you see truly accomplished and fulfilled are the people that listened to their calling and followed their purpose.

They FOLLOWED it.

If "purpose" was a north star and "self image" was a north star, which are you following?

…

Right now, the individual lives for attention and relevancy. We don't just seek it…we dedicate our lives and create an entire world to try and get it. It's so insidious, we don't even know it's happening. It's so commonplace, we don't think anything of it.

Even those that claim to be "woke" and "above" all of this. Those that are aware of social media and its effects, will talk about how "fake" it is. Those that have made some progress within their own lives. They have separated themselves from their old self. They've evolved from their high school or college immaturities and have shed their past like old skin. They've grown into their own, found themselves, and now live a life more authentic to them.

But they fall into the same trap.

Just more subtle.
More insidious.
Less easy to detect.
But just as important to identify, in hopes of true growth.

Aspiring musicians, artists, writers, directors, photographers and entrepreneurs. All of these identities come with intoxicating stories to live by, and with it, carry the potential to be steered away from the actual purpose itself. Each thinking that they are "unique", and ironically falling into the same traps as their counterparts. The story of "me", the story of "my journey", and closing off true growth.

This is not an attempt to delegitimize these archetypes and your identification with them if you do identify with them. But instead, this is an attempt to call your awareness to the possible contamination of your actions and their intentions.

How much of your time is spent working on your craft? How much of your life gets split off from this, and goes into reinforcing your own self image, getting attention, and being...unique? How much of your time is focused on your clothing, jewelry, accessories, aesthetic and LOOKING like you do those things? How much time is spent creating the image of you, and not...you? How much time is spent creating the perfect presentation on a social media platform?

Activists of all types fall into the same trap: Feminists, LGBTQ, liberals, conservatives, animal rights, environmentalists. All of these identities again coming with intoxicating stories to live by, and with it, the potential to be steered away from the actual purpose itself. Lost in the story of "me", the story of "what I believe in" and "our movement", and closing off true growth.

Just how much of your life is actually dedicated to equal rights, climate change, poverty and its actual goals? Or whatever it is that you believe in? How much of your time in the day is dedicated to learning, expanding your mind, researching alternative outlooks, seeing the shortcomings of your understanding of the world, refining your perspective, refining your character, gathering more knowledge and more skill, and being a more effective individual in the world?

And how much of your time is spent concerned about the aesthetic, your outfit worn, and the photo opportunities? How much time spent arguing and defending your self-defining beliefs? How much of your time is spent within your own self-validating echo chamber? How much of your time crafting the perfect witty posts and comments on the internet, yet doing very little else to help your cause?

Individuals of all types who have "woken" up, are you focused on the goal itself or a perverse version of it? Are you following your purpose or are you chasing something that rhymes with it?

Where are you on the spectrum?

Completely focused on your purpose or focusing on everything but?

You are somewhere on the spectrum.

Self-diagnose.

Only YOU know deep down if you're wasting your own time.

Relevancy and attention have become the new marks of success in society. And this reality influences your behaviors. Although you may even consciously disregard it from being important to you, relevancy and attention are currently societal values, and this seeps into your unconscious motives.

Whatever your purpose is, it's important that you WAKE UP.

Pay attention.

Pause. And listen. And watch. Look around.

Why do you do what you do? Are you doing it to its fullest? Or are you being steered away from your actual goal to instead satisfy your self image? Chasing attention?

You are human. Be aware. Be vigilant.

Many individuals who have more or less found what they want to do in life, are still hypnotized by the image of themselves as opposed to the actual work they want to create. They over-romanticize their life and try to control and micro manage their image and the story of "me". Obsessed with the story of "me" and telling their "truth". This self-absorbed focus will keep you in a cycle that is hard to create from, grow from, and live a meaningful life from. Taking your life on a detour towards self-indulgence. Your focus is split. You have immaturity that must be shed. Misplaced creativity. Unwise focus. Don't micro manage your image. Don't overthink it. Humble yourself and begin to live truthfully. Put your mind on your work, be a good person, and let everything else unfold.

If you are working on something creative, there's a certain amount of time you need to sit with your work. You need to be with it. In it. In that world. Your self-image will distract you out of it. Your mental preoccupation of others and of their perception of you, is a massive weight dragging you as you try to move forward. With this weight, you can still move forward in life, but only a fraction of your potential. If you wish to do something of great value in this world, quit focusing on your self image. Focus on your craft. Practice. Learn. Expand. When you truly focus on the work, you will then progress.

If you are working on a movement or activism, forget about the identity and beliefs you cling to. Instead of the group you choose to identify with, understand that you are a human first and foremost. Humble yourself. Spend more time learning from different teachers and perspectives. Expand your knowledge and wisdom. Don't waste your time pumping your own echo chamber. Don't waste time defending your own beliefs in social media feeds. You are better than this. Focus your attention on greater things.

No matter who you are and what you do, between your mind and the outside world, take yourself out of the equation as much as possible. Between your creativity and the outside world, ego is what stands between the two, and ego will strip away your work. It will strip your work of depth, of ingenuity, of passion, of true effect, and of real impact.

Take yourself out the middle.

Between your mind and the world, take yourself out of the middle.

You are a vessel. Allow your gifts to flow through you. Tap into them. Harness them. Develop them.

Do not concern yourself of your image. It'll only keep you distracted and your mind divided. You will lose potency in your work and authenticity in your character.

Focus on your work and align with your work. Both you, and your work, will then maintain its authenticity.

Your work cannot be something you are "interested in". It must be something you ARE. It cannot be something you only spend some of your time and energy. But MOST, if not ALL. This world must be fed if there is any hope for it to survive, thrive, and grow. In order to make any real dent in your field, any real dent in culture, it must be your PRIMARY focus.

Take the fast lane into your world.

…

Social media is the single biggest obstacle to success and fulfillment in this current age. It's the most prevalent source of our unhappiness. But it is especially distracting to those that feel lack within themselves and wish to have a higher sense of self, a higher social status, more attention and more validation.

Your day to day life becomes infiltrated. Your mind becomes more fixated and focused on getting a good photo or making a good post. It derails your purpose.

Managing self image is unwisely misplaced creativity. Social media, the medium in which you craft your self image, is unwisely misplaced creativity.

In social media's most optimal form for the individual, it is a tool. To create and inspire. To share ideas. To communicate and create connections. To share positivity, to share moments and to share laughs. And for this, it is great. Revolutionary. A great connector of cultures. A great connector of individuals. Social media can keep you buoyed afloat, with doses of inspiration and positivity when you need it. When you forget about the goodness in the world, it can re-mind you. If you proactively curate a positive ecosystem on social media. If you are conscious about your use on it. But even in its most optimal form, unless you have healed and do not crave highs for your ego as strongly, unless you are more disciplined, more busy with your goals in real life, and remain vigilant of social media's effects, you will get sucked into its negativity.

In social media's most common use, for the average individual, it has hijacked the mind. Its distracting nature has you wrapped around its finger. Whatever image you want to create, it will feed back to you the validation for it. You now have a place where you can receive attention and be validated for your own unique way of feeling better about yourself. Whether it be your physical beauty, your status, your material wealth, your creativity, your intelligence or your woke-ness, you now have found a place that will feed the self image you crafted, and make you feel good about yourself.

Social media has transformed individuals. Like an Achilles heel, the human brain has had one of its weaknesses exploited. The human need for acceptance. Along with this, it also exacerbates your wounds of insecurity and past traumas. Those that were looking for attention and acceptance, now found a bountiful source. Social media has created a very clear route to have significance. To feel like your life means something. You now have a way, an easy way, to receive validation for the idea of who you desire to be.

The damage that social media has inflicted on the average individual is so widespread, that addictive behavior, at least in regards to social media specifically, has been widely accepted in society.

We have normalized behaviors that should have never been normalized.

It isn't normal to wake up and the first thing you do is look at your phone and your social media platforms. It isn't normal to be hanging out with friends, and one of them, or more of them, are staring at their screen watching video clip after video clip. Post after post. Meme after meme. Scrolling. Scrolling. Scrolling. For 20-40 minutes. Or hours. Sometimes throughout the whole day. Every day. Wake up from your own trance and look at your friends. You are witnessing an individual's mind and willpower be hijacked. You are witnessing, in real time, an individual lost in their addiction. Stuck in a trance. Look at their eyes. Lostness. Look at their face. Look at their faces become drone-like. The malaise in their body. The lazy fixture onto their phones. This isn't normal behavior. And this has been normalized.

It isn't normal spending your waking moments searching for photo opportunities. Never experiencing life, but instead seeing everything happening around you as something you can potentially capture and present to the world.

It isn't normal to take dozens of photos of yourself and obsess about them. Keeping your eyes glued to your screen trying to figure out what photo, filter and caption combination will best represent the self-image you are trying to create and what will get the most likes.

It isn't normal to take your phone out at any lull in your day-to-day living. In the bathroom, in the car, in the elevator, walking to class or to work, standing in line, while eating.

It isn't normal to be at work or school during slow hours, on your phones mindlessly looking through social media. As if your life is on hold. Hours and hours of your life that can be used to build you up, instead, used to live in a self-imposed purgatory.

It isn't normal to want to work on something and you can't go 20 minutes without feeling the need to look at your phone.

The thoughts and actions of a junkie. This is the average individual's life. Addict behavior is the new norm.

...

Many men have found the easiest way for them to stand out, have uniqueness, be cooler, and get a chance at more status. They have found the easiest way for themselves to be more like the individuals they admire and want to be like.

Doing harmful things to themselves.

It requires zero intelligence, zero creativity, zero hard work, zero focus, and zero talent. The easiest way for them to feel like they are in the same cool circle as people that they admire is to do these harmful things to themselves. The easiest way for them to identify with greatness is to adopt these habits that some of their idols do. Take prescription pills recreationally. Drink lean. Do cocaine. Drink alcohol. Smoke blunt after blunt. Tote guns and adopt violent vocabulary and behaviors in an environment where it's largely unnecessary.

Listening to hip hop and the lifestyles of those in poverty, that don't know any other way of getting out of it, and glorifying this way of living.

Not seeing the beauty and honor of your own life.
Of your own origins, and your own path.

Just fantasizing others and living a life of pretend. Reciting lines about guns, shooting opps, dealing drugs, doing drugs, heartbreak of murders, of a struggle that is not yours. You've never shot a gun. You don't have opps. You do drugs to be cool. You've never lost a loved one from street violence.

You fantasize and glorify.

You don't seek greater meaning.

As millions of young boys try to escape this world, fighting within their own selves, trying to see a better life, having higher aspirations, moving through their community, trying to avoid bad influences, trying to find good influences, trying to build something of themselves,

you, being bored with the safety that your family has been able to build, in its subsequent mundaneness, seeking thrill, status and coolness, try to enter it.

Or at least dress, talk, and act like you are in it.

Nobody's thinking for themselves. Just copying what they see around them that is currently considered "cool" in culture, in hopes that they too can elevate their own status and lifestyle.

This is a lazy man's way to feeling significant.
It's the behavior that some of our idols participate in.
But this is a small fraction of who they are.
And it's the laziest in which you can move in their direction and be great like them.

Take all of this destructive behavior, transmute this energy, and direct it towards something of true significance.
CREATE SOMETHING.

Put all this energy into creation and accomplishment. Be aggressive in your work, not in the destruction of your own health. There's nothing cool about putting toxins into your body that are killing you. There's nothing cool about acting like you like killing other people and destroying families, or reciting the lines and attempting to embody those that do. Nothing.

Do not distract yourself with drugs and violence and the romantic image that may come along with it. Do not identify yourself with the destructive artist or the melancholic individual that nobody understands. Do not unnecessarily romanticize your life and your journey. These are all insidious forms of fear. The fear of actually facing your self in your totality, and achieving your potential. Actually facing your craft and creating. Intoxicating forms of procrastination. Intoxicating forms of "being somebody". Romantic and dramatic. Ignore them. These are not your final form. These are pit stops in the shedding of your ignorance. Keep going.

...

Many women have stumbled upon the perfect distraction. Mostly because it is so common and easy to replicate. If they sexualize themselves, they will get attention.

Envy from other women.
Lust from men.
Taking advantage of the insecurities of other women, and the lack they feel within themselves, that if these women were given the chance, would turn it off if they could.
Taking advantage of the testosterone-filled primal desires of men, that is so distracting for men, that if they were given the chance, would turn it off if they could.

By taking advantage of these two groups, you have ensured an audience.

Getting showered with praise and attention, not for anything you do, not for anything you created, but simply the body in which you exist in.

Women have the opportunity to be something so much more than their sexuality and their body. And many speak of the frustration of historically being belittled to nothing other than their sexuality and their body. But now, with all opportunity in their hands, given the chance to do whatever they choose, and move above and beyond their sexuality and their body, many still choose sexuality and their body to be their speciality in this world.

Not developing a skillset of worth that will move their family, their community, and the world forward, but developing a skillset around displaying their sexuality and body to the highest quality they can attain. Hyper focusing on their looks and their image, and surrounding all of their life towards it, in hopes to elevate their lifestyle to that of what they see their favorite celebrities do.

Working out for the enhancement of their body. Becoming professionals at painting make up on their faces to cover up what they see as flaws on their skin. Finding the perfect clothes to accentuate their positives and hide what they see as their negatives. Enlarging of the lips, chiseling of the nose, botox injections to reduce facial wrinkles, plastic boobs, silicon butts. Becoming professional photo takers. Finding the best angles and best filters for the best photo of themselves. The best caption to ensure the solidity of their cool, fashionable and sexy image. Adding more and more artificial layers to their self image, to further create grandeur. Their lives revolving around their appearance. Getting high off of this illusion of grandeur. Life becomes a 24/7 photo shoot, and nothing more.

And many women will use the guise of being a woman, and the exploration and liberation of their femininity and sexuality, to deflect any introspection or accountability. They may even use the excuse of us living within a patriarchy as the reasoning for why they must sexualize their bodies to create income for them to help themselves and their family. But this is further deflection of personal responsibility, all in the name to get "yours", but further feeding the status quo.

Instead of applying your mind and nurturing your own special gifts and talents, energy is now being oriented towards grabbing the lowest hanging fruit and calling it success. Misallocation of focus. Minds that can be used for greater things, but instead, found the quickest and easiest way in which they can receive validation and "feel" fulfillment. A wasting away of potential.

And this is en masse.

Millions of women, doing nothing, together. And it almost doesn't matter that millions are doing the same thing. You are getting yours. In your own little world, you receive your validation, you receive your compliments, you are envied and you are offered dates, you are able to travel, you are making more money, you are the celebrity you wished to become.

You are so much more than this.

Why care about your own appearance so much? Your body isn't even yours. It's the body you have been given. To use this temporary existence on this earth, to identify so heavily with something that you are put in, is the ultimate waste of your talents. To focus so much of your energy on the body you have been given to experience life with, instead of fully experiencing life and tapping into your gifts and talents, is a waste of precious creativity and power that the world so desperately needs right now.

This does not mean to demonize beauty. The beauty of humans is one of the aspects of life that makes living worthwhile. Beauty should be celebrated. But know where your time and energy is going and be honest with yourself. Be more than how you look.

If focusing on your image is how you choose to live your one existence on this planet, then this is what you have chosen. But if you feel empty inside, then this is a message being sent to you, that you are meant for more.

...

When individuals begin to achieve more success in their lives, and choose to stunt on social media, they are like hikers climbing up a snowy mountain, that now have reached a plateau and wish to set up camp and show people how high they have gotten. They are nowhere near their own summit, nowhere near actualizing their true potential... but they are higher than all the people that they were once with. And there's a lot of people below them. And they quit their traversing up the mountain, they quit all of their upward momentum, to peel off and climb out to the first plateau to get the opportunity to showcase their success.

Showing that you are at specific restaurants, events, parties, cities or countries. Showing what kind of people you are with. Showing what kind of significant material items you possess...a watch, clothes, makeup, shoes, your physical appearance, jewelry, cars, apartments. Posting constant stories to update people of your impressive whereabouts. Sharing the food you are eating, what places you are at and what you are doing.

Your constant mental occupation to express these things is the very thing that's keeping you at the level you are at, and stopping you from traversing to any higher level of success.

You are not focused on true growth. On being in the moment. On having real conversations. On seeing real opportunities. On more meaningful values.

Your mind is divided. Your attention scattered. With this immature mind, you will see no greater success. You will stay at the plateau you are at. Maybe more clout. Maybe more riches. But your existence, diluted. Work, diluted.

Although the amazing height you reached impresses all of those below you, everyone above you sees your true position on the mountain. True individuals that live by true principles...you don't have them fooled. In fact, it's completely see through. They know where you're at. Because they passed it on their way up to the summit. They know that your mind is divided. Your attention is divided. You're not TRULY focused on any particular craft or skill. You're not TRULY working on something of magnitude. You're not REALLY spending your time like THEY are spending their time. You two are not alike. One is the authentic version. And the other has the APPEARANCE of being authentic but lacks sustenance.

Don't peel off onto a plateau and begin to engage in showcasing your success. Don't peel off the path to TRUE success, to get the opportunity to show everyone your current level of success.

There's nothing wrong with having REAL genuine love and interest for things in your life and wanting to share it with other people. This is one of the funnest aspects of human existence…sharing your own passions with others. But what matters is where it's coming from. Really look within and figure out why you engage in these behaviors. Shed these distracting tendencies. Shed these ego desires. Shed your craving for attention, validation and recognition. Shed your desire to feel superior.

But don't just shed them. Shedding current motivations without having higher motivations, is futile. If you shed your current motivations, and are left with nothing new to motivate you, you will be sucked back into the powerful current of what once was. You will slide back into old habits.

Shed the current tendencies, but then orient your focus to a higher aim. Aim high. This higher aim serves as the armor that protects against the short-term desires and cravings. You can't just simply get rid of these behaviors that you see stopping you from becoming better. Prohibition has proven, in all levels of society, from the country down to the individual, to not work. Purpose, a higher calling, one that engages and stimulates you, is the key to the ridding of addictions to these distractions. This higher aim will give you divine-like clarity and focus. And this clarity and focus will illuminate the actions that you SHOULD be doing. And you can follow that path to higher success.

And as you move upward, you will begin to see the error of your old ways. You will see it in your past versions of yourself and you will see it in others around you. You will see how others are preoccupied with things that LOOK like success, but in and of themselves don't get them any closer to higher success. They are focused on APPEARING successful (being at a new fancy restaurant, hanging out with notable people, attending a fancy event, flying in a plane, being in a new city, owning a specific clothing brand, etc etc)...but they are not focused on ACTUAL success.

Understand that if your focus is in any way split between a plateau and a summit, people that are more successful than you can see this in you from a mile away. You can't fake it. Where you are at is unmistakable. You cannot hide it. Your true colors will always bleed. You can maintain it and try to not show it but it is futile. Do not waste your time trying to appear successful or cool. And don't chase higher and higher ways of appearing successful or cool. Dump it all out of your mind. You are wasting your time. Take your focus and put it towards purity and potency of your work. Towards being a truly good person and connecting with people. Towards higher actualizing of your potential.

Fashion is a good example. You see this with teenagers and young adults. Constantly chasing the cooler and cooler brand. Dressing in a cool brand and realizing that it is not actually cool and that a DIFFERENT brand is actually the "cool" brand. You think this brand is the coolest brand ever, but then realize that all the hype beasts wear it and it's "overplayed" and what is ACTUALLY cool is this OTHER brand. And then you realize yet again that it's played out and the REAL cool thing to wear is this other other brand because that's what all the coolest trending celebrities are wearing. Then you realize the REAL fashionable attire is this other other OTHER brand. It's a never ending cycle.

At the end of the day, you're still the same nobody that is chasing brands of clothing.

No real work created.

No real impact on culture or society.

No real significance.

You have accomplished the APPEARANCE of significance. But no real significance.

You're the same person, but now with cooler clothes, newly adopted cool behaviorisms, and a bigger ego.

No real change. No real growth.

And this is something that people at all levels of success are dealing with. This is not a poor nor rich man's battle. This is not a creative nor an uncreative person's battle. This is a human battle. It's universal.

There's people that were following their purpose, became big and successful, and once the distractions became too powerful, they began to follow their distractions instead. The musical artist that creates an amazing first album, and then their second and third album lacks that specialness that they were able to create with the first.

The higher you rise, the more enticing the distractions are. The popularity, the riches, the feeling of superiority. It's easy to lose yourself in this. So as you rise, you must meet these new levels of success with an equally as risen level of maturity.

As you make more money, you will have more ability to purchase pleasurable short-lived items. As you gain more power, you will have more ability to indulge in your vices. The more successful you become, the more readily-available destructive pleasures become.

Your true colors will be shown. And if you are not happy with who you see, it's time to shed yourself of this false skin and go deeper into the real you. Continue to go deeper, until you reach a depth that is untouchable from external influences.

In order to rise in your life, you must continue to sacrifice. Sacrifice until your life consists of only love, focus and passion. Focus on real impact. Real success. Don't focus on LOOKING like success. Focus on being a GOOD person. Not on being what you think is "cool". Do not split your attention. Focus on purpose. Focus on your craft.

Stay in your lane. Focus. Don't become distracted by others and their own performative dances that cover up the lack of connection to their true selves. If they are falling in pitfalls of copying others, pretending to be something they are not, being caught up with trends, being caught up with daily shallow behaviors, don't allow that to happen to yourself.

Do not follow the crowd.
They are lost, but know how to put on a great show.

...

Obsession with status, coolness, sexiness, and attention is driving this generation into depression, desperation, mental illness and insanity.

The individual is abandoning their real purpose in droves, and spending all of their energy seeking popularity.

Individuals that in their heart and soul, are engineers, chemists, educators, and environmentalists, are now joining the masses of "unique" individuals of fitness gurus, models, rappers, fashion designers, artists and influencers. None of these paths being inherently "bad", but many of these individuals are taking them for the wrong reasons.

It may actually be what calls to you and following these paths would be fruitful for both you and the world, but the majority of the individuals following this path do so not because of a true purposeful calling, but because they are tried and true methods of an increased social status and of attention. They are not listening to their true calling but instead being tricked by a superficial calling: being more significant.

"I want fame, I want a cool lifestyle, I want an aesthetic life that people envy" seems to be the unconscious thought loops of many. Every unique individual chasing the unique portrayal of their own unique life, to achieve...their own uniqueness. And in this pursuit, ironically, being quite ordinary. Replacing true creativity, realness, and rawness and putting in its place another cookie-cutter, self-indulgent individual. Another replica. People are trying so hard to impress others, that they avoid their own gifts, tapping into them, and fully expressing them.

In an attempt to stand out, we've only grown more predictable. In an attempt to be unique, in life's irony, we chase the most common ways of doing so. Everyone is an "artist", a "photographer", a "model", a "designer", a "creative". Everyone has a "cultured taste in music". Everyone has "aesthetic". Everyone is too cool to share and connect with people with less followers than them. Everyone is too cool to give a positive message as it would ruin their edge and mystique. Everyone is too cool to follow what is true to themselves. No great writers, artists, creators, inventors, or innovators. No great thinkers, leaders, statesmen, or philosophers. Just a bunch of people trying to look cool.

What's the difference between you in high school and you as an adult? Often there is little difference. You now operate in a bigger pond but still have the same mentality. Seeking popularity in high school has evolved into seeking fame in the world. Going to parties has evolved into going to clubs, lounges, and exclusive events. The clothing brands you wear has evolved.

Your demeanor and swagger has evolved. The aesthetic presentation of yourself has evolved. But you have not evolved. Your mind has not evolved. No growing maturity. No higher focus in life.

...

Social media and your self image is distracting all of us from doing anything real. Doing any real introspection, having real internal change, harnessing real talents, living a real life, and creating real pieces of work for the world.

The best way to describe this generation is we are all doing nothing, together.

We've left the depths of real life experiences. We've abandoned the present moment and the intimacy and preciousness within it.

Moment to moment, when social media and your self image is so important to you, your thoughts are continuously hijacked by the thoughts of how this very moment can be utilized to present something about you through social media. How this moment can be taken, repackaged, and presented to the world.

In this state of mind, the present moment is no longer sacred. Life is no longer meaningful.

While social media and your self image plays such a significant role in your life, there will always be a level of depth unknown to you. Your line of thought is always interrupted. Your experience of life is always interrupted. A depth of creativity that you will not know. A depth of understanding and wisdom that you will not know. A depth of experiencing life that you will not know. There are constant disruptions that suck you out of this depth.

We must continue the spirit of those that came before us, that pushed the fringes of what's possible. Push the edges of artistic expression. Tap deep into our own crafts. Chart new territory of the 21st century. Have courage. Have dedication. Move into the future.

Staying grounded in real life. Experiencing real life. Being alone with our own thoughts. Away from social media and from the internet. Being with our own imagination. Having real meaningful conversations with members present. Traveling and entering into different pockets of culture to experience more of life that you may not know. Following what inspires you. Learning and widening your knowledge.

Being so intertwined with life, being so engaged with the here and now, that you experience life fully. The way it is meant to. The ups, the downs, the lefts, the rights, of human experience. Focus on beauty and love. Art, music, literature, film, architecture, fashion, technology, people, relationships, nature, and life itself.

Your focus on social media and your self image stifles you and your creative process. Focus on your craft. Give it the attention it needs. Be dedicated, learn, ponder and imagine, create, make mistakes, take risks, grow, be inspired, open minded, learn more, work on your craft, collaborate, have meaningful conversations, refine your craft, create pieces of work and give them to the world, fall flat on your face, don't quit on your self, learn the lessons, refine your craft, become a stronger person, try again, continue to learn, humble yourself, expand your comfort zone, refine your craft, learn from others, listen to those that inspire you, share ideas, speak and spread positivity, focus on your craft more, give more of your work to the world, be supportive, build others up, live in the light of love. Create what is most true to you.

Modern day judgements and opinions mean nothing in the grand picture. Your self image means nothing in the grand scheme of time. History and God will be your ultimate judgement.

Be unconcerned of your image. Let everything surrounding your image fall into its own place.

Fall in love with life, focus on your craft, and be a helpful energy on this Earth.

Do not dilute your artistic life.

Live as close to your work as possible.

15

Chapter 15: Life maintenance

You'll never see the true capabilities of your existence, in the cycle that you keep yourself caught in. The 9-5 lifestyle. Working 5-7 days a week. Money, credit, debt, and bills. Hoping for higher raises, better hours, and higher positions. It's an illusion to think that if you work long enough and hard enough, that eventually you'll just slide out of this cycle and into a better life. This happens for a few select individuals, but it's nowhere near a consistent experience that individuals should rely upon. And it's an illusion to think that you can spend so much of your time and energy working, and simultaneously have the time and energy necessary for the new world you are trying to create.

Every day, working, commuting, cooking, and cleaning. Running errands and taking care of the responsibilities around your home, your family, and your own life. Busy. Tired.

All of this is life maintenance. The maintaining of your life's existence. Survival.

Don't get caught up purely in life maintenance.

Although it plays a crucial role in your life, solely doing this will result in stagnation. 1, 2, 5 years from now, your life will look virtually the same. You will be a bit older, everyone around you will be a bit older, you may be getting paid a bit more, you may have different favorite television series, and a new hobby or two, but your life remains virtually the same.

…

You're busy, yet you didn't do anything that day. You accomplished nothing. You didn't make any real progress towards anything better. No progress towards any higher vision.

You were busy. But did nothing.

How are you to figure out what you want to do in life in between you working, commuting, cooking, cleaning, recharging, and sleeping? How are you to move forward in your life trapped in this constant cycle? When will you have the time? When will you have the energy? How are you to find your purpose and chase it? Will you ever have the time and energy to feed that higher world you envision? Will there ever be a point in your life where you can abandon this vicious cycle of working a job you don't like, and move into that higher world permanently?

Life maintenance is important. You need a safe place to sleep and you need food on your table. But don't focus so much on the maintenance of your life, that you forget about moving forward in your life.

And don't live outside your means. Having a bigger home than you need, buying expensive clothing or expensive gadgets you can do without, and going out to eat or to other events that aren't necessary, will only lock you more into the necessity of working your job. You are only constricting the cycle you are caught in and giving yourself less room to move.

Maintain your life. But spend time moving FORWARD in your life. Read books, watch films and documentaries. Listen to interviews and podcasts. Study what interests you. Learn. Work on your craft. Work on your craft. Work on your craft. Eat healthier, meditate, exercise, and cut out stressors, so you have energy to create this space in the day for yourself, and have your mind operating at its full capacity. Give yourself time and space to actually THINK and FOCUS on a better life. Go on walks and think. Sit down in solitude and think. Your mind is the key to the creation of something better. Your imagination. Your creativity. Your genius. You'll never see your mind's true power caught in this cycle of only maintaining.

Spend time maintaining your current life, not for its own sake, but for you to have the opportunity to spend time on a higher purpose.

Begin to cut out of your life what you don't need. Begin to delegate what can be delegated. Optimize your time. Downgrade your lifestyle. Be smart with your time.

And now, with this new context, with your focus on your vision, whatever is left that you must do, your job, chores, and responsibilities, should be more bearable. After all, now there's a good reason for its existence. It's serving as the foundation for a better life.

And over time, you can begin to carve more and more time. Within this space you created, you may now have found your purpose. Begin to lessen the hours you spend working at your job. Become more wise with how you spend your time.

Eventually, you may get to a point where you feel you are ready to make the jump from your old life to this new one you have been creating. You can quit your job and proactively choose a major downgrade of your lifestyle, to allot yourself more time and energy to focus on your purpose. When you are ready to fully commit, fully commit.

If you're in the position and you have real work on this earth to put in, quit. You may be scared. Don't wait to not be scared. Move forward with it. Downgrade your life, make the sacrifice, and feed what's most important.

A normal job isn't going anywhere. You can always go back. But for now, give it your all. Give yourself a chance.

You leave a life of comfort for a life of adventure. All of the ups and downs. A life fully lived.

Following your dreams.

Quit your job.

You're not leaving to now do nothing.

You're leaving so you can finally do SOMETHING.

Your purpose should be your ultimate focus in your life. Not the maintaining of a life you don't even find fulfilling.

16

Chapter 16: Vices

Vices are not something that you simply remove from the human. Vices are part of the human condition. You don't have to have them. You don't have to go out searching for them. Individuals just seem to have a strong tendency towards having them, and tend to have particular ones for themselves.

Alcohol, pills, junk food, porn, weed, casual sex, video games, gambling, social media.

Things that you "enjoy", but know deep down may not be the greatest for you. It's a relationship within yourself that you have, with what is not the greatest for you...but it gives you something. It makes you feel better. It relaxes you. It does something for you.

Everyone has their own.

It's arguable that you cannot find a human that contends with the world, that is vice-less. It seems that vices are part of the human experience. Throughout history, they've existed in the corner of the human's eye to distract them from their purpose and a more meaningful life, for more immediate pleasurable emotions.

Life is hard. Relationships end. People die. Your surroundings change. Experiences fade into memories. And everyday you get older until you finally arrive at the end of the ride. It's easy to escape sometimes in an alternate state of consciousness where suffering temporarily lessens. Where we can forget. Where we can feel better.

Sometimes, you just feel you need to cope with just being a human on this earth and dealing with everything we must deal with. A cigarette. A drink. Or a stronger drug. Something to help us feel good in the moment.

Your vices have no bearing on whether you are a good person or not. Some of the greatest creators, kindest individuals, and most giving human beings this earth has ever seen, have had relationships with vices. Your relationship with your own vices, are your own personal internal struggle. Whether you were given in this lifetime easier battles or more difficult ones, is no indicator of the goodness of your soul.

The path the individual faces, while they are here on Earth, is a difficult one. One of uncomfortable evolution, letting go, and transformation. One of honesty, humility, and maturity. One of sacrifice, focus and discipline. And vices have always remained in the atmosphere surrounding the individual's day to day life, always there as a choice, ready to give you what you may want. Comfort, coziness, temporary happiness, temporary clarity, quicker creativity, alleviation from boredom.

It relaxes you from all the stresses of your day. It makes you feel good. It makes you happy if only for a moment.

It entertains you. It engages you.

It could be to punish yourself. To self sabotage because of fear. To self sabotage because of guilt. To numb yourself from what you feel you must face.

You can be using your vice to increase your sense of self. It gives you a certain aesthetic you want. What keeps many individuals attached to their vices is the romanticization of their vices. You've seen people you look up to use these vices, and even though they may have used them to maybe numb themselves, for creativity, it was popular at the time and they got hooked on it, or they didn't know any better during that era of history, you use them simply because...they used them. And you look up to them. In the lives of great creators, vices sometimes play a big role. We think that maybe if we do their vice, we will become more like them. Or at least, seem more like them.

You can be using your vice to numb yourself. We all have traumas. Everyone has pain within them. This is the human condition. And many of us hide from facing what is inside. We each have our own ways of distracting ourselves. Some of us drink. Some of us do pills. Some of us escape to video games. But we all try to keep our mind and our emotions busy. Running away from reality. Holding off processing emotions and trauma, like a child holding onto the door walls, refusing to take a bath.

The pain of being in an ecosystem can be so great in itself, that you numb yourself just to maintain some sort of sanity and peace within that ecosystem. You try to cope with being there. You may not inherently be addicted to vices, rather you use them in your current ecosystem to cope.

You may not be a depressed individual at all. But you're depressed in the ecosystem that you're in. The relationship you're in that you know isn't good for you. A job you're stuck at that you don't like. Being in a city that doesn't inspire you at all and has the kind of people, opportunities, and crafts that you like.

You don't understand how detrimental to your health your being in certain situations is. And yet you wake up and participate in it. Every day. You eat to numb yourself. You drink to numb yourself. You distract yourself from where you are, and you don't even realize it.

Given a new setting, you may have entirely new habits, for the reasons for your vices no longer exist.

...

How you want to live your life in relation to your vices, is ultimately up to you.

Is your vice something you enjoy? Are you able to focus on your purpose, live your life in harmony with your community and the planet, but also enjoy your vice?

Life is short. As long as you do not harm anyone, live your life the way you choose to. If your vices are the cause of an earlier death than when you would've died if you hadn't had those vices, understand that this is a trade off you are making. If this is how you choose to live your life, this is how you choose to live your life. Life is short, and regardless of how you choose to live it, whether as healthy and pure as possible, or as reckless as possible, it ultimately ends for everyone.

But before mentally giving yourself the okay to keep vices in your life, you must understand that vices may be taking away from you the quality of life you want, and the level of purpose you want to reach.

While you currently read this, you may have vices in your life right now. And you may not want to depart from them as they do something for you right now. They are not there for no reason.

And you like them being there. You enjoy its benefits.

But you may not be aware that you are engaged in short term treatment, but disrupting your own life. Feeling good, but suppressing your own movements. Suppressing your ideas. Suppressing your clarity and decision making skills and connection to a good future. You do not see the world you create for yourself, because you are accustomed to the lifestyle.

You do not know how more creative and present you can be. You do not know how much more aware and intelligent you can be. You do not know how enjoyable life can be.

You do not know how your life may reconfigure for the better. You do not know how many more people you can reach. You do not know who you can become, what you can create and the potential you may be leaving on the table.

And you most likely do not even know that you do not know.
These are just words you are reading, and you can't fully comprehend what you are missing out on.
It's a realm of existence that is unknown to you.
A realm of existence you may never have experienced.

...

Are your vices limiting your potential?

Does it detract from who you are truly meant to be?

Does it detract from the quality of life you know you want to experience?

Look within. Feel within. Pay attention. Listen to your higher self, and allow that to guide you. Be honest with yourself.

Is your vice taking more than it's giving? You may be sacrificing a higher quality relationship with your life's purpose, but you are so deep into your addiction cycles, you are unable to see it, or too numb to care.

You may be engaging in behaviors that are completely counter to your ascension. Engaging in behaviors that are pressing down on your soul. Your vices may be keeping you mentally dumbed down, emotionally unaware, and spiritually disconnected. And the letting go of your vice will raise you up to a level where you are now face to face with your purpose. With a more meaningful life. With responsibility. With real change.

And this is the very reason why you refuse to let go of your vice.

In fear of your greatness, in fear of living your life, in fear of actually facing meaningful work, you clutch to your vice, hide in a corner, and let time pass.

until your human experience ends.

...

Even as you gain success and happiness, at some point, it may be your vice that is holding you back from reaching the next level of life.

Go through periods of trial and error. See what your life is like with and without your vices.

Living life with your vices is rather easy. But If you are unable to do so without, this points to a higher problem of addiction, and going through an extended period without your vices is of even greater importance than you realize.

You have found something. It needs releasing.

If not to detach yourself from this addiction and regain control of your own life, to see just the kind of quality of life you are potentially missing out on.

In your hiding in your vices, you can be hiding from a greater life.

See what your life is like without alcohol. Without masturbation to porn or casual sex. Without your cigarettes. Without your weed. Without your pills you use recreationally.

See

The quality of your mind and your thinking.

The vitality and energy of your physical body.

The stability of peace and happiness.

The depth of your presence.

The connection to your gifts.

The meaning of your life and what you can do here.

You may be weakening your very own access to your own superpowers.

...

It's our generation's responsibility to break the repeated unhealthy ways of living human beings have been stuck in and elevate in our energy, lifestyle, and focus. We cannot continue these selfish cycles that keep ourselves down. We must process our pain. We must face ourselves.

We must see the fulfilling of our own potential.

Our generation's preoccupation with vices, like scared crew members on a ship in battle that have abandoned their stations to hide in the cabin underneath and pretend that everything is okay, we have abandoned our duty to mankind. We abandon our higher selves. We are scared. We often wonder what's the point of not indulging in our vices. Life is short, life is hard, and your vices make things a little better.

In any other time period, where life on earth didn't hang in the balance, living how you'd like and doing as you please, would largely be okay, granted that you did not impede on others and their livelihood. If you want to abandon your purpose, you could. You may not be happy, and your family, community and mankind may not benefit as greatly from you being who you are, but it's a choice that you could make.

But we do not live in this kind of time period. We live in a time period that needs every individual so desperately. We live in a time period that requires the rising of the individual's mentality.

It's on us to face reality. It's on us as a generation to lead and be on the cutting edge of culture. It's on us to ensure a peaceful, thriving and habitable future. It's on us to begin the transformation and healing of our people. It's on us, so future generations can live in a better place than we did. Mentally, emotionally, physically, spiritually, socially. Our entering into a new era.

It's on you to evolve and be greater, not just for yourself, not just for your community, but for Earth.

We will not be perfect. But we must begin to live a life greater than being a slave to our desire for immediately gratifying emotions.

...

Our generation is hurting. We are going through so much. There is so much weight on us. We are overwhelmed. And we don't know what to do.

The destruction of our planet, injustices around the world, homelessness, the degradation of our streets and cities. Our own pain and suffering in our own lives and our inability to afford a decent life. Working all the time just to pay for food and a place to sleep. Lost in what to do in life. Life for our generation feels hopeless.

You can see it in social media posts. You can see it in the statistics for drug use, alcohol use, depression and anxiety. You can see it in the video dairies of individuals talking about their struggles with their mental health. You can see it the pain in the homeless individuals on your streets. You can see it in your family and friends. Listen to our culture's music. The pain of our generation has been immortalized. The constant drug use, the fear, the heartache, the suffering.

We want to DO. Something within us so deep wants things to change so desperately. In our own lives. In the lives of our friends and families. In the world. But we run away from our purpose, and try to cope with everything that surrounds us. Try to cope with where we are in our lives and being stuck working a job we don't like. Try to cope with what our generation is going through. Try to cope with how messed up everything is. Hopeless. We just want to feel good and push everything else away.

The individual's addiction to television shows, social media, movies, and video games serve as a replacement for the true engagement with life. Escaping to artificial worlds for entertainment and stimulation. Not engaging with life...but this tends to fill the void. And not in a good way. But good enough. Playing video games and playing the character that faces their own journey, has an adventure, and lives their truth in the face of obstacles, because you are afraid to face your fears in your own life. Watching movies and seeing the heroes live their truth. Scrolling obsessively on social media, seeing others live their truth. Afraid to face your own.

The individual's addiction to masturbation and to porn. The excessive releasing of your sexual energy to feel good. A consolation prize for a life you don't like living. An incredible feeling. A repeated emotional escape, but extinguishing your passion for life. Releasing creative energy that creates life forms, and that, if harnessed within yourself, can create works and worlds, but giving it up, to feel a little bit better in the moment.

Casual sex working very similarly. An immature using of your sexual energy, but can be more easily rationalized. Masturbation to porn can feel very obviously like a giving up. But casual sex can be seen by men as conquest and impressive, and by women as liberation and freedom. But both still distracting themselves. A letting go of their power. Changing your personality, changing your day to day behaviors, to be attractive, and to get the opportunity for casual sex. Spending such a large portion of yourself on dating apps, shallow conversation, beautifying yourself, and chasing sex, validation, and empty meaning. Away from your work.

Casual orgasm itself, whether through masturbation or sex, seems that it empties you out. You become a shell of yourself, lacking the confidence, creativity and passion that would be possible if you cleared your sexual distractions and focused yourself. And if you are doing this repeatedly throughout the week, you are in a perpetual state of being a lesser version of yourself, and may not even be aware of a higher state you are missing out on.

The individual's addiction to alcohol and other drugs. Attempting to completely banish all negative emotions they are experiencing, and continuing to run away from what they must face. Smoking weed to forget about how much of a mess their life is, and how much they don't like where they currently are at.

The individual's addiction to junk food. Attempting to fill their life up with whatever good emotions junk food will give them. Even though it is only temporary, and they will feel bad afterwards, this is nothing more junk food tomorrow can't fix.

...

As we take steps into the future, as our technology advances, as our understanding of humans increases, our ability to create distractions that are more intoxicating, addictive, and pleasurable, will only increase. The quality and the availability will only increase.

Virtual reality porn. Virtual reality video games. Better graphics in movies and television. More and more choices of entertainment. More addictive pulls to social media. Better junk food. More available drugs.

And so this is a calling for the individual to mature. To focus their lives on what truly matters. To focus on their craft. To move into their own power at an even higher level. To live a better life and commit to this better life.

But when we have no mission, when we have no craft we are passionate about, when we have no higher purpose, when we have nobody to fight for, we give up and please ourselves.

…

Many individuals are bored. Going to school, working a job you don't like, and doing the same thing, every day, knowing that there is more in life that you want to do. You may feel like you have a purpose, and that there's real work for you to do. But if you avoid it, tension and stress will slowly build up inside you, due to you being so far off course of the life you are meant to live. The absence of a purposeful and engaging life, is the presence of boredom, frustration, anxiety, depression. And with the presence of these negative feelings, vices soon follow.

Many people are trapped in cycles of coping, and at any moment, can choose something greater for themselves and break the cycle, but they repeatedly choose what is within this cycle. They aren't happy with where they are in life, they aren't happy with who they are, and choose vices to numb the pain and temporarily feel better. But the very thing that they chose to feel better, only does so momentarily, and then soon after puts them in a lower place than they were before. And the next day, to cope with the person that they are being, to cope with being deeper in the hole, they choose the vice yet again to make them feel better. But again, it's only momentarily. And the cycle continues. Trapped in cycles of coping.

You can escape it. You can escape this entire life, and this entire path and reorient yourself to what is true, at any moment. But often, it takes the individual to be ready. You must be ready to leave your old life.

...

You know you are entering a new level when the old level becomes increasingly intolerable. You shed that level of your life. You shed the dead skin and you get closer to truth. Closer to who you really are.

If willpower is the only thing propping you up and separating yourself between you trying to live a positive life and your vices, you will eventually fall. Willpower is a powerful force in mankind, but it is finite. And it gets depleted. And all it takes is the perfect storm of suffering and you will relapse. Do not see your life as a constant attempt at trying to refuse vice's temptations. Trying so hard to not drink, to do drugs, to watch porn, to eat junk food. You will be busy all your life.

What will bring you out of these cycles of monotony and coping with your vices is healing, restructuring our lives, and moving forward.

Purpose.
Vision and focus.
Discipline and diligence.
Love and support.
Inspiration and calling.
Strength.

We must change how we see ourselves and stop expecting ourselves to be perfect. We must understand our own humanness.

We must have the strength to endure the pain of detaching from our old cycles, our old selves.

We must heal, cry, understand, and let go, so there is less need to numb ourselves.

We must remove ourselves from ecosystems that perpetuate our use of vices.

We must begin to not demonize our need for happiness and pleasure, and find healthy sources of them, so vices begin to release the power they have.

We must fill our lives with what inspires us and what we love. The people, the hobbies, the arts, the atmospheres.

And we must follow our purpose, so we begin to have an adventure to focus on, instead of the cheap immediate stimulation vices provides.

A cocktail of these experiences, all working in tandem, gets you out of your stuck-ness.

It's on you to evolve.
Move into your greatness.

…

Get rid of your consciousness altering vices so you can feel what you need to feel. Get rid of your alcohol, your pills, your casual sex, your porn, your junk food.

Stop holding yourself back.
Stop trying to hold onto your old life.
Stop avoiding the process.
Stop resisting your evolution.

You must face reality.
Allow your mind to be running on all cylinders, your body with vitality, and your spirit full of love.

Treat your mind, body and spirit with care.

Awaken! A sober soul lives with God.

There's relationships you need to be truly awake for, so you can see what you can do to make things better. You must be awake for the opportunities in your life. You must be awake to meet your purpose at its highest level.

...

Discipline yourself and endure the weeks of withdrawals. Endure the transition. The weeks of no longer having your coping tools that keep your emotional and mental wellbeing falsely propped up. Allow your pain to come out and surface. Process what has remained unprocessed within you. Allow your connection to God to strengthen. You need to feel what you need to feel in its totality.

You are healing.

Begin to face reality.

Have the strength to endure the pain of detaching from your old life. You're stepping out of the cycle of subpar living you have been caught in.

You are no longer actively distracting yourself from what God is trying to show you. You are no longer distracting yourself from your potential.
You are waking up to your presence on this Earth.
You are entering the continuation of your evolution.

...

Move forward.

Trying to not drink, masturbate, do drugs, or overeat, whilst sitting in your room and doing nothing, will make it next to impossible to succeed.

Leaving blank slots in your life where your vices once were, will only give rise to boredom. Replace this new time and space with adventure into your new life. You will begin to reorganize your existence into the higher version of you.

Find what moves you, and allow this to consume you. Your purpose will not only move you forward in your life, but simultaneously stabilize your life. Whilst you are focused, your life is given higher meaning. And higher meaning is healing to the human experience. It pours over the individual and soothes.

And continuously show back up after every failure and setback. Consistently showing up, and dedicating yourself to your path, chips away at your weaknesses, and builds focus.

Soon, your purpose will be the primary focus that your mind settles in. Soon, choices that are better for your life, choices that were once "forced decisions" that took willpower and discipline to do, will become choices you naturally make by default. Over time, these decisions will become more effortless and part of your character.

Having an adventurous focus and desiring a higher quality of living, begins the process of vices becoming powerless around you. Your vision becomes your new intoxication.

You begin to need willpower less and less to stay away from vices. You just naturally desire your vices less. You begin to realize that these vices are ultimately not part of the life you want. They are holding you back from living the life you want.

...

Become aware of the energy you want to live your life in.
And become aware of what drains your connection to this.

Some vices, when you do them, or do them in excess, you lose your ability to access your energetic sweet spot momentarily. For days, maybe weeks. And if you've made a habit of frequent participation with your vices, you may have never seen or felt your energetic sweet spot. Your potential. Always living life outside of your sweet spot. Missing the real depth you are able to access.

You can be living a life outside of the sweet spot, and never living in it...and never even know it.

Always on social media, caught in cycles of chasing a higher self image and validation. Always masturbating to porn, caught in cycles of exhaustion and depression. Always taking pills, caught in cycles of numbing and dumbing down. Always drinking alcohol, caught in cycles of recovery and refocusing.

Never allowing the momentum in your life to build. Never spending real time with what sparks your true curiosity and exploring life. Never allowing long periods of time in the depth of life, with deeper perspectives, thoughts and ideas. Never truly being with your own gifts.

You lack evolution.

Because of your lifestyle choices, you are never seeing the true gifts you may have. Maybe seeing glimpses, but so inconsistently.

You must begin to know how your energy is affected, and curate your life to where the sweet spot, becomes your home.

Become aware of the energy you want to live your life in.

And become aware of what drains your connection to this.

...

You may have needed to briefly live a life of imbalanced preoccupation with vices. One that was focused on pleasuring yourself. You needed to experience the unproductive-ness. The lack of richness and meaning in your life. The lack of fruit that you produce. The lack of what you can share with others. The lack of fulfillment.

You may have needed this. For now you are aware of how powerful the decisions you make are. And you can appreciate the good decisions you are making. You can appreciate the good things in your life.

You can appreciate the difficulty of facing your life without your vices, instead of giving up when it sometimes gets difficult. And it will get difficult. But you appreciate your sobriety and clear-mindedness. You appreciate the relationship you have with life, more than anything else.

From this place, and your awareness of you being in this place, wisdom arises.

You are finally identifying the repetitive nature of your life right now. And you are done repeating this.

You are realizing that the vices that numb the pain of what you go through everyday, are the very thing that numbs your ability to face your life and truly change your circumstances. With a numbing of your pain, comes the extinguishing of your power. You are done going backwards.

You begin to realize that the alcohol you drank, the pills you took, the weed you smoked, was something you used to numb yourself from the fact that you are not happy with where you are in life. You messed up. And until you stopped, did you now realize this.

You are clearing out the garbage that buried your soul. You are becoming more aligned with your purpose. You are growing in focus and strength. You are awakening to the god in you. You are claiming your seat of power and responsibility on Earth that so desperately awaits you.

…

Wake up and begin to choose your life. Begin to choose your purpose. Begin to choose the true adventure into your life. The true adventure of being on Earth.

Until you develop a consistent pattern of showing up to your purpose, and living your life purposely, and choosing to live more in this world than the distractions that pull you out of it, and doing this day after day, will you begin to live in your energetic sweet spot.

You must choose your purpose, day after day, to go deeper and deeper into this deeper quality of life.

Start to create positive drops and be kind to your future self. And eventually, your present self will start to experience the ripples of past positive drops. Then, every morning you will be waking up in the midst of past positive ripples and be more inspired to create more positive drops. This is the power of momentum and consistency. This is the power of developing true self esteem and trust. Creating a track record of being someone you love and someone you can depend on.

You are living in the energy you want to live in.

Even though it may be difficult at times, and you may be tempted at times, this is the direction where your new life is. And it gets better over time. Rationalizations will attempt to bring you back to your vices. But the more you don't cave in to them, the stronger you get. Your vices are not in control of your life. You are. And every day you practice mastery over self and do not cave in, is the growing mastery over your own self. A mental and spiritual freedom that cannot be experienced otherwise.

Master your energy. Protect your energy.

The daily feeling. The vision. The thoughts. The ideas. Your sweet spot of life. Excitement. Passion. Every day feels like a Friday. You are free on this planet. Creating the work you want to create. Enjoying your hobbies, developing your craft. Exploring the world. Having good relationships.

Remember your greatest energy, your favorite ideas, your most exciting story. The music that inspires you, the films that inspires you. Live in this energy. Discard what dilutes this energy.

Moment to moment deepen this energy.

Navigate this time here on earth in a way that you are in love with and engaged with.

Adventurers.

...

Begin to surround yourself with what really inspires you.

Over time, you will find yourself having healthier relationships with vices.

Some vices you may still enjoy, but you eventually no longer have a strong enough desire to use them, for what the vice does for you is not worth the level of disruption it would cause in your life. You enjoy the trajectory you are on more than the vice. You enjoy your life the way it is, more than the vice. And so you want your life to be good, rather than take whatever the vice would have given you. You can see a drink, and know that you may enjoy it, but not need it. You can be on the internet, and know that porn is there to type in and search up, and it would feel very good, but not need it. But this is largely because you are living a life that is worth living. You are excited for your life. You are on your purpose. You are passionate for what you do. You love the people around you. You are enjoying life on earth.

Some vices you lose your desire for them completely for you don't even enjoy their effects anymore. Like an old friendship, a job you worked at, or a city you lived in, these vices were with you for a period in your life, but eventually you parted ways. You transcended the desire for them. You leveled up and left the vices behind.

Some vices, you enjoy in moderation. Within your new life of committing to something greater, for some individuals, moderation with your vices is key. You have a weekly moment where you indulge in the junk food you crave. You allow yourself to occasionally look at sexual images, be inspired by the beauty. You are having dinner with people you care about, and would like to share a glass of wine with them. Temporary pressure relief valves in your life, as opposed to the complete elimination and unnecessary stress that may cause, keeps you focused. And makes you happy. Your time on this planet is limited anyway. As long as you are hurting no one in the process, give yourself the space to live the life you want to live. Do what you love to do. This is a large chunk of what makes life worth living. This does not make you any less of a good person. This makes you human.

...

But other vices, you may never really "beat" in this lifetime. You can't have moderation with them. A healthy relationship with them is not possible. Any form of moderation always finds its way to eventually becoming…"moderation". Slowly but surely, there is an imbalance in your lifestyle. The deterioration of your emotional, mental, and physical state. The disruption of your relationship with your purpose. You become someone you don't want to be. And you can't help but notice it happens over and over and over again. You can't seem to shake it. You can't seem to just do it once in a while.

Just one drink. Just one pill. Just one time looking at porn. Just one time having casual sex.

As that once becomes twice. And twice becomes three times. And soon becomes a vicious cycle you find yourself being tumbled around in. Any involvement with them breathes life into it, and it finds itself in your life. And what came back into your life so easily, may not leave so easily.

It causes a lot more harm than good. You desire them. You can't help it. But you know it isn't good for you. And you don't want to live a life constantly disrupted, regardless of how much you may desire them.

So you must commit your life to something greater than your vices. A daily commitment.

You must leave the ecosystem in which your vice calls you so much. Where you are bored and want to do it. Where everyone around you is doing it. Where you yourself are suffering so much there, that you feel the need to do it just to cope. If you must, leave the city, state, or country. Develop relationships in your life that you want to be better for, so your vices begin to dissipate in their importance. Have a purpose that means something to you, so the vices that you know would only distract you, begin to dissipate in their importance.

Curate a better world for yourself and live here. Where your purpose, good friends, beautiful landscape, passions and hobbies, healthy ways of transmuting stress, and everything that is good in life is close by, and your vices are further away at bay. In this existence, it's easier to be healthier. To be happier. To be more focused and productive. To expand and learn more. You live such a different lifestyle, these vices are energetically far off in the distance.

You vibrate in a different frequency.
And within this frequency, you can live in peace.

...

Be kind to yourself. Practice your focus every day. Tend to your garden.

Ultimately you are after vices, because you want to feel good.

If you eliminate vices that aided in your relief of stress, If you eliminate vices that added to your "joy of life", and you add nothing that relieves your stress or adds to your joy in life, this is a recipe for an inevitable relapsing into past vices. Your vices may be helping you sleep, lessen your anxiety, relax you. And to rid yourself of what eased your stress, and to leave this blank, is to bear too much weight.

You are only human. Everyone requires relief from the stresses of life.

The absence of healthy stress-relieving and emotionally-stabilizing activities, like exercise, meditation, going out into nature, spending quality time with loved ones, time with your passions, fun hobbies and games, playing, leads to you finding the relief of stress and the boosting of your emotions in other things. Often what will come more effortlessly, easily and readily available around you. Often back to your vices. Since this is what you have used in the past. The overconsumption of your vices is the self-neglected individual's route to happiness. And ironically, it doesn't even work.

Vices are an easy way to feel good right now.

Alcohol, drugs, porn, overeating.
You will want relief from stress. And you will get it. Some-how. Someway.

Do it proactively. Create a world for yourself where you take care of yourself.

With a bit of willpower, with discipline, with a higher pur-pose in life, with a supportive ecosystem, with balance, and with faith in yourself and the path, you can consistently choose the things that feel good but take more effort to unlock.

It's easier to drink, or do drugs, or watch porn, or eat junk food, or have casual sex, or post something on social media, to feel good. But you feel good, and get nothing else in return. You only make it harder for yourself for when you are in the same position again, to choose what's better for you. And the individual that continually chooses what's easy, stays in place. Like slipping down a muddy hill, you will not escape.

Choose what takes more effort to receive your good feelings. Choose what may not be so immediately pleasurable, but ultimately feels good. A subtle, at peace, satisfying, good.

Instead of a frenetic, junkie-like, eventually wanting more, good.

This is maturity. This is evolution. This is what unlocks a depth of life. This is what unlocks a deeper relationship with your craft.

...

Do not forget the joys of life. You will miss the point of life entirely.

Do not ban every activity that has nothing to do with your purpose. Do not create prohibition around activities whose only reason is your enjoyment. This will create a more rigid, stressed you that, ironically, may be less productive than if you still had some activities you enjoyed and relaxed you.

Don't demonize everything that feels good. Don't demonize your need for relaxation, as you are demonizing your humanness.

Feeling good and enjoying activities, adds to your enjoyment of life. It makes you happy, more easygoing, more lighthearted, more relaxed and fresh. Activities that have no other purpose other than enjoyment, has one of the ultimate purposes in life. Enjoyment.

Ensure you are focused and your life is purposeful. But do not martyr yourself unnecessarily.

...

Maybe we are meant to live life as our imperfect selves, and navigate our time here with the best of our abilities, work on our craft, and enjoy our time here, until it is time to move on.

Vices or not, the world awaits your acknowledgment of the god within you.

17

Chapter 17: Procrastination

Pay attention to the decisions you make. You are either moving towards your vision, or you are living a life in which your vision is still an idea in your mind. An idea in your mind that will be acted upon at a "future date".

You are either making decisions in which you are actualizing your vision in this reality, or you are making decisions that perpetuate the reality that your vision is still an idea.

Do not lie to yourself. Do not allow the present moment to be filled with you pushing away your Truth. Pay attention to your mentality.

...

A procrastinating individual is one that has a vision of what one can do, of what one can be, but is choosing to stay in place instead.

They are misaligned. Their mind, body, and spirit are not aligned.

Procrastination births suffering in many different forms. Setting in motion the act of not doing what is most important to you, you are setting in motion a ripple effect of suffering. Another day passes by that you are not who you want to be. Another day passes by that you put off the very things in the present moment that can start moving your life in that direction. You stagnate. Cortisol and adrenaline pumps in your body. Your muscles tense. You're more agitated. Your physical body, your appearance, your relationships, your peace of mind, your happiness, everything begins to get negatively affected. And to save yourself, instead of doing the work that must be done, you chase after vices and other distractions. You are sitting in your own mess, and trying to cope with that fact.

The horrible feeling of procrastination seems that, because you're not getting moving and getting going, is the individual's way of unconsciously aggravating itself so you *can* get going. And if you don't move forward, as you sit in your own procrastination day after day, you create more and more suffering in the spot in which you stagnate. The Universe has built within the individual a way to ensure we move forward.

You know you have something you need to work on, and in the 21st century, it's so hard for us to get going. We're so...comfortable. It's so hard to get the ball rolling and to do what we need to do because we're just so comfortable. We're very, very, very comfortable. Our lives are set. It may not be that great, but it's not that bad. We got good things going for us. And to voluntarily knock ourselves out of this comfort, risk what we have going for us, and to start actually doing, takes a lot of motivation. Takes a lot of SOMETHING to get going.

When you look externally. When you look at your family. When those you love struggle with addiction. When your family struggles with money. When family members and friends die. When you look at your community and its problems. The homelessness, the crumbling infrastructure, the monotony of life for most individuals. When you look at your city, state, and country. When you look at the world. When you look at these problems, and you put a spotlight on these things, you study it, you look at the pain and suffering that's occurring, and you really, really take it in…gears start moving. Perspectives start to rearrange and gears start moving. And you begin to change. And it becomes increasingly more difficult to squander your time and be the version of your self that is the most basic form. Your sense of urgency increases. Your sense of meaning and purpose increases. You can no longer tolerate your own self loathing and laziness. You grow impatient with your own small immature desires. You can be contributing something positive to this world.

And now you are undergoing the evolution of becoming the version of yourself that will.

…

In the space between you and your purpose…once your purpose is known… this is the territory you must chart.

This is where you must work.

In the absence of effort, all the negative and undesirable in life will have their volume increased. Because you are disconnected from your purpose, disconnected from your meaning, you are disconnected from life.

Floating… stagnating…in the ocean of life.

Don't search to get put on.
Stop searching for more inspiration.
Stop trying to create the perfect routine.
Quit waiting until you have the right tools.
Quit waiting for a better time.
Face your work.
You will continue to live the same life.
Your days will look the same.
Living in the same spot of ideas remaining ideas.
You continuing to live the same reality, procrastinating.
You have to take action on your ideas. You must WORK. Live in the messiness. This is where progress is made.

GO and DO.

You will receive the exact information you are looking for. What you continue to emotionally search for, is hidden behind the work you are avoiding.

...

You're in a small world. Small habitual cycles.

Identify the repetitive cycles you are caught in that you continue to participate in.

Are you continuously trying to "save" people that don't want your help? That don't even want to help themselves?

Do you go in relationships, having someone else to engage all of your time and energy, to feel like you're doing something in your life?

Do you spend a lot of time "gathering ideas and inspiration", but not a lot of action?

Are you in school because you have a vision of how the degree you earn here plays an essential role? Does your schooling act as a stepping stone toward where you want to go? Or are you in school because, momentarily in your life, everything feels under control and predictable. School has set expectations and you are familiar with how it works and you feel safe in this environment. You "feel" like you are moving forward, but in reality, you are pushing away life for 4 more years.

...

Your passion, your purpose, the thing that you want to do and keep thinking about but are avoiding. That is where life is now. That is where you will find a proliferation of energy, enthusiasm, focus, and passion.

You will not find life in your old life. Happiness. Fulfillment. Satisfaction.
None of these things can be found there anymore.

These higher qualities of living are in the activities you must do. They lay in the behaviors of the you you know you are supposed to be.

You will continue to suffer and feel empty until you move forward and begin to do that which will bring life out of you.

Go, do.

18

Chapter 18: Self development

Self development is a level up from where most individuals come from. You went from not thinking about your life at all, and letting your life slide right by, to turning your attention onto everything regarding your life and how you have been living. With the awakening of your consciousness, you have given birth to a powerful spotlight and you now shine a light on all of your actions, behaviors, and thoughts. And this allows you to navigate your life with more power than you ever have before.

But beware of getting distracted from your path.

What began as a tool for life, for many individuals, self development becomes a place where you mentally camp and make a home. It's no longer a tool to help build their life, rather now, it often replaces life. It's a way of thinking that stays stuck in between you and the experience of life itself. It gets in between the intimate connection of your human experience. You get stuck in managing your life instead of living it.

In your new lifestyle of self development, you are always searching for, and expecting, perfection. Obsessed with the perfect routine, perfect habits, perfect diet, perfect body. Chasing this and trying to get everything done in the most ideal fashion. You are so overly concerned with doing everything right, that your purpose lays there, abandoned. The richer experiences of life, abandoned.

When you are so invested in getting all of these aspects of your life perfect, life passes you by.

Forcing yourself to read books you have little genuine interest in for the sake of "knowledge". Eating healthy foods you don't like for the sake of "health". Doing activities that don't engage your spirit, for the sake of the "optimization of self". And punishing yourself when you cannot do these things, things that you do not even enjoy, consistently. All in the name of "self development".

...

Beware of higher forms of procrastination. Reading book after book, listening to podcast after podcast, watching videos nonstop, trying to gain a bit more information. These ways of procrastinating are more easy to rationalize as what you are doing has some merit to it. After all, you ARE learning something. And this makes it harder to identify within yourself than the more obvious reckless forms of procrastination, that you are wasting your time.

Earlier on in your journey, doing these activities was a step forward in how you used your time. As opposed to consuming entertainment that serves little purpose other than entertainment, you are now learning. But at some point, it now becomes procrastination.

You are still putting off what's most important.

Watching informative videos may teach you something, but is it the most important thing you can be doing right now? It's heading in somewhat the right direction...somewhat the right general area... but it's not precisely manifesting what you are looking for. Just how much self development content must you consume before you elevate your life and begin to live the life you continue to think about?

Keep a watchful eye on your avoidance of your purpose.

...

You are not in servitude to self development. You can't read all the books, master all the hobbies, and do every healthy habit.

So you must focus on what calls to you the most, and understand that making the decision is inherently sacrificing others. There's a lot that you can do in this life. But you can't do it all.

You must decide. You must live your life proactively and move forward with purpose.

In a way, you are scared of life. Scared to live your life and embrace the fact that you are not here forever. Scared to accept that you are a human and you have flaws, and you will live your life, from the beginning to the end, with your flawed humanness.

For many individuals, the developing of oneself transforms into an obsession of control. Disguised anxiety of death. Trying to run from the inevitable. Trying to figure out what are the routines and habits to get the MOST out of life. Trying to figure out what are the best foods and exercises for the most longevity of life. Trying to figure out the perfect schedule to get the most out of their purpose. All the while, they avoid life. They become managers of life. Not experiencers of life. Afraid of the finiteness of life, and in this fear they try to control, but end up missing the whole point of life itself. It's to live it.

Busy trying to perfect a life that will inevitably end, regardless of what you do. You cannot avoid the inevitable. You cannot hide from the inevitable. You cannot prolong your life and defeat the inevitable. The inevitable, is inevitable. Death will come for you.

So live life in the moment. Live life right now.

Don't waste your time optimizing everything to 100%, when you can get it to a good level and move on with your life. Ironically trying to get everything to 100% perfection, will make you more unhappy than people that forget about it. You will be more stressed than people that forget about it. You will be less productive than people that forget about it. But you are stuck in the trance of optimizing your life.

You can't focus on your inner world forever.
This defeats the purpose of playing the game.
Focus on playing the game.

...

And more than anything, don't judge yourself. The majority of people in self development cannot move forward due to an inability to create momentum and flow in their life. Because of constant self-judgement, constant self-criticism, and constant obsession with what is "best" and what they "should" do, they are never able to be in the flow of life and live. This introspection and desire to change one's unhealthy behaviors and to better oneself, started with good intentions. But as time goes on, this constant introspection and self-criticism becomes a way of living and a way of being. They have habitualized and normalized self-judgement. These are the new predominant thought patterns. Constant comparison to an ideal, perfect version of themselves. And this causes them to unknowingly reject the stream of life.

And in this stream, is where many of your gifts are found.

...

Comparing your daily actions to an ideal version of how things can be, helps regulate your behavior and ensures that you don't waiver too far from your own values and goals. A small amount of this is healthy. But the obsession of self development creates extreme amounts.

Causing constant burn out, relapsing, and unhappiness. But acting as if they are happy. They are grinding in life. And life becomes just that. A grind. No fluidity. Only difficulty.

In this grind, you are unable to get in the groove of things. Unable to truly immerse yourself in your work, in your life, and enjoy it. When you're living so rigidly, and living so according to what you THINK is what you should be doing, you neglect the process of your actual soul. This is where the magic is. This is where the greatest creators live.

Wise words, diets, regimens, schedules, recommended habits. Cold showers, yoga, running, lifting, lemon water, avoiding social media, gratitude journal.

All these things are IDEAS. They serve as ideas for you to TRY. Do not attach yourself to any particular habit. This is neglecting your soul's own true process.

Obsessing over these habits is the very act that is taking you out of your actual true power. You are distracting your SELF.

…

There comes a point in developing yourself, where you must begin to filter the advice of the millions of voices from self-development on "how to be", with your own, now growing, wisdom.

You must begin to listen to your soul. Listen to what feels right for you.

And when you listen to others, you do so proactively. You listen to the wisdom of others as you go along *your own path.* It doesn't consume you. Rather you are focused on your purpose, and living your own life, and the momentary breaks to listen to wisdom from others helps your own progress.

It's a choice you make within your day to listen to what someone who you admire has to say.

It's a choice you make within your day to be a student to who you see as your mentors guiding you along your own journey. Whether it be for meditation, relationships, language, a craft, or life itself.

And you may have periods in your life where you feel it's time for introspection and reflection, and you spend less time doing and more time learning, thinking, and adjusting.

Follow your own path. Don't follow anybody else's. Figure out your own way of facing life. Navigate your own time and space here on earth. There is only one you. And you must treat yourself in ways that only you will know.

19

Chapter 19: Perfectionism and micromanaging

There's no such thing as you being perfect. Never will be. You will not attain it.

You may read this and logically understand this. But your actions may show otherwise. You may still be trying to "get" perfection.

You will learn this lesson eventually. Time, frustration, unhappiness and repeated unwanted outcomes will teach you.

It is time to let it go, and live your life.

...

Understand that perfection is unattainable. Imperfections, traumas, insecurities, pain, live within us.

We are who we are.

In chasing perfection, you will continue to put in tons of effort, all in a futile attempt to run away from who you actually are, and the progress you can actually be making.

Understanding your humanness, and not denying your own humanness, is a fundamental component to a rich human experience.

You wanting to say all the perfect things. You wanting to create the perfect things. You wanting to make no mistakes and feel the sensation of perfection.

Know that you chasing a perfect you will be like a dog chasing its own tail. There will be no end. You will do this until you die. And the life you will have lived will be that of compiled years of you rejecting the human experience.

Rejecting humility, rejecting real learning and progress, rejecting who you are, chasing an idea of who you thought you could've been.

...

Realize that when you finally start doing, that it's going to be messy. It might not match the vision you had in your mind. Maybe not initially. You may not feel ready. You may feel insecure. You may feel like a fraud. You may feel like you want things to be perfect, and feel like you aren't able to fulfill that feeling. But you are moving forward.

You may make mistakes. You may embarrass yourself. You may be judged. You may doubt yourself. But you are moving forward.

Do not obsess over perfection.

When you obsess over perfection, you begin to move slower, you begin to become more hesitant, you begin to doubt yourself more, you begin to make less decisions, your days become filled with procrastination. You want your work to be perfect. And you, are human. You are not perfect. You know deep down, you are not perfect. So you become scared to contend with your work. You distract yourself. You begin to stagnate.

When you obsess over perfection, you pollute the atmosphere within your mind. You think that whatever you are currently doing, is not enough. That you, are not enough.

Even though you may be exactly where you need to be.

You, and this idea of perfection that you are holding onto, is the very thing that keeps you from moving forward, becoming what you want to become, and creating what you want to create. You think you are resisting movements and keeping yourself from falling into a trap, messing up, or failing. You think you are holding onto something near and dear that you are CON-VINCED will move you forward, but the very thing you are holding onto is what will ensure that you stay in PLACE. You have become a proactive force in your own stagnation.

You are not giving yourself space. You are not allowing yourself to be a student of your craft.

You don't allow yourself to make the inevitable mistakes. You don't allow yourself to take chances and learn from them. You don't allow yourself to be curious about life.

You don't allow yourself to be in your own energetic sweet spot, and truly contend with your work. You don't allow yourself to be present and focused on your work. You don't allow yourself to play with ideas, to use your imagination, to create, to learn, to try new things, to progress.

You don't allow yourself to actually try your best.

You are continuously ignoring the real progress you can actually be making. You creating. You refining. You learning.

Instead, you are a distracted being.
You abandon the creative process.
You abandon the edges of your own creativity. You abandon your humanness. You abandon contending with life.
And sit, in the idea of perfection.

...

You are scared.
You have the perfect vision of the perfect creation. This is your gift.

But you are scared to mess it up. You are scared to ruin it. You are scared that it will not be what you want it to be.

Accept that you are scared.

But understand that you can't stay here forever. You must MOVE.

You will be here your whole lifetime.

Holding onto your perfect vision.

But never creating it.

You must LET GO of the idea of you being perfect. Let it GO. Put it aside.

Do not hold any longer. Let go.

Let go and allow yourself to go down the stream of life.

You must work. You must show up to your canvas. You must create.

...

You must humble yourself. You must accept that it will take time for you to develop your craft to be able to create at the level you want to create. It takes time to find, and live, in that energetic space. This is truly knowing your craft.

There's lessons to learn along the way. There's nuances to understand. There's more vivid ways of expressing your ideas that will be discovered.

When you start moving, the idea you see and feel and act on, although you may not feel capable of truly curating it to the level you want to, connects you to the next idea, and that idea connects to the next idea. Every step forward, you are developing your craft. Every step forward, you learn how to articulate and express more accurately what is within your mind. Every step forward, you learn.

And as you move, as you continue to create, as you continue to learn, and you stay focused, you get closer and closer to what you envision.

This is the process.

The vision you have. It is a gift. But this is not for you. It is just coming through you. This is the gift for others.

The gift that is for you, is the evolution you undergo when you are in the process of creating what you envision.

The wisdom and life lessons you learn along the way. The sharpness of your articulation through continuous learning. The ability to express yourself in the craft you chose. The ability to dive deep into the human experience and truly bring things out of worth. The imagination and creativity you get to enjoy and play in. The grace that flows through you. The happiness and joy of contending with life. The appreciation for your time on earth.

...

You can be anxious. You can be depressed. You can feel insecure. You can feel like a fraud. You can feel like you're not good enough. But this does not mean that you can not put your mind to something, and do something great.

You are human. Accept your humanness. Accept yourself. Many individuals are ruining the magic of life by chasing perfection and optimization.

You will not figure it all out in this lifetime. Accept this.

Creations on Earth, are otherworldly. And they are completed by those that commit to their completion, in the face of all their own humanness.

Those that are humble. Those that are patient. Those that stay focused. Those that continue learning from others. Those that continue developing their craft. Those that learn about themselves and evolve.

They are completed by the individuals who, in the face of wanting to be perfect, allow themselves to be vulnerable, and to go through the process of creating anyway.

...

Wake up and show up to your life. In the same way that those you look up to, do.

Allow the thoughts of perfection to do whatever they wish. Along with your fear. Along with your anxiety. And insecurities. And every other negative emotion and thought. If they want to join you for the ride or not, it is not of your concern.

Regardless of their stance in your life, wake up, everyday, and create.

Understand that you will not be perfect. You will not feel perfect. Allow it.

You won't feel at your best all the time. Allow that too.

Just show up. And continue to show up. When you show up, even though you may not feel your best, and you go through what it is you were scared to go through, you are now in a new reality.

You are a more determined you. A more focused you.

This focus, over time, becomes the most powerful energy in your life.

Courage with contending with the uncomfortable is built over time.

Your vision, is built, day by day.

...

You can't see how things will turn out.

You don't know how what you want to create will be created. You don't know how you will become who you envision yourself becoming.

You don't know the journey ahead. And you micromanage like you know the path. You don't. By attaching yourself to the idea of everything being perfect, you keep yourself from the process of life.

Instead, follow what feels right. Let the story unfold. Uninterrupted and unbothered by your current self's ignorance and limited knowledge.

Doing what's right in front of you, and riding the ride.
Go with the flow of your existence. Your path is laid out.

Letting go, and allowing yourself to work, will take you further than you can possibly imagine right now.

Listen to the music that inspires you. Watch the documentaries that spark your interest. Work how you want to work. Focus on what you want to focus on.

Much of the abilities that you desire to have, are found in the lessons in the process of moving forward.

Be humble, be open, listen to inspiration and continue to move forward.

Change, regardless if you think it's good or bad, is the very thing that separates you now from your completed work. And you judge certain changes as good or bad, but you have no idea what your evolution looks like.

You must be your true self, in the face of the unknown. You must be your true self, even though it may be judged, criticized, or you yourself are unsure of its strengths. But you must trust the process. Be yourself. And this will begin to open the doors you have been seeking.

Be aware of what inspires you, and live in that space.

Everyone has their own fundamentals they must adhere to.

Honor yourself.

Nobody is above the process of cultivating their own gifts.

We all have to trust ourselves in the face of the unknown.

...

There is no perfect path that is unanimously accepted by all as the true path to success. There is no path that exists that we can all share. One that includes all the decisions you must make, all the habits you must have, all the places you must go and all the people you must interact with. This does not exist.

Every individual is different. This is the great challenge for mankind. Everyone has evolution within them that they need to face. You must walk your own path in life.

And with the gathering of knowledge through your experiences, through your growing wisdom and awareness, through the listening of your intuition and spirit, through your envisioning and focus, and through your having courage and working on your vision, your own path will be walked.

You will never know if the path you choose is the best one. Let go of needing to know this information.

If you stay humble and continue to learn, if you continue to pay attention to your growing wisdom and awareness, if you continue to listen to your intuition and spirit, if you continue to envision and focus, if you continue to show up every day and put in the effort, and you are living life in the moment, moment to moment as it unfolds, you are on YOUR path.

You are on the greatest path that you currently have the ability to be on.

Trust the unfolding. And let go of everything else.

...

Turn off the tv. Put away the social media. Be alone with your mind. Listen to the music that energetically moves you. Imagine. Envision.

Begin to craft with your mind. Begin to move thousands of pieces into their energetic spaces.
Suspend your self doubt.

Trust in your vision.

Commit to your vision.

Show up to your vision.
Wake up, believe in your work, and work.

Allow yourself to make mistakes. Allow yourself to be embarrassed. Allow yourself to be awkward. Allow yourself to not know everything.

Continue moving, continue trying, continue learning, continue refining, continue creating.

This is where the best you, awaits.

This is where you best serve earth.

20

Chapter 20: Internet and technology

For many individuals, your phone is ruining your life. Your constant use of the internet is stealing the life that you are meant to live.

The internet, and the mindless wandering of it, is the biggest hijacker of purpose in the modern day individual.

In this mindless wandering, you may stumble upon bits of wisdom and knowledge. You may progress. You may learn. But this pales in comparison to becoming proactive when using the internet and using your mind with purpose.

...

This period of history and the humans that are in it, are experiencing the heavily unregulated, wild west of the birth of this new medium. This incredible new creation. We're learning how to use the Internet, together.

But simultaneously, we are living in the modern day gold rush. The gold is the individual's attention.

The internet is young. The first generation. It's the Wild West. Raw form. Little to no regulation in favor of the people. Little to no regard for the well-being of the individuals using it. Many of those in charge of the corners of the internet have the primary goal of profit in mind, not your sanity, and not the cohesion and thriving of the earth.

Profit is primary, and the consequences of how the money was made is not of their concern.

The majority of businesses are doing their best to capture your attention, hold your attention, monetize your attention, and continue holding your attention, by any means necessary. With little to no regard to how it's affecting you as a human being. They'll use fear, divisiveness, outrage, anger, shame, sex, envy, jealousy, anything they can to keep your attention.

You stepping foot into the internet, you are stepping foot into a world that in every corner and crevice, you are poked and prodded and lured to watch, read, consume. To spend more time consuming what they are offering you.

By any means necessary.

Regardless of what it is doing to you mentally.

Just because something captures your attention and you end up doing something that you didn't necessarily want to do, doesn't make the thing that made you do that, evil or have malicious intent. You can just have a lack of focus and a desire to distract yourself.

But are there companies that are more intrusive and immoral than others in their attempt at grabbing your attention? Of course. As time progresses, we need to have a serious discussion in how this may be regulated, and if it should be regulated in the first place. Where should we draw the line? Where should we begin to take the individual's wellbeing into account? How do we ensure that we don't unnecessarily limit freedoms? It seems that in this Wild West state of the internet, those with the money and power have utilized the internet and the understanding of human psychology and emotions, to exploit the individual and poke at their knee-jerk primal reactions to respond to fear, sex, and validation, to allow them to dominate the internet and dominate many humans psyches.

Although this is clearly wrong, and there must be some sort of middle space where ways of grabbing our attention is regulated, and the mental sanity and health of the individual is respected, we must not wait for a future time and place for this to happen. We must exercise this ourselves. We must not wait for others to master themselves and rise in their consciousness and morality to improve the state of the internet, rather we must master ourselves and master our own usage of the internet.

...

The individual's unhealthy relationship with the internet has stolen a massive chunk of this past decade's potential. Potential in creativity, in innovation, in moments of happiness and love. We've lost a large chunk of our mental well-being and our peace of mind. We've lost a lot of our humanness. We've lost so many inventions and creations that could've been created. So many individuals' creativity, tainted by their self image. So many individuals' lives, stunted by constant consumption.

This is a phase in humanity where we are addicted, attached, ran by, this new invention. It's new. In this past decade, we didn't know how to navigate it. What a healthy relationship with it looked like. What addiction and feeding mental illness looked like. Now, we're beginning to know.

What we see emerging is the importance of a healthy relationship with the internet. The amount of time spent on the internet. Where you go on the internet. And what you are doing with what you learn on the internet.

We now know just how powerful the internet can be. Depending on the individual, they can be more aware, alive and living a more purposeful life, or be more empty and distracted.

The internet can be a portal into culture. A portal into knowledge. A portal into your expansion and refinement. A portal into developing your mental equipment for your autonomy and freedom. A portal into raising your own consciousness. A portal into exploring different skills and crafts, discovering your purpose, and learning more deeply than ever before with your purpose. A portal into connecting with real creative innovators and doers. A portal into being part of positive communities.

Or it can be portal into the continuation of your stagnation. A portal into more distractions. A portal into a constant state of unhappiness and stuckness.

It depends on you.

The mastery of your relationship with the internet, is the turn of the tide. Not just for you, but for many individuals. In the ending of your leaf in the wind relationship with the internet, in these ashes, like a phoenix, in your choosing to be intentional with your time on the internet, your own power and creativity emerges.

The beginning of a newly invigorated relationship with life. A closer relationship with your purpose. A better reality to live in. A happier you.

And this turn of the tide in your own life, multiplied throughout society, is the turn of the tide in mankind.

...

Your excessive and immature internet usage, with its immediately gratifying nature, you scrolling and consuming, erodes your capability for deep focus, deep thought and patience. You are left lacking the ability to live deeply and experience aspects of life more deeply. Your attention span is sliced and diced, until soon, focusing on anything over a few minutes becomes a battle of will.

Things that have been created with deep thought, and are meant to be observed, experienced, consumed with deep thought, you look right through with no detection of its depth.

Works of art, peaceful music, a moment in nature, a conversation, a documentary, a film with less theatrics but with a meaningful story, a book of any form.

When you come across any these creations, creations that are meant to expand your experience on earth, you and your frenetic and erratic mind cannot settle into the experience. It's too busy, at an extremely heightened level, seeking for another quick high. Something that is as stimulating as the rest of your immediately-gratifying mental diet.

In the same way that a junk food diet will have you not able to detect the sweetness of blueberries, your constant consumption of memes, photos, video clips, news headlines, comments, articles, posts, will have you not able to detect the sweetness and depth of life.

Even silence, and your own imagination, isn't stimulating enough for you.

You are confined in your own stupidity.

...

Many kids and young adults are stuck, living their life on repeat, with the same memes, posts and stories on social media, shows on streaming services, videos and vlogs from their favorite subscriptions, and online video games. Never expanding and experiencing real life. Never reaching depths that came so much more effortlessly for past generations of humans. Underdeveloped social skills. Underdeveloped confidence. Little to no time with their own imagination and creativity. Little to no time with experiencing the wonders of real life. Little to no adventure with their time here on Earth. But the perfect scroller and consumer.

And older generations, who once experienced a depth of life with the natural mental freedom of having no internet, now too live on the surface. Many parents absent in their own families, leaning so much more into their social media profiles, and the *presentation* of their families. Obsessed with impressing friends, associates, old classmates, and distant family members. Reading inflammatory articles online and being filled with fear and hate, unable to see the spell they put themselves in. Reading news from sources that are far from legitimate, and developing a more bleak and negative personality. Playing mobile games for hours, as their real lives around them resemble that of an unkempt, browned, garden. Avoiding their responsibility and abandoning the position they are in as the elders of the planet. Pull the technological syringe out of you veins.

...

Individuals of all generations, so involved with everyone else's lives, that they truly forget about living fully in their own. Watching their friends live their lives. Consumed with the everyday life updates of their favorite celebrities. An obsession of watching others experience their own adventurous lives, instead of making an adventure of their own. Sitting. Scrolling.

Living your life in the stands and watching people in the arena, living life.

Waking up, picking up your phone, and immediately getting sucked into the internet, and beginning feeling nasty within yourself, scrolling and scrolling and scrolling, and not being able to shake this stuckness.

Unhappy with life. But going to sleep. And waking up and doing it again.

You don't give yourself the chance to water and nurture your own life, and see what can come of it. The depth and richness that's possible of your own life experience, goes avoided.

...

And in its most harmful form, will have you falling into an echo chamber based off of your own fears, and radicalize yourself.

Blindly consuming and sucking down the internet, the news, and social media, without any self mental check. The equivalent of an individual on the weekend drinking too much alcohol with nobody around him to check on him, and he himself not understanding what he is doing to himself. Just caught in the flow of the moment. His emotions moving him around like a rag doll in the ocean. Just scrolling and consuming. Going deeper into their own rabbit hole.

With the emergence of the internet and the access that it gives us to a wide net of information, we have individuals traumatizing themselves.

Do not consume and suck down the internet, the news, and social media without any mental check of whether you are doing so, too much.

Sucking down information that is often packaged in a way that is not meant to truly inform you, but to summon the most emotion and attention out you. The most fear, the most outrage, and the most division. This is what drives up profits, and so this is the aim for many of those that deliver this information.

Not to inform, but to stir emotion from within the individual.

You do not have any of your information challenged by your peers. And if you do, you spend your time trying to convince them, instead of trying to listen. You do not have an open mind seeking to understand. You grow in your paranoia. You grow in your hatred for specific groups. You think you are right and everyone else is wrong.

You think you are waking up and becoming wise to the world around you. That you are rising higher and higher above everyone else and figuring the world out. In reality, you fall deeper and deeper into a rabbit hole of ignorance.

Living in fear. In fear of other people. In fear of the future. In protection of your life.

Enough time has passed for us to be able to discern the differences amongst individuals that use the internet heavily and immaturely and those that do not. It's becoming clear the individuals in every day life that are drowning in fear from endlessly consuming the internet. They leave their home and walk in public in fear. Terrified in conversations with strangers, waiting for the wrong political thing to be said. Scared of the individual that walks past them, drives next to them, or interacts with them in public, that represents the "other" demographic of people they see on social media. Tense waiting in line at the supermarket. Jumpy to any behavior that resembles the clips they've seen on social media.

Just what exactly are you doing with this information, if anything at all?

Not do anything to change your own life, or try to improve the state of your community or society with your constant consumption of current events, but rather to feed your own mind and further agitate yourself. To have a battleground in your own mind and further reinforce who is good and who is bad. To unknowingly further feed your addiction to feeling fear and anger.

You think that you are above the ability to be agitated, because you are aware that there are forces out to agitate you. All the while you are still being agitated right under your nose.

Constant scrolling, scrolling, scrolling. Addicted.

...

In a way, the internet has less to do with itself, and more to do with us and our own states of mind. We create it. We consume it. We use our own attention and choose what we do with it. We make our own decisions. We feed the good. We feed the bad.

Right now, the internet is a mixed bag. For every argument that takes place, there is someone else in some other part of the internet, learning something for the first time. For every article spreading fear, there's a podcast or video speaking about hope and love. For every post that tries to be cool, there are posts that try to be humble and connect. The internet is a melting pot of different life experiences. There is ignorance, there is intelligence. There is love, there is hate. There is joy and connection, there is anger and division.

Our attention to certain corners of the internet, gives those corners of the internet strength. Our behavior on the internet, reinforces a certain dynamic and way of carrying yourself on the internet.

The state of our own consciousness, and our own relationship with the internet, multiplied throughout society, shapes the internet.

The more we see the responsibility we have as individuals, the more we mature. The more we mature, the more we align with our purpose. The more we align with our purpose, the more focused we become in our day to day lives. And as we are living purposeful lives, the higher of a tendency to use the internet with good intention increases.

Distractions expose themselves. Inflammatory headlines expose themselves and become less enticing to click on. Cesspools of arguments on comment threads, forums and social media become less enticing to participate in.

You are able to navigate the internet with more ease.

The more we mature, the higher of a tendency to use the internet with good intention increases. The more we use the internet with good intention, the more beautiful of an atmosphere the internet will contain.

As we evolve, the internet evolves.

…

When you humble yourself and focus, you begin to develop the ability to access a whole entire new territory of creativity and intelligence, never before accessible to common people, and large parts of this new territory never before discovered in mankind.

Programs that allow you to enter new territory within crafts. Architecture and creating new designs. Music and creating new sounds and collection of sounds never before heard to mankind. Programs that optimize work within crafts and allot more time and energy to be used for deepening your expertise within the craft.

A wider array of information, creative ideas and inventions, introducing never before seen perspectives and ideas into the human mind.

New philosophical understandings with the access of all different corners of the world and their discovered wisdoms within their own cultures. New stories being shown to the world with the exposure of almost all areas of society.

New scientific discoveries from minds going deep into the endless fountain of research, data, and information, and being given to the world.

Communication and collaboration becoming immediate and seamless, allowing the formation of projects, creation and execution to become not only tangible to the average individual, but possible. A creator you admire, is a message away. An individual you wish to work with, is at your fingertips. A team you envision, is only awaiting your connecting and constructing.

The digital world, when niches of it have been mastered, offers the individuals that master it, never before seen perspectives, ideas and abilities.

The creators that are able to live in the real world and dive deep into the digital world and maintain themselves, and have an empowering relationship with the mixture of the two, will bring into this planet never before seen gifts. Different fields of mankind receiving new creativity.

Use your mind. Travel to the internet with intention. Creators, innovators, inventors and artists of the 21st century are mapping new landscape never experienced before.

...

It seems that the internet is a key part of our evolution. It makes sense that with human's creative abilities, given enough time, we would have found a way to hyperconnect with each other all over the globe in real time, and for all of us to be able to connect to a great source of information. Perhaps, almost all the information we know as humans. A place where all humans can connect to each other, despite our physical distance. Speak to each other. Listen to each other. Watch each other. Learn beyond imaginable. Share our artistic creations. Love each other more closely. Laugh together. Share ideas. Communicate more closely.

We are faced with so much more than ever before. To understand more of cultures. To understand more of the universe. To understand more of this life on earth. We are facing ourselves, with awe.

The internet has, for many people, become the catalyst in which helps facilitate their awakening.

Mankind is evolving. The individual is evolving.

...

Use your mind wisely. Use the internet wisely. Focus your mind. Do not get distracted.

Develop the ability to come onto the internet, use it for its purpose, and leave. Use it while it is useful. And leave when it begins becoming distracting and unenjoyable. Pay attention to how you feel within. Pay attention to your focus when on the internet and the moment you get distracted and begin to fall into a haze of clicking and scrolling. Develop a powerful conscious awareness of your self and your use of the internet. Curate your experience with your technology.

And develop a desire to live a higher quality of life with a higher state of peace and happiness. Over time, you will find that you naturally desire to spend less and less time on the internet. You see the fearful headlines, gossip filled stories, or sexual images but there is little to no pull. You are not interested in wasting your time on the internet. You are engaged with your real life, and when you choose to use the internet, you are in and you are out, and back into engaging with your real life.

Master your self and master the internet.

...

It seems that the internet feeds psychological disorders and disruption in man. Whether because it's being used incorrectly, incessantly, or used at all, we do not know yet. Maybe it's only because of its current form. Maybe the effects would be similar regardless of the form, because it has less to do with the current form and more to do with the very nature of the internet. The endless amounts of information and content available. The constant stimulus. The power at your fingertips. The weight of decisions on your shoulders.

We are too close to the advent of the internet to know. This is all brand new to us. In retrospect, decades from now, it will be much more clear. But right now, everything is muddied.

In the future, the relationship between the internet and the human mind will be widely studied and understood. This era in particular will be of great interest and heavily examined, as this is the era in which the internet was birthed, and humans, in their innocence and naïveté, commingled with it in ways that in the future will be seen as so obviously foolish, unhealthy and destructive.

...

Maybe the internet continues to get more algorithmically dense and intense, and reaches a point where the human mind is, more or less, owned by the Internet and those who run those algorithms. Even more so than today. A level that we currently cannot fathom.

Always intoxicated by short term immediate interest. Always having your insecurities poked and prodded. Always having your sexual desires constantly inflamed. Always having your ego stirred and needing to purchase and consume more things to feel complete and level up in your life. Always having your worst fears proved right about other groups of people in the extreme posts you see.

Maybe the internet is a train headed for disaster, and it's bringing millions of mental psyches with it.

We do not know what the future holds. It's a gamble. We can only do our part.

In our own lives, having a healthy relationship with the internet, and doing our part of healthy production of content and healthy consumption of content. Be mindful of what we put out unto the internet, and be mindful of what we do. Be mindful of how our emotions are being poked and prodded. We must refuse to participate in the sensationalism, fear inducement, and outrageous spins, whether posting it ourselves, consuming it, or sharing it. We must find the spaces that are true, the spaces that have intelligence, open mindedness, empathy, and a dedication to looking at all perspectives and finding what is closest to truth in the midst of all the nuance, and stay in this reliable space.

Have positive influences. Individuals that are reliable processors of information. Kind individuals. Fun influences.

But more than all, understand that going outside, spending time with people in real life, and going into nature, should be fundamental parts of our existence.

Take time away from the internet. See how your life is with much less time on it. See if you have been distracting yourself from a deeper quality of life you have been seeking. See if the time you have been spending on the internet has been in reality you getting sucked daily into a state of nasty comfortable addiction to discomfort, when all you may deep down really desire is to go outside, explore, and live life with nature, with hobbies, and with friends.

In our own families, doing our part to ensure the internet is used maturely to the best of our abilities. Limit the time available for our children, and limit the access they have. Ensure their experience of the internet is filled with learning opportunities, exploring their own creativity and imagination, learning skills and crafts. And the entertainment consumed is wholesome and contains lessons in values and virtues, but also allowing entertainment that is humorous, ridiculous and keeps ourselves playful in life. Ensuring that they have a good balance of internet usage, and real life fun, play, outside exploration, hobbies and crafts, and learning.

And with our own power in our own specific field of expertise, ensure healthy sustainable business practices with social media.

Or just not use it at all. Maybe it'll be wise to leave the internet and protect your psyche. Perhaps we should spend less and less time on the internet, and more time with real people in real life. This may have untold healing effects to the individual of the future.

Or maybe you should stay on the internet, stay connected on it, produce and share content, and have your finger closer to the pulse of modern day culture.

Or maybe the answer is some sort of nuance within all of this. Maybe new innovators of this century will see the distortion of this digital landscape, and offer their own creations to help balance it. New internet pages, apps and social media platforms that don't seek to manipulate the individual for its own gain, but instead keep the individual's wellbeing first and foremost in its framework. And perhaps this caring of the individual's wellbeing is what keeps individuals using their particular creation in the first place. The future is that of unity, love and caring for one another. We crave this. Not just in real life. But with our experience of the internet. Given real objective news, not sensationalized clickbait that injects us full of fear and division. Occasionally offered products we may be interested in, not bombarded with thousands of products with every click and scroll.

It seems that the individual has already begun their great migration to the light. There seems to be a deep subtle hunger for common sense, genuine individuals, and real life. A hunger for wisdom. A hunger for respectful discourse. We are beginning to pay our attention to real conversations, long conversations, on podcasts discussing all perspectives, as opposed to fake one-sided perspectives from most news. We are spending more time outside. More and more people are leaving apps. There is a shift that we all feel needs to happen. And we are all doing our part.

Ultimately, you must do what feels right to you.

21

Chapter 21: Rise

It seems that we're all searching for a richer quality of life. And we can't seem to find it.

Our generation wants something different than what we are currently experiencing.

We put our headphones on, and head to school. Hoping for better days.

We show up to our jobs to make our money. Tired. Hoping that things can change.

Millions of young adults searching for their purpose.

Searching for a way out of their misery. Looking through culture, through music, through art, through film, through crafts, soaking up whatever they find that resonates with them. Researching throughout the internet, trying to find how they can create a better life for themselves.

Millions of people sick of their same old story, and desperately wanting something better, but feeling hopeless.

Millions of individuals, of all ages, living their day to day life, with potential.

...

At some point, on some day, you will realize that the most important thing for you to do, carries the least amount of life force in your life. You give it the least amount of your energy. You distract yourself. And while this is the case, you will stay exactly where you are in life.

If you know the direction in which you can grow, then it is your duty to go in that direction. If you know what you must work on, it is your duty to work.

...

What you are using to distract yourself, must end. Social media, alcohol, porn, your self image, video games, internet, drugs, junk food, television.

The whole world you created can be a distraction. Your job, your hobbies, your girlfriend or boyfriend, your friends. One big elaborate distraction you've made, to hide from what you are meant to do. As you tell yourself reasons as to why you cannot move forward, of course you're in pain. You're living an existence that isn't meant for you.

You have ideas. You have visions. You have dreams. Within your mind lies the keys to a greater life.

Not just a greater life for yourself, but a greater life for those that directly surround you.

Your family.
Your friends.
Your community.
Your pocket of Earth.

By holding yourself back, you hold everyone back.

You have been given the ability to bring light to those directly surrounding you.

And yet you do nothing.

A better life for your parents, for your friends, for your coworkers, for your neighbors, was supposed to come through you.

You are supposed to be the vehicle that brings that light into their life. Whether it's through example you are supposed to lead for them. Or through the words and knowledge you are supposed to share with them that gives them a deeper connection with themselves. Or through the positive, focused habits that you start to do that gets them reflecting on their own habits.

Or through the resources and connections you are able to bring into their lives. Or through the positive conversations that make them feel supported and feel like they can aim higher in life. Or through the love and happiness that you begin to embody that you can share with them. Or through your work that inspires them. Through what you invent. Through what you build. Through what you create in this world.

But you choose to do nothing.

Work the same job. Go to the same bars. Play the same video games. Watch the same shows. Eat the same junk food. Obsessed with yourself on social media. Drink the same alcohol and do the same drugs.

You've let fear win. And all of these distractions that you involve yourself with are your consolation prizes. The life of someone who's quit.

Of course you'll feel miserable.
Depressed.
Anxious.

Like a traffic jam due to an accident, you and everyone surrounding you are bottlenecking in the highway.

You are bottlenecking your own life and those around you.

You're stagnant. And because you are stagnant, the people you were supposed to help are stagnant. All because you choose not to handle your own life.

You must correct your course of direction.

...

With the claiming of the responsibility you have with your time here on this planet, comes great power. You are honoring your life.

Follow your purpose. You will begin to connect to the truth within you. You will begin to connect to the deep energy we are all connected to. Your life will reconfigure and restructure. This is where your peace is. This is where your genius unlocks.

Although it may be scary and unknown, this is where your life is meant to be lived.

You cannot escape your potential. You cannot hide from it. And once it is known, your reality has changed.

Once your potential is known, YOUR REALITY HAS CHANGED.

You can go back to old activities, but you will now do these old activities with the awareness of what you know you should be doing instead.

You must face what you must face. There is no amount of distractions that will change this. You can continue to live in your distractions. But you will live your life here. And then you will die here. And that will be your life. You either die in your distractions. Or die on your purpose. You will die one day. The choice is yours.

You are meant for more.

Your path is forward.

...

Your purpose is your particular human being's medium in which how you will raise your consciousness. Your purpose is your particular human being's medium in which you will begin to change your life, and continue to change your life. It's the core asteroid in which the rest of your soul gravitates around and soars through your evolution.

In order for your life to move, you must face your purpose. Your focusing on your purpose, transforms you. As you wield your purpose, your purpose wields you.

To create what is the next form of what you are, to give to the world what you are meant to give, you are called to rise in as you are.

Your soul is seeking evolution.

A meeting of you in your human form with god himself.
While you are still alive.
Face to face with your craft.
Living life.
Living the adventure.
And continuing to live in this light.
As close to the light as you can live.

…

You departing from a life of distractions, and entering into the life you are meant to live, is bittersweet.

Difficult.
But you know something profound is happening.

These days, weeks, months, years.
You are in a transition phase in your life.
The maturing of who you are.

The first weeks of eliminating bad habits and departing from that lifestyle is a special kind of suffering that many cannot endure. Or at least they think they cannot. It's a special kind of suffering in which the absence of your common distractions, introduces waves and waves of uncomfortable emotions. Anxiety. Frustration. Boredom. Dissatisfaction. Incomplete. Angst. Anger. Sadness. Pain.

You are finally facing yourself.
You are moving in the right path. You are growing.

In the newfound absence of your distractions, you will experience all that you have been avoiding with those very distractions. You will see reality.

Embrace the discomfort. The high highs of new clarity. The low lows of the absence of what you've used so long to numb the unhappiness of your life. The ways you've numbed your existence on Earth.

Embrace the lesser self within you that thrashes around emotionally, seeking to go back to your old ways. Embrace it. Endure it. Go through the days and weeks. Do not falter. Love yourself. Be patient with yourself. Sit with what you've avoided. Process it.

Let go of the emotional weight in you.

Surround yourself with healed individuals. Connect with healed energy.
Surround yourself with those you love and that love you. Connect with loving energy.
Meditate. Breathe deeply. Close your eyes. Stretch your body. Connect with yourself. Connect with god.
Go into nature. Sit by the ocean's waves. Sit under the stars. Connect with the universe.

Talk with people. Open up. Connect with expansion.

Listen to healing music. Film scores, orchestras, chants, music with heart and soul in it. Cry. Lay down and let go. Process. Connect with healing sounds and vibrations.

Focus on your purpose. Connect with your higher self.

You are going through a metamorphosis. Stand. Be strong. You're not alone. Your ancestors watch over you. Millions are going through the transformation with you. Our generation is with you. You are loved.

Let go of your hands' tight grip off your vices. Don't hold onto your vices and coping mechanisms. No more numbing yourself.

Be awake. Fully experience your emotions. Don't be in a constant altered state of consciousness. But in the purest state of consciousness. Sober. Stand, naked, awake, in the face of life.

Let go.

Life itself will wash over you and heal you.

This is what transforms you.

Commit. Endure the pain. It will be difficult.

But there is light in the other side.

...

When you're not making the moment-to-moment daily movement forward in your life, you have nothing to hold onto to keep you inspired and focused. And your life behind you will seem more appealing. Because there's comfort, and "good emotions" there. And you will move backwards. Cowering into the past. Past relationships that you know you outgrew. Past jobs that you know you are wasting your time at. Past vices that you know are keeping you stuck. Past ways of living that are no longer for you.

Do not sit and try to abstain from everything "bad", and do nothing. Trying so hard to not distract yourself. Do not stand still. Move forward.

Work on your craft, physically exercise in the forms you enjoy, consume nutritious food that you find delicious, meditate and enjoy the peace of mind, spend your time consuming real knowledge and thinking, spend time with who inspires you, listen to the music that contextually designs your life elegantly, go outside and spend time with the world, get out of your comfort zone and do what you wish to do.

Spend time being who you truly want to be.

You are moving. You are now energy in motion. You will experience trust in yourself. You will begin to love who you are.

You will experience more joy. You will experience more peace within your mind. You're experiencing new energy in motion.

These new emotions of fulfillment, will be your daily fuel. Morning reminders of a better life ahead. Your true path ahead.

...

You may veer away from the path from time to time.

Know how to get back on the path. Know what puts you into focus, and know what puts you out. Live true to this. Through commitment to your purpose, you will endure many lessons. Through trial and error, you will learn what brings you closer to your path and what brings you away.

Find your inspiration again. Live in it. It's a space you can live in, that always awaits you. You must find that space. The music, the environment, the routines, the ways of thinking, the limited conscious use of the internet and where you go, the ways you spend your free time, the city, the neighborhoods, the interviews and discussions with creators with focused energy, being around certain people. Be amongst elevated thinking. Be amongst positive energy. More than anything, sit and face your work.

It's on you, once you know the richest energy, to live true to this.

Make this place, this vibration, your home.

...

Re-commit to this energy, and remember that although less immediately-gratifying in the pleasurable spike way, it gives you a deeper sense of happiness and fulfillment.

...

Your commitment to what you envision, in the face of all of your ups and downs, in the face of your self-doubt, in the face of available distractions, is what opens the door to your new world.

...

There's many different directions to take your life. There's many different fields of thought to enter. There's many different consistencies of thought to commit to. There's many different habits and lifestyles to have.

And you only have so many days on this planet. You cannot choose it all.

Your sacrifice to have what means the most to you, is every-thing else that you could've been in the same moment in time. The lifestyles you gave up. The vices and pleasures. The persons you could have been.

You must decide what means the most to you, and what your life will be about. What your life will consist of.

You can't do it all.

You must choose.

In the face of many available options and paths, when you are living a life committed to your purpose, you choose richer experiences. You are resonating with richer experiences.

You wake up and realize your limited time on earth. You listen to music with true depth. You have thoughts with true depth. You have meaningful conversations. You work is focused.

Your world transforms.

…

You can be exactly where you want to be creatively, if you allow yourself to be.

It's a power within you that is always available.

Believing in yourself is a beautiful energy.

In your relentless choosing of your purpose, over time, you grow. In the present moment, faced with the many different choices this life has to offer, and you choose your purpose, you grow. Day after day, week after week, month after month, year after year, faced with the many different choices this life has to offer, in your continuing commitment to your purpose, you grow. You are believing in yourself and what you are capable of. Your reality is reconfiguring and restructuring.

Your commitment to your dream, allows you to eventually step foot into your dream.

...

Live a life of integrity.
For your perspectives to not be diluted.
For your visions to be strong.
For your understanding and wisdom to be true.
For your actions to matter.
For your work to mean something.
Live in the space of creativity and deep thought.
If only for a brief moment in time, you get to experience the full expression of you.

...

Focus on your work.

Music, art, writing, architecture, science, technology, politics. Speaking, teaching, humanitarian needs, designer, director, entrepreneur, inventor, engineer.

Whatever it may be, the world needs it.

Listen to your soul, focus on your craft, and work. You will access your own genius, and give your gifts and your greatest self to Earth.

Embodying our own greatest self is the very tip of the spear of change in humanity.

22

Chapter 22: Move forward

Move forward.

You don't have to remain admiring.

You can become like the people you admire. You can be someone you are excited to be.

You don't have to remain having your dreams, visions and ideas locked in your mind.

You can make them into reality.

...

All of your energy into your purpose, is what will take you to the level that you never thought was actually attainable.

Allow yourself to lose your mind.

The feeling of losing the grip of your mind is what allows you to fly.

What you may think is you losing the grip of your mind, is you losing the hardened structures that has been keeping you stuck. The loosening of these structures is you losing your mind. But this is what allows you to fly.

This is what gives you freedom on Earth.

Feel your mind. Let go of the resistance. Feel the tension. Let it go. Let yourself be free.

Completely lose all mental barriers. All mental limitations. All disbeliefs. All the reasons why you think you can't move in the direction you envision. Lose your need to impress others. Lose your need to ensure you are accepted. Lose your need to manage your image and be cool. Lose your need to ensure you look good to people you know. No more micromanaging these thoughts. Lose these thought patterns.

Let go.

Listen to the music that inspires you. Feel your energy dancing, cleansing, restructuring and creating space for ideas and visions.

Face your work. Move deeper and deeper into your creations. As you focus your mind on your work so deeply, you are leaving these old limitations and thought patterns behind.

You are losing your mind. Do not be afraid. Let go. Focus your mind. Move towards your vision.

...

Having your vision and committing completely to it is not just advice for no reason. Showing up daily and entering this space accesses this magic element that can't be accessed otherwise. Your mind will begin connecting in ways that you cannot currently understand. You will hear music differently. Hear wisdom differently. See life differently. See your time differently. You'll behave differently. Your mind will begin to operate differently. You will create differently. And you will move forward differently.

You have a certain energy. It's special. Your life energy, while you are so focused, while it's so infused with your purpose, you are exactly where you are supposed to be.

You are now participating in the dance that the universe has offered you, the moment you came out onto this earth as a baby.

...

Knowing that there is no turning back, your mentality will enter a completely untouched place. You are committed. This energy is irreplaceable. It's the very energy that takes you to where you want to go.

Like a ship setting out to sea in the new world long ago, you are setting out to sea and moving into a new world creatively.

With your courage and your vision.
You have chosen the life you will live.
You are now entering uncharted territory.

No matter what levels of discomfort you experience, whether fear, insecurity or self doubt, whether a shortage of income or not having a place to live, when discomfort arises, inevitably, in any shape, you are committed, you are courageous, and you keep moving forward.

The curation of you is undergoing.

These chapters in your life, and your focused movement through them, forge you.

...

The more focused you are in your life, the more you are focused on creating, on studying great works, on studying your field, on truly living your life, the more gems you will find that will unlock the next level within your mind.

You will go deeper into creativity. You will go deeper into understanding life. You will go deeper into the human experience.

The true depths of human experience. This is where genius resides.

The depths of collective consciousness.

The depths of understanding the significance and preciousness of the humans that are currently alive on this planet.

The depths of understanding our place in human history, what has led up to this present moment, and the trajectory of where we are heading into the future.

The depths of understanding where we are at as a people, so you can create something culturally and spiritually relevant and resonant.

The depths of seeing what is needed for mankind's growth and seeing how you yourself can craft, invent and create.

The depths of seeing that which resonates with the human spirit itself.

This is where masterpieces are created.

In a scattered mind, in a mind where you are one foot in and one foot out, there may be moments in your life where you see glimpses of this deeper world. The world that the greatest inventors, artists, geniuses, writers and statesmen have lived. But, because your mind is scattered, because you lack duty, because you lack the understanding of your precious time here, because you remain undisciplined and unfocused, you'll quickly be bungee'd back up into your own scattered nonsensical ignorant world. You care too much about yourself.

What would become of you if this energy was focused?
Grow up.
Face yourself.
Face your work.
Elevate your relationship with life.
Elevate your relationship with your purpose.
This is evolution.

…

Understand that the universe is trying to guide you to your greatest life. You must listen. It is on you to curate.

Your vision. What you see that is possible. What you feel is possible.

This is the life you can create at the peak of your human life experience.

And this is your greatest offering to this planet and humanity.

You have your own energetic sweet spot in life, waiting for you. Listen to what inspires you. Pay attention to what brings real positive emotions from you. This is your tool for navigating your journey on this planet. The work you're creating, the music you surround yourself with, the setting, the people you connect with, the ideas shared, the thoughts, the architecture, the food, the art, the books, the time spent, the mental material taken in.

Live in the space meant for you.

…

Don't leave the gap between you and your potential remain abandoned and untouched.
Fill the gap.

Belief is the key. Belief is the password. You must believe in yourself.

Whatever it is you are meant to do, belief plays a fundamental role in its manifestation from your mind to the earth.

Your power directly correlates with your belief in your dream. The more belief you have in yourself and your dream.

Believe in yourself but develop yourself. Belief in self with no development of self is a path to delusion. Belief in self with development of self, and a commitment of being open and learning, is a path to the creation of your work. Your soul's progression.

Work on your craft. Open your mind. Learn. Humble yourself.

Do you understand what would happen if you just believed in yourself? The idea of yourself?

What you can give to the planet?

The ones that achieve a lot in this world are just people that believe that they can. They choose to do so. How dull would life be without the works of J.R.R. Tolkien or William Faulkner? William Shakespeare or Mark Twain? Bill Evans or Charlie Parker? Bernard Hermann or Piero Piccioni? Alfred Hitchcock or Stanley Kubrick? Federico Fellini or Akira Kurosawa? John Steinbeck or Charles Bukowski? Paul Cézanne and Paul Gauguin? Georges Seurat and Albert Einstein and Niels Bohr? Edwin Hubble and Marie Curie? Alexander Graham Bell and Nikola Tesla?

And all of the great minds who came after them that were inspired by these individuals, using them as a map to navigate their own creativity and meet their own ideas. Using their story as inspiration as fuel for them to move forward in their own life and create their own work. Using the great pieces of work they created as a stepping stone to go further into the same field, building on top of what they created. Using their great pieces of work as ingredients in their own, to create something unique to their own mind, and unique to their own generation.

This experience on Earth continues...

Meet your own ideas. Live in your own energetic space. Devote yourself to your craft. Create what is deep within you. This is how you contribute to culture.

Masterpieces do not fall unto Earth. They are crafted by man.

23

Chapter 23: Your uniqueness

You are living your own experience of life. You have your own uniqueness.

Realize that only you experienced your own teachers of life, your own parents and upbringing, your own material read and watched, own hardships, own lessons, own passions, own perspectives.

The question is, when YOU connect with the universe, what do YOU create? What is YOUR response to life?

The Individual is what will change things. Parts of a better future for us all, are locked within the individual's mind. You have no idea how powerful you are. And awareness of this power, is the most important piece of information for the individual of modern day to know.

Listen to great music. Envision your ideas. Feel your own power.

This is your gift.

...

YOUR focus. YOUR expression. YOUR influence. It matters.

The power that we seek to come forth into society and make changes, is not inside AN individual, but within THE individual. And this includes you.

We are full of power. It is our birthright.

You are born in tune with God. Born a breathing, living, expression of something so much greater. Born a conscious creator, with imagination and creativity and ideas in your mind, and the ability to create in your fingertips. Born with the power to give structure to what is within the mind, and bring unto this Earth. It's up to you, to recognize this and start living by it.

...

You do not exist separately from everyone else. You are not an island.

You are connected with others. An energetic fluid unseen, tethering us together. Your close friends. Your family. Your neighbors. The random daily encounters with other individuals living their own lives.

People need YOU. They need what you are pressing out into the world. You have an energetic imprint. You have influence. People see you. People hear you. People feel you.

This is reason enough to be at your most authentic. At your most expansive and giving. At your most engaged. At your most focused on higher things that matter the most.

Where will your focus be?

Do not allow the opinions and judgements of others who do not understand, or your doubts and fears of being yourself, or anything else, affect your energetic fluidity, your connection with life, and the energetic flow you are meant to live in.

Live in your own energetic space. Being who you want to be. Confident in who you are. Passionate for what you love. Passionate for your time here on earth.

You living in this space, inspires others to move into their own energetic space.

Your confidence in your own unique expression, pushes others to have confidence in their own expression. Your passion for what you love, pushes others to be more open and passionate for what they love. You loving yourself, and loving your life, and choosing what is true to you, inspires others to begin to truly love their own life and choose what is true to themselves.

You are carving a path in the energetic landscape, that those that surround you, may begin to follow. Through you seeing and believing a better life for yourself, they begin to see and believe a better life for themselves. They see the path you are taking, and they see that path begin to illuminate in their own life. They see your relationship with life, and they see that they too can have a similar relationship with life. With your accessing of a deeper true self, you show others the possibilities of them accessing a deeper true self for themselves.

Your life matters. More than you know.

...

Be who you are.

Obsession with how someone else did something, and their own success, and how good their life is, will take you away from your own uniqueness, your own journey, and what you can offer the world. You are not seeing the richness of your own experience. What path you could potentially carve out for others.

You are exactly where you need to be.

Who YOU are. THAT is the life you are meant to live. THAT is meant to carve the path.

Know that you are young. Even if you are of older age, if you are alive on this earth today, you are young.

Many have come before you, and have passed on. And you sit here today, young, as you are still alive. New to life, new to this time here in history, and new to what surrounds you.

Know what came before you. Know what surrounds you today. And know where you want yourself, and the world, to be headed.

Really understand who you are, what you are, who you are becoming and where you are going. What you have done thus far. What you are currently working on. What you will create in the future. What you want to be. How your energy feels. What you want your life to mean. Who you are on this earth. The idea of you. Not the idea of your ego. But you as a project. Being a fan of yourself. Being someone you love being. Living a life you love living.

Fall in love with you. Fall in love with the idea of you.

We are all separate individuals, but we all energetically fall into streams of different types of individuals, all converging into finding some sort of higher way of being. All with our own ways of spiritual exploration, rising of our consciousness, the development of creative power, and navigation of life on earth. Searching for happiness. Searching for purpose. Searching for peace.

And if YOU are able to make it out and create a beautiful life, this gives everyone like you, and everyone that resonates with you, hope. A path. Those that share similar experiences. Similar thoughts. Similar insecurities. Similar fears. Similar upbringing. Similar creativity. You are not alone. There are more like you than you think. You matter.

Be you. Whoever YOU are, be you.

And you will inspire who you are meant to inspire.

Those that are meant to see you, will see you. Those that are meant to hear you, will hear you. Those that resonate with you, will resonate with you.

Some may not resonate with you or your work. You are not for them. You are different types of individuals. They resonate with others. They are inspired by others. Their path in life is different. They will receive the messages they need to hear for their own growth, through different means.

Some may judge you. Do not be deterred. They are living within their own limitations and prison. They judge many, including themselves. They are stuck in life. Do not take it personal. Continue being you.

But those that resonate with you and your message and your expression. Those that would resonate with what you create. Those that surround you and pay some of their attention to you. Those that see part of themselves in you. Carve the path for them.

...

Pay attention to your birth and the specific state of society surrounding you.

Pay attention to your birth and where you are in the timeline of history.

Pay attention to your era's wants and needs.

Pay attention to your own gifts, creativity, ideas, and calling.

Your life is unique.

An individual like Malcolm X, with his birth into his specific state of society and the timeline of history. With his upbringing and experiences involving poverty and suppression of individuals that looked just like him. With his years of solitude in prison to self reflect, read books and grow his awareness and knowledge. With his growing wisdom and selflessness. With his attentiveness to his era's wants and needs. With his gifts. With the belief that someone ought to help. With his courage and leadership. The lane he took was almost inevitable. To become the individual he became that we know today. It was written into mankind.

Artists. Musicians. Activists. Philosophers. Social leaders. Inventors. Innovators. They are the personalities that form as responses to the current state of society. They are the solutions to mankind. They are what lead us forward. Curators of energy on this earth. Energy in their hands. Awake.

Breaking free from a mediocre job. Feeding their life into their purpose. Focusing on their craft. Focusing on their work. Attentive to their era in time. Attentive to what the people need. Letting their ego go and realizing their time here on earth is not forever. Understanding that, in a way, they are already dead. And they give their time here to the highest aim. In the face of all that may surround them and judge them, they are themselves. Listening to their calling. Listening to what pulls them. And holding onto the ride. And letting go of everything else. Trusting the path.

Honoring their uniqueness.

Be you. Know that you staying true to who you are, matters. Listen to your calling. Figure out what exactly it is that you will contribute to culture and to the planet. And aim for it. You are not here forever.

24

Chapter 24: Creating

At some point in your life, you must ask yourself.

Are you a passenger or are you a creator? Will you be on the sidelines of this period of time on the planet, riding the waves of what's created by others, or will you contribute with your own abilities? Summon your own waves? Get out of the stands and go into the arena and face life? Refine your own gifts and see what you are able to create? See what good you can do for the world?

If you are a creator, eventually, it will be time to create.

...

At some point, you need to start clearing the excess and clearing the distractions. It's time to summon what is within.

The modern day individual is surrounded by infinite information, everywhere, at all times. If you stay in this place, you will repeatedly be disrupted in your progress, and effectively neutralized as a creator.

There is always more information to learn, and knowledge to gain. New interviews, new podcasts, new documentaries, new research. But staying here, you will drown in it.

There is always entertainment you can consume and areas of culture that you can expose yourself to and be inspired by. New music, new art, new literature. But staying here, you will never cultivate your own voice.

There are always current events to inform yourself about. To stay up to date in what's currently happening in culture, in your country, in the world. But staying here, you will only move with the waves created by those around you, and never make your own.

When it's time to create, when it's time to start focusing on your work, you must start to go within, where the outer world cannot touch your focus. There's a time and place to listen to people. This isn't the time or place. There's a time and place to focus primarily on researching everything under the Sun, expanding your knowledge, and shedding light on all the areas of your own ignorance. This is an important part of your growth. But it isn't that time or place.

If you pay attention, and you allow your intuition to arise, you will know when it's time for your work to be your primary focus in your life. There's creativity, genius, and wisdom being birthed through your own consciousness. It needs your attention. It needs to be nurtured.

There is no other mind like yours. Each individual has something unique to offer the world. Each individual has a completely unique collection of genetics, upbringing, passions, skills, and experiences. The songs you listened to, the videos you watched, the books you read, the conversations you had. Your own creativity, taste, likes and dislikes. Your own particular choice of colors, sounds, words, and perspectives. Your own ideas and concepts. Your own thoughts. Your own dreams. Your own visions. You developed your knowledge and wisdom over the years. You expanded your comfort zone and experienced more life. You focused your energy on the areas of life that deeply resonates with you. And all of this together creates a unique perspective that is unreplicable. Everything you experienced, whether known or unknown, within.

All of this together fosters something deep within you, and brings into your awareness what you are meant to create and bring to life. Your own lane. Your own gap in culture that you know deep within you must fill. You know what your niche of your field needs, what your community needs, and what mankind needs. With your focused aim on your own particular work, you will create what you know must be created. This is your purpose. Your mind is unique. There is only one and there will only ever be one.

And this is your gift.
There's great power in this.
We need you.
The world needs you.

Allow yourself to go within to do your best and create. To the best of your abilities and skill. To the best of your current knowledge and level of awareness. To the best of your creativity and courage. Go within your own flow. Go within your own world. Give yourself the space and opportunity to go into your own mind and create the best piece of work that YOU can create.

What you create, with your focused mind, is a brush stroke from God.

...

As you get closer and closer to the realization that it is time to face your work and create, your pull to distract yourself, and numb yourself from the greatness you face, will increase.

Alcohol, drugs, casual sex, porn, video games, junk food, social media, endless scrolling of videos and shows. Everyone has their own particular way of keeping their attention preoccupied and away from what they must face. They are keeping themselves stuck. Scared to move forward. Scared of uprooting what they've built so far in their life to take a chance on something bigger. Scared to put in the time and energy, and not have anything to show for it.

Scared to fail and be embarrassed. Scared of not being who they envision themselves being able to be. Scared to succeed and enter a new world they do not know. Scared that they are entering a world of better creators, and they are not good enough. Scared that they will enter in this new world and run out of whatever gift they do have. Scared to be heartbroken. Scared that it's all just pointless. Scared of the unknown.

And as they keep themselves stuck because of their fear, they are in pain. They are stuck with where they are at in life. Doing the same things every day. Although they fear moving forward, staying where they are at is no better. Staying stuck hurts. And so they cope with the pain by increasing the distractions.

You are entering a significant transition phase in your life, and the turbulence of your day-to-day will only intensify as long as you avoid moving forward. You can run and hide in your distractions and live today in the sameness of yesterday and the day before…or face your work and evolve.

Face your work. Away from everybody. Away from everything. And work.

You facing your work begins the transformation you crave.

The transformation you've starved for.

You leveling up in ways you've dreamed of.

Focus purely on creation.

As you feed more energy into your creation, you simultaneously go deeper into the exploration of yourself. You are creating your work, and *discovering* yourself simultaneously. You are learning more about who you are.

You are also creating your work, and *creating* yourself simultaneously. The more you focus and go deeper into your work, the clearer your vision for what you are meant to be in this world, gets.

Your work, and you, move hand in hand.

As your work matures, you mature.

As you mature, your work matures.

Give yourself the space, and focus on what matters. Allow your life to evolve, your work to be physically created, and for you to become who you are meant to be.

...

Patience and understanding that it's not enough for you to have the right alignment internally, and to take action upon it, and receive feedback, but to continue to do this over and over and over and over and over again. It's not momentary pressure, but the sustained pressure that creates the diamond.

It's not momentary focus that creates your work, but sustained focus.

Time plays an essential role in the creator's process.

In the philosophical sense, time serves as a barrier of entry. It serves as a gate. The ones that are worthy must continue on with the process. And not just simply be in it…that's not enough. But be in it and be ENGAGED in it. Sustained focus, engagement, and enduring the whirlwinds that your human will whip up in the entire process. The thoughts of failure, the self sabotage, the success barriers, the self esteem issues, the anxiety, the pain, the heartache, peer pressure, the judgement by others, cognitive dissonance. Many will fail to pass the gate.

It takes developing your skill to a sharper and sharper level. It takes making mistakes and learning from them and developing a better understanding of yourself and of life. It takes developing your craft and learning greater and greater ways to express your ideas, and more and more accurately manifesting what you are thinking. It takes time to learn the creative language you wish to speak. To know what ingredients and tools you need. It takes time to feel some semblance of "figuring it out." And it takes time to refine your craft, create your piece of work, and have something of value to give to the world. Be patient. Continue learning. Stay committed.

What separates the individual with no mastery and the individual that has mastered their craft, is time.

Time, and the experience within it. It takes time to see and feel the nuances, that the individual with no mastery cannot even conceive of. It takes time to make what once took all of your conscious effort, to become part of you and become automatic. It takes time for your mind to open and higher levels to reveal themselves to you. It takes time to build your confidence. It takes time to become who you've always envisioned.

Time is IT.

And so knowing that time is a necessary part of the equation, and being able to STAY ENGAGED in your craft, and STAY in the time that must pass, in order to actually manifest what you are creating, then patience becomes the most powerful trait to have.

You must stay in time. You have to continuously be in time sustaining what it is you are trying to create. You must have patience.

You must love what you do. You must feel called to do it. For love is the only thing in the world strong enough to keep you steady throughout this whole process.

You cannot do something for thousands of hours without love fueling you. Beyond discipline, love will keep you focused. Love will keep you working hard. Your passion. Your obsession. You feel no choice but to continue. Through the ups and downs. Through the difficulties and obstacles. Through the plateaus. Through the self doubt and fear. Through the judgements of others. Through everything. And on the other side, rests your created work.

...

Creating is a patient process. There is an eb and flow, that cannot be sped up. There is only so much output possible in the day. Time, and the adversity within it, is the great filter for what will remain unrefined and unreleased in the mind and soul of the individual, and what gets created.

Understand the journey you are embarking upon. That you must show up. Sit with your work. There are days ahead. Months. Years.

You must show up to your work and chip away at it, through the sunshine and the rain, the good days and the bad, when it's easy and when it's hard. It takes sustained effort and focus to enter the new world you envision. It takes showing up. And showing up again. And showing up again.

Your work is what serves as the leading force that brings you into the new world.

Abandoning your work is abandoning the new world. And laying stranded in your current one.

Many creations are kept within the human mind, not worked on, unreleased. Many other creations began to depart the human mind and become physically created, but were left abandoned somewhere along the process. Left on a desk, in a room, on a hard drive.

It will get hard.

When it gets difficult, continue through the hard work.

You must go through a lot of emotions to complete your work.

Do not allow your idea of the perfect piece of work, intimidate you into thinking you are not ready to show up to your canvas.

Do not allow your idea of the perfect piece of work, intimidate you into not continuing your work.

These emotions that you feel with your work, that keep you from doing your work, are part of the process of you creating your work. You must show up and face your work and face yourself, regardless of these emotions. This develops the confidence in yourself that you will take with you for future stages in the journey. This develops the faith in yourself and your abilities. You don't see how powerful an experience it is to feel these emotions, and to continuously show up anyway. This is PART of creating. This is PART of you becoming who you are meant to become. Over time, you and your commitment to your work, will be more powerful than the negative emotions attempting to keep you from moving forward. Your focus transforms you.

Feeding your time, energy and attention into your work, is the greatest fuel for departing from your old world and moving into your new world. If you wish to level up in the ways you envision, your work must be your main focus, upon which the rest of your obligations of the day, orbits.

As soon as you know the direction in which you want to go in your life, wake up everyday and remember it. Your highest aim in your life, gives you the greatest context to live by.

Remember the work you are trying to create.

Remember the greats you look up to, and listen to the highest quality gem-like words they speak.

Remember the highest quality design of your vision.

Show up and create. Some days you may like what has been created. Some days you may not. Showing up every day is what matters. Showing up every day, the diligence, the tenacity, the unrelenting ability to not give up, the faith, the love, is not just a part of the process to get closer and closer to what you envision. It's the fundamental ethos. It's the spirit.

Show up to what you are doing. You cannot wait for inspiration to come. Although it may come occasionally out of nowhere, and it's always nice when it does, this is not nearly consistent enough to complete your body of work. You must show up. Show up to your work. Chip away at your work, little by little. Get things going. Think. Work. Move things around. And allow what will be generated within, to be generated. The more you show up, the more you live in your work, the more accurately you will be able to design what is within your mind. Do not wait for inspiration to come to show up to your work. Show up to your work first. And allow inspiration to come. And follow this.

Follow inspiration. Stay in its light, follow, trust, and continue to work.

...

Listening to others' thoughts and judgements will interrupt you. Caring about others' opinions will interrupt you.

Put others' thoughts about your work, to the side.

Put others' beliefs about who you are and what your capabilities are, to the side.

It's on you to go deep within and face yourself. Give this dance some time.

And over time, as you truly begin to form what you have been envisioning. As you mature and grow. As you develop your skill with your craft. As you dedicate your mind, heart, and soul to your work, and begin to truly create your work at the highest form you can possibly make it. As they begin to see and feel your work for themselves. As they see other responses to your work. As they see those that they respect, admire your work. As they see the effects that your work is having. As they see the results your work is having. As they see you grow and become something bigger than you were before. They may begin to come around and see what you have been seeing.

But do not wait for them to see what you see while you are still in the process of realizing it yourself. Don't expect anybody to share your own belief of what you are capable of, when they are only exposed to a portion of who you are. They do not see what you think. They do not see what you dream. They do not see what you are creating. They do not see your relationship with God. They have not felt the energy you are experiencing. They do not see who you are becoming.

Don't wait for people to approve of what you do. Don't wait for people to validate your path and who you are trying to become. Be it. Feed the world you are trying to create.

Understand that when you go within, listen to your self, and go with your own flow, you are not permanently shutting down outsiders and their words and views. You are not trying to shut everyone off and create your own echo chamber, in which you are an absolute creative genius and everyone who disagrees is ignorant. You are trying to shut everyone off and move into your own world, and for once, get the chance to see who you have the potential to be and what you have the potential to create. You are temporarily going within to face yourself and create the best work you can create.

Enough consuming. Enough taking in criticism and feedback. Enough learning. Enough micromanaging your own life. You have enough ingredients. You don't need any more. Go within. Create.

Pieces of work are burped up by individuals on earth through time. Art pieces, works of music, books, designs, innovated works, inventions, birthed throughout time that resonate with the generation and serve its role. Creations that serve as remedies for culture's current ailments, that solve problems, that stand as new beauty for people, that inspire individuals in new ways.

The incredible pieces of work throughout history have started EXACTLY where yours started. In the human mind.

Entrust your own taste. Believe in it. Go deeper in it. See where your intuition takes you. Listen to the music that interests you, watch the movies that interests you, curate your life according to what you think is beautiful and what you want to focus on. See where your love takes you, when you listen to it.

And work on what you truly envision.
Facing your work, the territory is unmapped.
Listen to the universe. Follow your intuition. Follow your heart. Follow what calls you.
Allow yourself to be you.
This will begin to map your own creative territory.

...

Your energy is everything.

Your sweet spot, your resonance, is where your greatest power is. Where you are able to see and feel more deeply. Where you are tapped in, think clearly and create.

You must find whatever unlocks the positively experienced moments in your life. What brings enjoyment, peace of mind, deep engagement. Higher levels of you. Higher levels of creativity. You must learn about yourself and fill your day to day life with what brings you into this space.

Everyone is different.

How can you work towards what you want to accomplish, if it's miserable every step of the way? Do not force the work out of you. Listen to the whispered secrets of your experience of life. Listen to the inspiration. What brings subtle happiness into the background of your life. What brings more effortless ease and focus. Where your vision is vivid and you can touch it. This is where you are meant to be.

...

You don't know how your best work is created.
Give different ways of living and working, a real experience.

Don't confine yourself to how you "think" you are supposed to create. Don't confine yourself to how others create and force this model unto yourself.

You see others recommend that you have a clean workspace. What if your mind thrives when it's messy? You see others with a regimental structure. What if your mind thrives from the randomness and spontaneity of day to day life with no structure?

A cup of coffee may speed your energy up, increase your anxiety, to where you cannot grasp your own resonance. Or a cup of coffee may slowly float you down into your own creative resonance and get you thinking, feeling and working in the right space of mind.

Alcohol may disconnect you from it. A glass or two may loosen you up to where you can more effortlessly work on what you need to work on.

In the same way it takes time and experience to learn the sweet spot of playing an instrument or performing a skate trick, it takes time and experience to learn how you should approach yourself and how you work with your craft.

You must figure out where your best self resonates. The sweet spot of yourself.

Knowing what inspires you and helps you think and feel more deeply, and what keeps you on the surface. Knowing what helps keep you focused, and what distracts you. Knowing when to continue working and ride your momentum and when to take breaks.

It takes time and experience to know yourself. This is half the battle. You are learning how to navigate yourself and the creation of your work.

A day of creating good work holds messages of how you can connect to your own genius and create again. The structure of the day, the music you listen to, the time you woke up, your thought process, your emotional navigation within yourself, your mentality. Pay attention to what fosters your greatest connection. Working in a certain place, in a certain atmosphere, or around a particular time of the day. Having a drink by your side of your liking. Eating before you work or waiting until after you work to eat. Phone put away, the right ecosystem, the privacy, wearing specific clothes, meditating. Tobacco as you go for walks, and ponder. A pint of beer after a day of hard work. Listen to these messages. This energy, is your energy. This is your gift. This is you.

You are becoming more in tune with the energy that will create the great work you envision. You are beginning to live in this energy.

Showing up every day will teach you everything you must know. You will learn the subtle nuances of accessing the sweet spot within yourself. You will learn how to guide yourself to the fountain of creativity within your own mind. To that energetic space that awaits you. You must listen.

Close your eyes. Listen to the music that resonates with you. Pay attention to how you feel. Feel your energy. Feel and know yourself beyond words. Know yourself at a deep level. Allow yourself to be yourself.

This will become your home.

…

There are messages in a good day of work. Listen to these messages. You are learning how to connect with yourself.

But go with the flow of today. Humble yourself, live in the present moment, and work on what is in front of you. This energy is a fundamental part of the sweet spot of yourself.

If you created good work, and the next day begins, don't try to recreate what happened yesterday. Today is a new day. Trying to recreate the magic of yesterday will have you following old inspiration. Yesterday was its own day. Today is its own day.

Do not wake up and go to the past. Wake up and live in the present. Attempting to recreate yesterday, you will not have the magic of yesterday. You were living in the present and going with the flow yesterday. Today, as you chase yesterday, you are not living in the present and going with the flow.

If yesterday you were excited, and today you are more mellow, allow and follow that. Do not chase excitement and resist what you currently feel. What you currently feel today, and you allowing what you feel today, is leading you to today's magic.

Today's lessons, today's ideas, today's progress.
New territory.

Wake up every day, humble yourself, live in the present moment, and work on what is in front of you.

...

Focus on your work. But remember you are human. There is only so much juice in the lemon in the day to squeeze. Replenish yourself. Moments in the day, and moments in the week, you can, and perhaps should, live your life outside of your workspace. Be simple. Enjoy the riches of this Earth. Watch a good film, read a good book, walk around the city, explore in nature, go into different rabbit holes in culture, have enlightening conversations, relax with friends, have a good laugh, exercise your physical body, think. It takes time and experience to know when to replenish yourself, and how. Learn what nourishes you and fills you with joy and inspiration, and live by this. Learn what leaves you empty and lacking, as if you never stepped away from your work and took a break, and lean back from entertaining this.

Know yourself, not just creatively, but lovingly.

...

In the beginning, ego and egoic ideas may inspire you to move forward. Make you passionate about how you see yourself, how others will see you, and all that you can receive for yourself.

But ultimately, you must get out of your own way. You are blocking the deepest quality of work you are able to create.

Self importance destroys the precious essence of your craft and interrupts the quality of your thinking and feeling. If you truly want to create the greatest work you can possibly access, you must remove the idea of yourself from this process.

If you dressing in cool ways inflames your ego, then purposely wear more simple clothing. If you talking in certain ways or about your work inflames your ego, then speak more humbly, speak less, or do not speak at all. If you posting on social media makes you think more about yourself and how people perceive you, share less on social media or temporarily let social media go entirely.

As you hold onto your ego, there is a flow of energy that is unreachable to you. Get out of your own way. Let go. Focus purely on the deep energetic space.

Listen to the music that speaks to you and that you hear, feel and receive at a deeper level.
Close your eyes.
Be still.
Breathe deeply.
Think of your limited time here on this earth.
Think of your place in the timeline of history.
Think of your creative mission.

Connect to your deeper energetic space.

The more you visit this space, the more you will evolve.

You will read words at a deeper level. You will hear words at a deeper level. You will hear music at a deeper level. You will see other humans at a deeper level. You will see your own life at a deeper level. You will understand and feel at a deeper level.

You are going deeper into the human experience.

Live in this space.

...

Over time, you can come out of your workspace and get feedback. In particular, from people who you respect, with lives with which you respect, who created work that you respect, or with minds and creativity in which you respect.

You can reach out to those who love you and know you to a certain degree. You can reach out to those who know what you are trying to accomplish. You can reach out for feedback from people in general.

In any case, see how individuals with their own minds and their own perspectives, see your work. You can show them in different stages of your creation, in a finished draft, or when in your mind, it is completed. This will help you see your work in different angles. Take their perspectives with a grain of salt, as they are not you, and only you know what you are truly trying to create. But understand that they may see what you don't, and this may play a fundamental role in your evolution.

Their perspectives may serve as new ideas that you can implement if you feel it is true to your work. Their perspectives serve as new information that, when meeting your mind, may begin to generate new ideas that neither you or them thought of before.

Humble yourself. Listen. You are learning your craft more deeply. You are receiving real feedback on what your current abilities are. You are learning what within you needs refining. You are learning what within your craft needs refining. You are developing your abilities. You are becoming more comfortable not being liked by everyone and standing on what is true to you. You are building your confidence. You are sharpening yourself.

These open conversations may be key for you to create your work to the level that you have envisioned.

...

As you create, focus on your own work and what you truly know. The creative language your life knows most intimately. What you resonate with so powerfully. That you currently wish to speak.

Know your lane and stay within this. Know your current area of expertise. Close your eyes. Know what you can and cannot articulate in this current moment. Know the territory to the left and right of your lane, the territory in which you are still learning. And know the territory that is much further out, that you currently know little to nothing about. All of this contrast will illuminate your path and the exact gap in culture that you are meant to fill. Know what your community needs, what your niche needs, what mankind needs.

Expanding your lane into areas that you do not know, is the quickest way to begin to doubt yourself and your abilities and to create what is not as authentic to you, what you do not truly know and lacks sustenance, or at a level that you are not satisfied with your current understanding and ability in the craft.

Expanding into these areas that you are interested in is good. It's progression. This is how you learn. This is how you understand more of life and grow. This is how you master multiple domains and be able to speak what is within you accurately. But you must do it when it is time.

As you are creating your work, stay within your realm of maximum effectiveness possible. Stay within your lane for the maximum creative dent you can make within this era of your lifetime. What you are currently able to conjure with your best abilities.

You only have so much time on this planet. Focus your efforts wisely.

And in time, when you are ready, expand and move into the next project within your craft. Move into the next craft. Move into the next calling.

For now, focus on what's in front of you.

...

Sometimes continued time with your work isn't the answer. Waking up everyday facing your work and working, even through stress and frustration. Sometimes you must develop distance between you and your work.

Let your work breathe. Let yourself live life and breathe. Sometimes space, rekindles your relationship with your work, sparks new creativity, and allows breakthroughs in your work. Go out into nature, go on a road trip, go on a run. Spend days, weeks, out in the world. Allow your mind to be free for a while. You'll know when to come back to your work.

...

At some point, you must realize that you have exercised your capabilities to their maximum capacity. This is what you are able to do at this point in your life. You have pushed your creativity to the edges. You have exhausted your own current potential.

At some point, you must realize that you have created to the best of your abilities, and let it go.

You can continue taking longer and longer to work on your own creation. You can do this until death. You can always improve in your skills, and try to make things better. But you can do this until death.

You must realize you have exhausted your current potential, be proud of yourself, and let it go.

Sometimes, artistic creations feel less like an architecturally sound and completed project from which you derive a sense of fulfillment, and more like a project that you think could be better, but it has decided in itself it is complete, and from which you derive a sense of relief with a touch of sorrow.

Perhaps, a complicated mixture of it all.

...

Creative work is not meant to be kept within forever. It's meant to be given to the world. Eventually, you must bring what you created, to the surface. Allow yourself to release your work and stand by it bare naked. Do not be afraid to release your work and stand by it, as this is fundamental to continuing your growth. The withholding of your work, is the withholding of your evolution. Enter your trial by fire and earn your badges of honor. Sharing your work is the sharpening of who you are. Who you become, and the effectiveness of your craft, is earned. There is a process. Trial by fire.

When you begin to create and release your work, you enter the public stage. The world stage. A new territory.

Judgement comes with the territory. Expect it.

Hate comes with the territory. Expect it.

Unadulterated love and praise comes with the territory. Expect it.

Good or bad, stay grounded in your own world.

Know that you will hear extremely bad all the way to the extremely good. People thanking you and people hating you. People saying you're a genius and amazing and people saying you're stupid, crazy and lame. Regardless, empty the charge that others' opinions have of you, and stay grounded.

You will receive feedback on your finished work in time. Take your ego out of the middle, and take in the information that you are receiving. See the universe's response to what you have been doing. See people's response.

Be humble. Be open. How does it affect people? Is it having a positive outcome?

Is it getting people through their day? Does it help them gain a more empowering perspective? Does it inspire them? Does it make them laugh? Does it help them process trauma and pain and cry? Does it entertain? Does it make them think? Does it inspire people to get closer to being who they are meant to be? Does it make people dance and be filled with joy? Does it tell a story that moves people? Does it solve a problem? Are their lives better or easier?

Is what you created, HELPING? Small or big, Is it making our experience together on this Earth, better in its own unique way? In this great era of history, understand that your work can be feeding the continuation of our spiritual stagnation, or do something positive for people.

Your creative work does not have to be a powerful philosophical piece of work. There's many creative ways to contribute to the world.

Take the feedback. The good and the bad. Let it be processed over time. Understand more of your direction. Continue to grow. Live your life. And when you feel called back in, go back within and create. Now, with new ingredients. Higher levels of thinking. Deeper understanding of yourself, of life, of your craft. Follow the new ideas that are birthed from your new place in life.

...

You may not know something is a true piece of work until some time has passed. In the moment it's being created, even the creator channeling this work may or may not know the gravity of it. And even in the era the work has been released, even if it is appreciated as a true piece of work, the extent of it may not be realized until more time has passed.

The effects of some work may take years to be seen and felt in the ways that truly capture the full creativity and essence of what was created.

As the years go by, and new generations experience the creation, the creative impact continues to expand. With new humans, in new eras, with new experiences, with new information, new perspectives are born. New eyes. New ears. New minds. New ways of receiving and internalizing work.

As the years go by, the generation that experienced the creation when it was released, with now more time passing, now sees and feels the creation with more context. As time passes, the piece of work stands in its place in history vividly. Its ripples are now experienced. Its deeper effects on culture are now experienced. Its influence on the individual is now experienced. Its impact on other creators and their access to their own genius is experienced.

It may take time for some work to be seen and felt in the ways the creator felt. It may take time for it be fully received and fulfill what the creator felt within, many years ago.

Creators are trapped in their place in time. Limited by the inventions they can work with, information they can learn, and individuals they can collaborate and create with.

Do your best within the time that you are in. You are in this era for a reason. You are part of this generation for a reason.

...

There's very little actual creators and doers.

A bunch of talkers, idea-sharers, perspective-regurgitators, complainers and finger-pointers.

A lot of people in the stands, judging, critiquing, consuming, having opinions, but not a lot of people in the arena, creating themselves, trying to solve problems, trying to refine their own abilities and offer something greater for the world, trying to help. They themselves not taking that journey into unmapped and uncharted territory into their own creative world.

Go deep into your own craft. Be of service to humanity.

We are ALL creators. We all have genius within us. Listen to your calling. Create.

Use the planet as a canvas, in which you will paint your great art piece. Use collective consciousness as a block of marble, in which you will carve your great sculpture. Use life as a blank page, in which you will write your great novel and paint paintings in others' minds with your words. Use your own human spirit and what sounds true to you, to create sonic remedies, new empowering fuel for the mind, and powerful energetic homes for other humans to live in and focus in. Use your own soul to speak into existence the emotions that of mankind, and of consciousness, is feeling. Express the deepest truths of our time here.

The focused minds of earth are the human collective consciousness' deepest divers.

When you reach deep into your own creative bag, you are reaching into the bag we all reach into. It is the universal human experience. The human spirit. It is what ties and binds us all together. It's the deepest home we have. It's what we all come from and from whence we will all return.

The deepest energy.

When creating, what you create isn't "yours", but that of the collective. It's something that deeply resonates with many.

You have been the one to have birthed this creation, but it is not "yours". You are the vehicle for which this creation shall come from the depths of the human mind and soul and surface on to this world. But it is not "yours". It is man's.

The deepest truths of our generation…
Of where our minds are at in the present moment…
Of what we need, and may not know we need it…

You don't know the answer. You cultivate the mind that receives the answer. You don't know the creative nuances.

You cultivate the mind that receives the creative nuances. You commit to your own greatness and the difficulties that come with it. You practice the craft for thousands of hours. You are diligent in practice. You humble yourself and learn from others. You are wise with who you listen to. You are open minded, let your ego go, and allow yourself to expand into uncomfortable territory. You develop confidence in yourself. You dedicate time and energy into refining your work. You become a more eligible vessel to birth the earth's gifts. You become one of the universe's entrusted vessels.

It is not anybody's job to understand and appreciate your work. It is only your job to do what is aligned with your soul.

It will resonate with who it is meant to resonate with.

Everything that you do, everything that you are, everything that you create, through your fingertips, is the accumulation of history. It's the leading edge of this human experience on earth. The 21st century. Universe is pushing you into new directions. And you moving into new directions, is mankind moving into new directions.

There are new energetic ingredients in your fingertips. It is the 21st century. We have never been here before.

Listen to the universe.

The universe's ideas are being created within your mind. Give birth to them.

YOU are the vessel for these ideas. Listen to your genius.

Chart new territory. Invent. Innovate. Create.

You must listen and express.

...

You are not promised creating the perfect piece of work you wish to create. You are not promised riches and fame. You are not promised the success and accolades you may visualize receiving as the public's response to your creations.

You are promised a more meaningful path. Spending your days chasing what matters to you. Spending your days creating what matters to you. Spending your days being surrounded by what matters to you.

The daily process of conjuring and curating. The pursuit of manifesting what you envision. A deeper relationship with life.

Getting better at focusing. Getting better at creating. Getting better at your craft. Becoming a better energetic portal for the deep universal source we are all connected to, and your chosen craft here on earth.

Each and every one of us becoming a devoted conduit for our own respected crafts. Creating to the best of our own abilities. Helping life on Earth in our own way.

A helpful energy on this earth.
A creator.

25

Chapter 25: Further along your purpose

Don't fumble your focus and miss your vision.

Don't take your blessings for granted.

Wake up everyday and repent.

Everyday is a new day.

Everyday is a new you.

Everyday wake up, humble yourself, give thanks for your existence, and focus on what matters.

...

Everyday be thankful for your existence here.

Everyday be thankful for another chance.

No matter your religion, walk in the light of god. Walk in the light of the higher power that brought us here.

No matter your origin, no matter your beliefs, you can walk in the light of the higher power that is above the human form.

Consciousness. Dreams. The Universe. The stars. Wake up and walk in that that we cannot fathom. Understand the preciousness of your time on earth.

…

Life is constant.

You are an active vessel.

Every day you must show up and remain humble. Let go. The more you let go of your ego, the more space you have for the universe and it's creativity and wisdom to flow through you.

Commit to your values and do not forget them.

Any day, you can begin the process of becoming more bitter, more resentful, more selfish, more focused on yourself, and less focused on doing good.

Any day, you can begin your descent.

Any day, you can begin to close off access to your greatness.

Putting your ego to the side is a daily practice. Humble yourself. Focus on your own progress. No competition with anyone else. Humble yourself. Love yourself. Meditate. Learn. Listen to others. Focus on the good you can do. This is a way of being.

Any day, you can become better than you were before.

Any day, you can create with more fineness and clarity.

Any day, you can become more infused with the present moment.

Any day, you can live in a higher state of love.

Any day, you can become wiser.

Any day, you can glow more.

…

Do not let the accolades distract you. Do not allow more opportunities distract you. Don't sell your vision for the consolation prizes that you may be offered along the way.
Move wisely.
It's very easy to get caught up in nonsense.
Stay humbled. Focus on the work.

…

Protect your energy. Protect your access to your own creativity. Protect your mind and your own positive thoughts. Protect your self care habits.

You must make yourself exclusive. Don't give yourself to just anyone.

Don't have conversations with everybody. Don't spend time with any and all people. Develop self awareness. Pay attention to how you feel around certain people. Make sure you surround yourself with good people. Guard your time.

…

You cannot rest on your laurels. You cannot work hard, and get to a certain place, and now sit on your throne. You must always be a student. You must always be toiling. Washing and wringing the clothes, tending to the garden, walking up and down the dirt road, creatively.

You must keep your humility. You must keep your work ethic. Always study and learn. Read. Watch films. Go into nature and think. Go into your workspace and create. This is not something you do temporarily to gain success.

This is a place you choose to live your time on earth inside of.

This is a quality and consistency of life you choose to have. The quietness of little social media, entertainment, and conversational noise. The solitude of you with your own mind.
You choose to live in this space.

...

Go on a walk. Grab a coffee or tea if you'd like. Go on a run. Go on a drive. Sit down and think. Go on your porch, balcony or rooftop. Put yourself in the place where your mind is best able to release all of the day's worries and float up and float up and float up and see your life and it's trajectory.

What are you doing in life? Where is your life going? Are you moving in the direction you want to go? How are you spending your time? Are you spending it wisely? The 24 hours in a day you have every day, are you truly using it to the best of your abilities? What should you do this week? Next week?

This month? Next month? This year? Next year? The year after? What about your whole life? What should you do with it?

There's a reason why sometimes things haven't aligned yet and it wasn't your year to truly elevate to the place you wanted to elevate to. Reflect. Take a step back. Know the cycle of habits that you must let go in the coming year. Know the direction you must evolve into. Know where your mind must be at. Where your time and energy goes. Who you must spend time around less. The sacrifices you must make. Some of what you consume must be let go. There are decisions you must make.

Make them.

You need an element of this in your life. Spend hours of doing this every week. These moments will give you information that nothing else will. No person, no thing, no book, no video, no conversation. Nothing will give you the kind of information you'll receive in these moments of solitude and introspection.

As soon as you figure out what you need to do, go do it. Zoom back down into your life, and with your newly adjusted way of living, start taking action. Go do. In all of your wisdom and in all your ignorance, move forward. Start moving forward with the best of your knowledge and the best of your abilities. Start moving forward with confidence and courage and face the challenges ahead of you with your shoulders rolled back, eyes forward, grit in your teeth, trust in yourself, and love for the world.

26

Chapter 26: Your Greatness

Understand the lands we walk. What the individuals that came before us had to face. The work they had to do. The constant difficulties. Mapping out the territory of the earth.

Those before us developing towns. Building roads. Farming for food. Scientific discoveries. Inventions and innovations. Using their minds to invent better ways of living for themselves, for their communities, and eventually for mankind. Facing an unknown earth.

Now it's in on us, to take mankind further.

Now we have infinite power at our fingertips. We have the internet. We have the ability to connect. To collaborate. To work on what means the most to us. It's on us to rise in our responsibility, and do our part. Represent our generation of individuals. Help our community. Help culture. Help earth.

The earth is more known and better understood. We have better tools. We have more knowledge.

But so much lies unknown. We still don't know where consciousness comes from and how we have this awareness but so many species do not. Where dreams come from and how they work. Space and the universe remains a mystery. So much of our oceans remain a mystery. There are an untold number of species living amongst us still yet to be discovered. We still aren't sure about our own species' older civilizations. We don't fully understand human health optimization and longevity. What happens after death remains a mystery. Whether this is one stop among many, or this is just a sliver of life we got to experience, from which once death arrives, we will return back into the weaved fabric that is the universe. Whether those living on Earth are the only living lifeforms in the universe. Space and the planets distant from us, sitting there, waiting as our and our descendants' final frontier.

WE STILL DON'T KNOW WHAT EXACTLY IS GOING ON HERE.

We still don't know how all this works. Why we are here. What exactly is going on.

Mystery surrounds us.

Homelessness. Poverty. The pollution of our oceans. The usage of plastic. Mental health. Substance abuse. Division.

Problems that need solving surround us.

There's incredible art works yet to be created. Paintings, writings, sounds, films.

Artistic perspectives and moods uncreated surround us.

There's incredible inventions yet to be created.

We have more water, more food, shelter. We have a better foundation of living to survive, and more solid ground to give ourselves space, nurture ourselves, use our minds, and create.

...

Every individual should be following their own purpose. Finding fulfillment in their own lives. Finding their own happiness. Helping their community in their own way. Adding to the richness of our time here.

Not everyone has to achieve "greatness within culture", or "world renown status" or "massive success".

There's merit to every single person's existence, no matter how small and no matter how big. If your existence is a net positive to the world, is all that truly matters.

But if you feel like you are meant for something great, truly great, it's on you to listen.

...

Ultimately, your own experience of life is as deep as you want it to go. But you need to focus your whole being on going there.

You must go deep.

If you wish to focus your life's efforts in becoming this, then you can.

Every generation of humans living on this planet has greats amongst them. Individuals on the cutting edge of time. Shifters of culture. They are the people that will change much of the trajectory of mankind.

There's been incredible human beings for hundreds of years. With every generation, there's always some in the batch.

The leaders of change in this world.
The tips of the energetic spear. The creators of the future that we are all stepping into.

Inventors. Artists. Musicians. Directors. Writers. Philosophers. Architects. Designers. Speakers. Business owners.

Geniuses. Shifters of cultures.

Leading their own specific niche. Leading through their accomplishments and what they overcome, inspiring others. Leading through teaching and sharing ideas. Leading through their creations, and directly improving the lives of others. And leading through how they live own their lives.

Dedicating their time on earth to something beyond themselves. Dedicating their being to solving their field's problems. Doing something different, at the highest level they can possibly reach.

The modern day flowering great, who, no matter how appreciated, is always under-appreciated, who live their days trying their best to move society forward, who live their days working deeply, doing the best they can with their time on earth, and enter unexplored creative territory, is the future's mythological and praised ancestor.

Martin Luther king Jr. within social structure.
Tupac Shakur within music.
Virgil Abloh within fashion.
Pablo Picasso within art.
Robin Williams within comedy.
Charlie Chaplin within film.
Nikola Tesla within science.

For in the future, their actions become more clear. Their life becomes more clear. Their mission becomes more clear.

Their sacrifices becomes more clear. The territory they charted becomes clear. What they accomplished for mankind with their time on earth, becomes clear.

Individuals who temporarily achieved greatness with their time on Earth.

...

Most people think that they can't accomplish their dreams, achieve any greatness, or become greatness, when there are endless examples of people doing exactly that. Individuals breaking out of monotony, boredom and normalcy and becoming great. List 15 great people that you admire. Now research them and look at their personal life and upbringing. Where did they start? Who were they at one point?

You'll see people from lower, middle and upper class all becoming great. Living in the ghetto, living in the the average suburbs, or living in prestigious neighborhoods, becoming great. Black, White, Hispanic becoming great. American, European, African, becoming great. With a single mom, a single dad, or both parents, becoming great. An only child, or with many siblings, becoming great. Fat, skinny, man, woman, becoming great. High school dropouts, high school graduates, and those with degrees from universities, becoming great. Children of amazing creators and children of everyday laborers becoming great. Healthy or disabled, becoming great. People with insecurities and fears that learned to live with it, and people with complete confidence, becoming great. People that thought too much of what other people think, that thought that they weren't special, that thought who am I to be great, becoming great.

Read autobiographies. Watch documentaries. Watch interviews.

Do not continue living in your own self-deluded, comfortable bubble where you can hold onto this idea that it's not possible. It is possible.

Demystify the gods. Humanize the greats. Realize that what they have achieved is not some sort of distant anomaly, but rather, a part of the built in normal function of the human experience. It's a space that is accessible for humans on Earth, with real dedication.

Realize your own potential.
When looking at successful individuals, look at their story.
You're watching an individual's evolution.

The same evolution that is waiting to occur within you.

...

Look in the eyes of the greats that live today. The same human emotions you experience.

See their journey. See their stories. Look in the mistakes they make. Look. They are imperfect. They are human.

Look in the difficulties they lived.

Look at their own obstacles. The deaths of close ones. Hardships. Incomplete families. Homes of struggle.

Little confidence. Unsure of what to do. Unsure of their work. Unsure of what they should do in life.

Hard work. Persistence.
Blood, sweat, and tears.

Doubt in themselves.

But persisting. Choosing to believe in themselves.
Believing in their vision.
And working towards it.

The greatest fighters had nightmares of losing.

The greatest writers doubted their work.

The greatest filmmakers didn't know how they would finish their projects.

The greatest public speakers and performers would be sick before going on stage.

The small homes great creators were born in.

The rejections many of the greatest creators have had.
The insults. The hurtful comments.
The doubts and limitations thrown at them.

Read memoirs. Read notes. Read autobiographies.
Watch interviews, watch conversations, watch films.

Understand that the greatest individuals that you yourself look up to, have stories of fears and anxieties. Do your research. Read their stories. Watch their videos. Listen to their own experience of life and how they had to come face to face with fears.

Penniless artists and inventors. Broken homes and poverty. Uneducated but with a passion to learn.

Henri Rousseau began truly painting seriously in his 40's and worked small jobs in his 50's, working at a small newspaper, and playing violin on the streets, as he painted new works. John Ford played in hundreds of pictures, and did small contributive jobs on set, as he learned his craft, eventually beginning to film his own pictures, producing dozens of works before truly harnessing his craft. Ernest Pyle studied journalism, traveled, and developed his ability to write over decades.

Throughout your journey, over the years, go back to this knowledge, and allow it to give you motivation to navigate your own life and know that you are not alone. You have your own story to tell. You have your own journey. You have your own obstacles. At the end of the day, we all are human, experiencing the same human emotions.

The great individual you look up to, had their origins. You have your own origins. We all share the same experiencing of having an origin, and trekking through life, living this adventure.

You are in the same position as them.

With your own story.
With your own gifts.
With your own skills and passions to refine.
With your own energy to curate and focus.

With your own dream to create and step into.
With your own territory to chart.
With your own contribution to culture.

You are on this planet equally. You are on this planet just as much as they are.

The human experience.
Temporary in time.

...

Take your life seriously.

Believe in yourself.

You have no idea just how great of a contribution to Earth you can make.

You matter.

Everything you touch in your own life.

The people you walk past. The people you interact with. The people, around the world, that may resonate with you, but don't even know you yet.

The ideas within your mind need love.
They need care.

Commit to doing your greatest.
Don't be ashamed.
Don't be embarrassed.
Moment to moment, in your environment, be the beacon of light.
Focusing on your own greatness, doesn't take away from others. Don't feel guilty.
Don't lessen yourself.

The most extraordinary of gifts are locked within the most ordinary of humans.

With their insecurities.
With their fears.
With their doubts.

Under a hard childhood.

Under an emotional life.
Under not knowing if they should continue going.

It is your duty to yourself. It is your duty to your loved ones. It is your duty to your community. It is your duty to the ones you have lost.
And it is equally, your honor.
Every day you are here, it is a gift.
Every day, it is your honor, to be able to show up, and be the greatest you can be.
To do your own part.

Believe in yourself.
Believe in who you are.
Believe in what you are.
Believe in yourself the same way you believe in those you look up to.
Believe in your own connection to greatness.

Regardless of your current level of knowledge and ignorance. Regardless of your current level of talent and skill. Regardless of how developed your craft currently is. Regardless of the current clarity of your vision.

If you feel the inkling of greatness within, choose to commit your life to greatness.

Choose to be a student of life.
Choose to understand the world.

Choose to see how you can best serve.

It all begins with a conversation you have within yourself of how you will live your life.

Being great, is not something you are born into or not born into.

It's not something that happens to others, and not to you.

It's not something that you don't have a choice in the matter.

It's a conversation you have within yourself.

You choose to be great.

You have one go.

...

You are just an expression of the times.

You cannot help but live in the times you live in.

Stuck in your period of history.

Stuck as a human.

But knowing this, although limiting, is not entirely so. It's not necessarily limiting, even though you now know your limits. You are bound to this era of time. This is where you are at.

Now, go do.

...

You're a human being dropped into this period of the world's history.

Study your field. Study your craft. Study your history. Study man.

Understand, to the best of your abilities, how the present moment that you are currently living in has been shaped by individuals, events, inventions and wars.

Understand where we are currently at. Understand the problems we currently face. Understand where we are heading as a people.

You paying attention to culture, paying attention to your community, paying attention to mankind, you will slowly begin to understand where you are. You will slowly begin to develop a better awareness of what exactly is missing. Of what people need. Of what is required to help facilitate growth. Of what is needed artistically. Of what is needed creatively. Understanding where you're at, is key to creating something culturally, spiritually relevant that speaks to the collective's core.

The key to greatness is the time in which your creation sits in.
The key to greatness is the space in which you exist in, and how you operate in the face of this.

The sounds…
The words…
The curated works of art. The inventions. The designs.
The ways to move. The innovations.

...

You are not divorced from its current events.

Every period of human history was standing on the shoulders of giants in terms of technology, innovation and creation. And every period of human history had its problems, trials and tribulations that it was facing. Whether as individuals, as a race, as a country, or globally.

In the 21st century, we have ours.

You need to be aware of them. In order to be the greatest self you can be in this lifetime, you must be the best self you can be for the community and world that you are infused with. Become aware of what your community needs. What the world needs. And how you may best serve the world. What is YOUR gift.

If you are to be great,

You can't be creative in a void. You must know your surroundings, to chart new territory. You must know your surroundings, to know your ingredients. The creative artists always created and contended with current events and the world that surrounded them. The time they existed in. The era of history they were dropped into.

Vincent Van Gogh painted. Showed the every day man, the peasant, arguable the most humans of human, in their real light. The beauty of earth. Victor Hugo fought for social causes, capital punishment in his drawings. John Steinbeck wrote of labor exploitations during the Great Depression. John Muir wrote about the beauty of nature, and fought to establish national parks, and have it be protected. The writings of Leo Tolstoy of nonviolent resistance inspired 20th century figures. Nipsey Hussle through music moved the masses to educate themselves, live with integrity and make something of themselves, through the poverty of their times. Bing Crosby's voice and tunes going through the radios, boosting the moral of American families in World War II.

Your work does not need to be so in your face.
You can create, and have it be nuanced.
Subtle.
The atmosphere your work sits in.
The ideas you may allure to.
The sounds.
The stories.

But know the world you are in.

Live within this juxtaposition.
Create what is true.

...

You are thrusted into the world. Thrusted into existence.

As you listen, as you learn, as you get older, as you experience more of life, as your wisdom grows, as your awareness and presence grows, as you mature, you become a grounding force.

You become more conscious of your moment to moment influence on the planet... start to carry yourself accordingly.

Live your time here on earth, in the deepest level you can reach.

Focus on the greats. Keep your attention on greatness and what greatness does. How greatness lives. What it looks like. How it feels. How it breathes. How it exists on Earth.

Let this help guide you.

Treat your time like the greats treat their time.

Have the circle of concerns as such.
Thoughts as such.
Patience as such.
Focus as such.

Moment to moment, you must exalt yourself over your own smaller thoughts, habits and fears.

Live in the momentum of you being face to face with your dreams.

How are great individuals and creators so magical...

Only when the individual drops everything, and listens to their own soul, will his life transform.

...

Forward movement.

What is unanimous of all the great warriors, statesmen, fighting men of great battles, artists, philosophers, is forward movement.

Courage in the face of death.
Living with fear and moving forward.
Moving into uncharted territory for their descendants to follow.

Clearing the dangerous path, knowing how much risk they are putting themselves in. Judgements. Threats. Changing the narrative. Innovation.

Introducing new paradigms.
Introducing new designs.
Introducing new artistic perspectives.
Introducing new experiences.

Introducing new moods.

Moving forth in life, not for themselves, but for their community.

For their loved ones. For mankind.

Leading the charge of their generation into the unknown.

Being an inspiration for future generations to look up to, as did great leaders in past generations did for them. Being a beacon of hope.

There is little time squandered in self-preserving thought. Any of the kind, is dismissed as immaturity and selfishness.

This time, your time on Earth, is used to move us forward.

Honoring those that came before you...
those that came before your time, and lived their life in dedication to something greater than themselves.
In dedication to you...and they didn't even know you yet.

...

Where would we be if Martin Luther king jr instead of focusing his efforts on equality for all, spent his time riding the waves of the 50's and 60's spending his time at concerts, jazz clubs? Where would India be without Mahatma Gandhi? Where would South Africa be without Nelson Mandela? Where would we be in the present day without George Washington and those that constructed the constitution?

Where would the world be without these individuals?

Heroes do what's needed.
They want to live their own life too.
They want to enjoy their time on earth.
But they use their life to do better things.

Courageous humans.
Noble humans.

Heroes are always needed in time.

…

You cannot be nostalgic and stare at the past.
For every era that you look to, the individuals within, could have looked beyond itself.
Humans with never-ending fixation of the past.

Every era has something special within it. Every era experiences its own current day.

You are in an era.
You can look into your own era.
And do the present day's work.

Look around you.

Look at the artists you share this earth with.

Look at the present days circuses, peanut galleries and distractions.

The present day trends of being.

Present day hardened opinions.

Territory uncharted.

Gaps in culture that need filling.

What do people need?

...

Marcus Aurelius facing, in his day, a modern Rome.

Vincent Van Gogh greatly studied the works of Rembrandt, who lived 200 years before him. And we are here, in this time, almost 200 years after Vincent Van Gogh himself. Who may be looked at in this era in the same light?

Artists of today.

Innovators of today.

Times keeps going.

Great works always needing to be done.

Authentic lives always needing to be lived.

Chapter 26 1/2: Creating 2

People try to be creative, and it's lame.

They try to be revolutionary, but nothing in their work is new.

No new territory explored.

No unique thought.

No experimentation.

No creative synthesis of all the work you study, and input of your surroundings.

The same perspectives as others in your field.

The same opinions shared with the person next to them.

Same surface layer desire to be seen as revolutionary.

Revolutionary in title only.

But none of the creative energy of one that deserves the title.

No real work made.

Simple designs on t shirts.

Same albums with simple verses.

Fake deep in interviews and social media posts.

"Fashion icons".

Same simple desire to discuss your own process and be seen as a creative genius.

Calling everyone who is uninterested in your shallow work, a hater.

No real impact. But acting as if they are individuals of great innovation. And people around them lifting them up as if they are.

Lacking talent.
Lacking real hard work.
Lacking time in the deep energetic space...focused.

So many people. Lacking sustenance.

Everything. Everyone. Lacking sustenance.

Why are we impressed by horrible ideas?
Why are we impressed by lazy craft?
Why are we impressed by personality-less creators?

"Vintage" clothing.
Calling every clothing a "piece".
Calling every song a "record".
Taking photos of art work to display some sort of artistic aesthetic expression. Faux artistry. Aesthetic by association. Not even really caring for the art, but rather seeing it as the possible added mystique and allure to their own ego.

Using names of painters and designers to increase your own uniqueness.

Record players in apartments for visual aesthetic.

Buying tattered clothes, or with splattered paint, to have the appearance of someone with more character and living their life, instead of developing character yourself.

Using old film recorders to make their videos resemble artists of past times, offering nothing necessarily new, but using this aesthetic as their main piece of creative unique contribution.

Appearances at cafes to faux deepness.

Walking fast around the city in mystique clothes, expecting to draw attention and have people be curious about you.

Drinking cool low key but trendy beers, not for the enjoyment, but for the appearance.

Listening to songs that don't really truly resonate with you, but because they are popular.

Chasing an accepted image.

Chasing validation.

Chasing admiration from strangers.

Trying to impress other humans you are sharing earth with, in the many nuanced ways you discover. Abandoning real creative impact, and adopting the desire for relevancy and acceptance from the current passerbys of earth.

Instead of following what's true to you.

Starving for what feeds you.

And this is among the individuals that are decently socially intelligent, creative, and have a decent work ethic.

Remaining on the periphery of your own creativity… of the sounds, the textures, the visions, the ideas, that truly resonate with you. That take you deeper into what you have to offer the world.

Getting caught up in trying to appear cool.
Getting caught in a lifestyle.
Away from themselves.

No real character. No real personality. No real creativity.

The people we are on earth with today are dull and boring.
Nobody really wants to do anything. Nobody really lives interesting lives. They do not dare to venture. They do not dare to be bold. Rather they want to look like they're doing something.

Like they are someone of value and rarity.
Like they do cool things behind the scenes that you do not see. Trying so hard to be different.

But their routines remaining simple.

Their lives remaining similar to everyone else's.
As everyone is doing this.

They're simple human beings.
The version of themselves they are being, is simple.

No real risk taken in their lives. No real sacrifices and letting go of what's holding them back. No real time with their creative selves. No real surrounding themselves with creative works that inspire their own ideas. No real time filling their mind with creative ideas and perspectives. No going for walks. No contending with ideas. No real time with their work. Creating work, creating work, creating work.

Doing. Practicing. Embodying. Refining.

No hours of deep thought. Multiple ideas, flushing ideas. Coming to resolutions with perspectives. No new revelations. No new epiphanies. No new discoveries. No new territory.

The same territory as the "creative" next to them.

Staying safe and working at their job.

Doing the easiest things to stand out, but thinking that they are ahead of the curve.

Half their thoughts are spent thinking about how they look and how people are judging them. Walking past mirrors on the streets, always having to look over and get a glimpse of their appearance. Thinking about so much junk.

Hours at a job they don't like. Hours commuting and distracting themselves. Hours looking at dumb stuff on social media.

The way the modern day individual interfaces with life on earth, is more basic than many care to see inwards and admit.

Basic thoughts.
Basic conversations.

Basic behaviors.
Basic routines.
Basic ideas.
Leading to simple work.
Nothing revolutionary about you or your work.

Living a simple life, with simple work produced.

...

The earth has become one giant —

The commercialization of the earth itself. As if it's one big mall. We sully the earth and the human spirit, with every billboard we prop up throughout the countryside.

Every new building built with the cheapest of quality materials, in the most mundane and casual design.

With every regurgitated film with the same regurgitated plot. Repeating what real creators of the past have toiled and explored themselves.

With every actor that spends their time building up their own brand with every social media post, story and interview, instead of living a real artists life in solitude.

With every artist that spends their time scrolling on social media, posting, so much energy keeping up with others, so far away from the creative space within their own mind.

With every writer that works behind an office desk, bored, continuing their life of boredom.

With every musician with a similar sound to the musicians surrounding them, refusing to release their real work.

With every team of creators, churning out projects as rapidly as possible, skimming over real taste, to compete with the speed of social media.

With every sentence lazily spun up. With every melody settled upon. With every idea left on the shelves.

The space of real creativity, the space of real craft, goes avoided.

...

Put down your phone. Close your eyes. Dream.
These visions, is what makes life on earth, so precious.
This is our own great adventure.

Becoming what we envision. Creating what we envision. And living our lives with this beauty in our hearts and minds.

Letting it surround us. Letting it be how we see. Letting it be how we touch.

Letting it be how we interface with life on earth.

Close your eyes. Keep your mind on your art. Let go, and drift deep into the textures and sounds of your ideas.

This is the world in which you waltz in.

…

Powerful works, capture the essence of the human spirit. Makes us feel something real. Love. Sadness. Sorrow. God. Anger. Heartbreak. Missing someone. To process emotion. To process themselves. To feel understood. To feel touched. To understand the world around then. To understand themselves. To understand their path in life. To cry. To see different perspectives. To feel love. To feel powerful. To feel the significance of our era. To feel the significance of relationships. To truly appreciate nature. To feel inspired. To feel the ability to accomplish.

We are starving for real work.
Just everyone giving up. Tired.

We need creators, and real artists, and real individuals living authentically in their own lives, for real works to be created, and for real works to come out into the world.

…

We don't have to look into the past to admire.

We don't have to reminisce.

We don't have to sit stagnant and stare to the few real creators of today.

We don't have to try to fit in the social scene, and live a life we don't even find genuinely exciting.

We don't have to protect a reputation we deep down can't care less to maintain.

We don't have to stay working a job we hate.

We don't have to follow the roads others take.

We ourselves, can embody the great artistic spirit of man.

We can explore.

We can spend our time creating.

We can spend our time contending.

We can embody what we want to see.

We can create what we want to create.

Adventure!

Grab a coffee! Grab a beer! Grab a cigar!

Go outside! Explore the world!

Live your life!

Do not hide away. Do not be afraid of death.

Be afraid of hiding away from life!

…

Set sail!

We are not here forever.

Let us be adventurers. Artists. Explorers. Scholars. Inventors. Engineers. Writers. Designers. Actors. Directors. Musicians.

We all have something within us.

Let us not sit idly by. Rather, live as close to creativity while you are here. Live a good life. Live in a nice place, but live as a peasant. Create faster. Be furious with your creativity.

Live in the energy of the greats.
Live in creativity.
Wake up and create.
Go down thoughts and ideas.

…

You feel it in your skin, bones, mind, heart, and soul.

As you walk down the street. As you make more decisions in your life, focused towards your work, and truly becoming who you want to become. As you work on your craft. As you study the greats. The life you live.

Your focus. You entering new realities.

There's something special, very human, about not knowing everything. That's part of the journey.

You won't know all the nuances of what you're trying to create. Of the phase of life you're moving to.

But you must move.

Meet your work in the same way the greats before us did!

Meet your work with the same spirit the greats on earth before us did!

Explore new territory.
Live in your craft!
Live a life on earth!
Live a life worth living!

Set sail!

...

Ernest Hemingway.
What was he doing in his 20's.
You choose to become a writer.
To become a writer, you must become a writer.

What was Ernest Hemingway doing in his 20's. Writing.
What was Jean Michel Basquiat doing in his 20's. Painting.
What was Pablo Picasso doing in his 20's to 80's. Painting.

Working.

In the world.
Truly deep in their mind.
Thinking, creating.
Working.
You must work. Every day.

Vincent Van Gogh, left to work in Paris. Painting from sunrise to sunset, while his contemporaries would often stop after the sun went down. Using the little money he had used to purchase more canvas, eating very little. Bread, coffee, and absinthe.

Living an adventure of a life.
Jack Kerouac. Charles Bukowski.

Traveling. Exploring your own country. Driving across country. Seeing fellow countrymen. In the same way Mark Twain and John Steinbeck traveled the country. Big Sur and the mountains. The towns. The rivers.
Be the modern day adventurer.
Go to national parks. See the beauty of earth around you.
Living life. Broke with no money. No idea what to do next. But living life, and exploring.
Discovering the world.

Billy Wilder. James Stewart. Ernest Pyle.

Excellence in your craft. Capture the mood. Design what you envision.

Live in a small room. Sleep on a couch.
Put yourself in the position to succeed.

Your 20's are sacred. They're the time to figure out your life.
To learn. To explore. To write. To create. To learn crafts.

Be human for a while.

Be a normal everyday man. Experience what it is to be like everyone around you. A countryman. A waiter. A farmer. Working construction. Garbage. Struggling with rent. Figuring out who you are. Working. Studying.

Developing your sharpness.
Learning how to navigate the world.
Developing social and emotional intelligence.
Develop a sense of responsibility. Develop a sense of duty to your country.
Learn to be innovative and have self reliance.
Dependable on yourself.
Learn to be a good student. Humble yourself.
Become articulate. Find your own sound.
Find your own rhythm to life.
Find what gets you to wake up and live life with the proper ferocity that it is meant to be lived with.
By god man, live!

This is your time here.
In the same light of great artists of the past.

The same trees and the same stars.
This is life on earth.
This is our time to experience life.

Entering real conflicts, war zones, coups and protests.
Be amongst homeless.

The cultural hubs of the planet! Where innovation is alive!
Paris, London, Milan, London, New York, Tokyo, Los Angeles.

The countryside! The untouched beauty of the earth!
Where memories and tales permeate the air.

The historical places.
The current fascinating places of culture!

Nashville, Sacremento, Mobile, Memphis.
San Diego, Detroit, Philadelphia.

The small towns. The back roads.
The origins of our nation. The roots of our culture.

Late nights. Early mornings.
The rich neighborhoods. The poor neighborhoods.
Wander the cities. The cafes. The bars. The fashion stores. The restaurants. The liquor stores. The comedy clubs. The underground pool halls. The old film cinemas.

Real artists. Real painters. Real writers.
Creating in your own studio.
Tinkering in your own desk, inventing and designing.
Notes everywhere. Papers. Ideas.
Your workshop.
Designers. Architects.
Sitting with their work.

Wandering through museums. Seeing the relics of our ancestors. Seeing the art work created by individuals who focused their minds, refined their crafts, lived in this space, and brought to earth physical pieces of the human consciousness.

Through the internet, you can sit with artists.

Surround yourself with genius and ideas.
Surround yourself with physical pieces of creativity.
Surround yourself with books, artworks, and your paper and pencil.
Surround yourself with films, documentaries, and interviews.

...

How do you know if you are it? If you are the one? If you have something special? If you're different? If you have something new with value to offer the world?

You don't.

If you are the one to create something revolutionary?

If you are someone who will create something that over time, will be respected, admired, and held as a cultural entity? A cultural cornerstone? A cultural masterpiece?

What is experimental for an individual in his day to day life creating his work, becomes a classic piece of work in the future for generations that are raised under its influence.

A real piece of work.

A sleeping giant. Toiling and creating every day.
Unaware of the importance of your work.
Unaware of the future.

You leave this to your audience.
This is not for you to know…

…

Your work will be unbearable if you don't believe in yourself.

Believe in your self. Believe in your work. Believe in your own connection to greatness. Believe in your ideas. Believe in your creativity. Believe in your craft.

And if you don't, dedicate your self to your craft until you do. Study your craft. Live in it. Surround your waking hours with it. Practice. Create.

Live in it, until that's all you know, and that's all you breathe.

Then you will believe in yourself.

You'll know your craft through and through. You have self awareness and know yourself. You are a good student to your craft. You have developed your skills. And over the years, you've gotten closer to the genius that's within everyone. You've dedicated yourself. You didn't listen to your distractions. Day after day, you chose your purpose.

And the universe opened its doors to you.

Then your work will be your home.

It will be your fountain of youth. It will be where you feel most alive. It's the place where the greatest individuals can pick up fruits and bring them back to mankind.

The greatest books.
The greatest films.
The greatest albums.
The greatest inventions.

You go into that creative land,

Day after day.
You go into the land and come back.
Bringing back fruits,
Piece by piece.

Unfinished work.
Building architectural masterpieces.
Eventually having a finished work to give to mankind.

...

Some of the greatest actors, have duds as films.
The greatest musicians, have songs that don't translate well and were a complete miss.
Some of the greatest painters have unfinished artwork around their studios.
Some of the greatest musicians have hundreds of unreleased songs.
Some of the greatest comedians bomb.
Some of the greatest inventors failed over and over...

It is on you, to show up.

It's very difficult to capture the essence of life.
It's very difficult to capture precisely what you envision.
But as a creative individual, it is your duty to try.

You will fail sometimes.
But you may get close sometimes.

And this is the splendors of life. This chasing.

All we have is the pursuit.

Your dedication to your craft.
Your slow walks in the neighborhood. Your deep thought.
Your curiosity and wonder. The sun. The trees.

Your mere humanness, in the middle of it all.
Contending with ideas.

…

Our time here on earth, if one was not from here, would arguably see this unknown place, this small floating blue-green dot, as one gigantic creative workspace.

Humans all over the planet.
Built with an imagination.

The ability to dream.
The irresistible desire to dream.

In one gigantic obstacle-filled planet.
With gigantic obstacle-filled personal lives.
Each of us challenged.

Each of us with our own flicker of consciousness.
With our own temporary time with it.

Facing the unknown.

What are others doing in the face of the unknown? What are you doing in the face of the unknown?

Life is short.
You're sharing time on earth together.
You're alive together.

…

You live your life, knowing that you won't be able to do everything.
Many experiences will be left on the table.
Be brilliant.
Be an effective individual on Earth.

…

Face your work. Meaningfully.
And create.

A work of the human spirit.
A work of the artistic spirit.
Charting territory not of physical destinations on this green earth, but of something naturally within every man.
Charting the territory that is of our birthright.
The creative space within the individual.

Do with your writing what Vincent Van Gogh did with art…

Do with mathematics what Marlon Brando did with acting…

Do with architecture what Bernard Hermann did with orchestra…

Do with film what Charles Dickens did with literature…

Do with engineering what Walt Disney did with animation…

Do with business what Albert Einstein did with science…

Do with landscaping what Duke Ellington did with music…

Do with fashion what Frank Lloyd Wright did with architecture…

Do with music what Orson Welles did with cinema…

Sit by the candle light.
Dream in ways our ancestors dreamed.

27

III.

A new existence

Chapter 27: Self care

At some point in your awakening process, as you become more conscious of yourself, you begin to become more in tune with your own mind, body and spirit. You begin to feel your own experience of life more and more. And you begin to feel the stress. You feel the tension. You begin to feel when you are in your energetic sweet spot of life where you are feeling good, at peace, healthy and at ease. And you begin to feel the moments of when you are brought out of it, and into a more uncomfortable, unhappy, space of existence.

Over time, you begin to notice the contrast. The repeated experiences begins to illuminate just why you are feeling the way you feel. You become more sensitive to what is causing it.

The sickness certain foods are giving you. The building discomfort and unease within your body of sitting down all day scrolling on your phone and not moving around. The negative mood being around certain people puts you in. The stress of being bombarded with advertisements and materialism. The anxiety from spending hours every day of your life at a job you don't like. You are awakening to the world around you.

And you are beginning to realize you are living with a body that has not been taken care of.

…

We're living in a time of increasingly expeditious awareness. Truth is surfacing. Fast. About other cultures and races. About what we're told by our governments. About healthcare. About drugs. About our climate. Our own traumas. Our family's traumas. Our culture's traumas. Everything is rising to the surface.

And in response to that, anxiety is increasing. Stress is increasing. Monotony in pointless jobs are becoming more evident and less capable of suffering through.

And in response to anxiety, stress, and monotony increasing, our abuse of outlets and ways of numbing ourselves increases. Marijuana. Alcohol. Prescription drugs. Video games. The image we create on social media. Consumerism and purchasing materialistic items.

There's a shift among us. It's breathing down our necks. It's encroaching. We must shift. Change is near. Within us, and within our society. It's a massively tumultuous time to live in.

This is an era of great change that will be looked at as the maturing of the individual.

All of this pain is rising to the surface. And at our current level of wisdom and consciousness, our immediate reaction is to blame someone for it.

And we would be right. We know that many of the systems that we live and participate in daily, do not care for the common people. We know this. It is no longer farfetched, but common knowledge. We are broken, misaligned, unhealed versions of ourselves. And it will stay this way. Too many people in positions of wealth and power, benefit from us being broken. The systems that we live in and participate in daily, are not built for us. It is not built for the benefit of the individual. It is built for the benefit of a few select individuals. And it will continue to operate this way, unless these few select individuals with the wealth and power to change these systems have transformations in their own consciousness.

Fear is pumped into the news. We are taught a victim mentality and told to blame other groups of people. They feed on our insecurities and exploit them. We are punished and thrown in prison for our addictions to drugs. We are fed horrible and unhealthy food in our schools. We are told to take pills instead of being taught about nutrient-rich foods, exercise and fasting. We are fed constant advertisements that manipulate us. We are one medical emergency from complete bankruptcy. We are not respected and cared for as individuals. We are not treated with care. We are squeezed and sucked of our energy.

Because real change that would transform our culture is largely dependent on the transformation of the wealthy's consciousness, we may be waiting for a while.

We can no longer wait.

Although this must change, and over time with our own purposeful actions it will, we must stop waiting for corporations and governments to improve themselves to alleviate our own pain and suffering. We must stop waiting for something to change, and begin the change.

We must put our focus on ourselves. We must begin to take care of our own energy on this Earth. Our own mind, our own body, our own spirit. Self care. Real self care. Loving ourselves, taking care of ourselves, and taking our own being into our own hands. This is what we have the power to do. Right now in this moment. Right here where you sit. And from here, every day, moving forward.

It is time to begin to claim that power. A new emerging relationship with ourselves. An updated relationship with ourselves.

...

Most individuals are operating at a small percentage of their actual capabilities. Because of no goals or vision set and real movement towards them. Because of overwhelming levels of anxiety and stress, with no understanding of why, and no attempt to address it proactively. Because of constant preoccupation with work, school, and obligations, and no time spent on developing mental space from all of this through meditation and exercise. Because of constantly eating foods that drag your energy down.

The average individual, with so much potential, becomes neutralized. Stagnant. Frozen in time and space, due to their lack of self care.

Creatively stuck. Physically heavy and tired. Mentally all over the place. Emotionally overwhelmed.

...

You think you are angry. That you are inherently an angry person. That specific people are angering you. That certain situations are angering you. But in reality, you are not engaging in self care. You think you are angry, but you haven't exercised in days, maybe weeks, so you have pent up energy and adrenaline within you. You don't meditate or give yourself time and space to center yourself, so you get aggravated more often from moments throughout your day that really shouldn't.

You think you are depressed. But in reality, you are not engaging in self care. You think you are depressed, but you just haven't gone outside in days. You are glued to your phone, and don't take your eyes off. You don't have any hobbies that excite you. You don't socialize with people or spend time doing things that actually interest you.

You think you are an anxious person.
But in reality, you are not engaging in self care.
You think your life is miserable.
But in reality, you are not engaging in self care.

You are neglecting yourself. You think you are inherently these things, but in reality, you are just not taking care of yourself. You are skipping out on the self healing therapeutic mechanisms built into our human experience. And to do so, is to live life unnecessarily more difficult.

In the autopilot nature of your existence, it's much easier to wake up, go about your day and look around and blame things for your agitation.

Don't look at your surroundings for the reason you are so anxious. So depressed. So angry.

Look within and see if your actions are of someone that is actually taking care of themselves.

...

There's universal habits that, when done daily or a few times a week, carry tremendous benefit for whichever individual that does them.

What exactly they are, how you do them, and how often, is subject to change and is heavily dependent on the individual's preferences. But doing these habits nonetheless, is arguably the most intelligent thing one can do.

Nature and sunshine. A good hike, a good run, a good trip into nature, is more nourishing for the mind, body, and soul than you can possibly imagine.

Meditation, time and space away from others and being in solitude, therapy, breath work, fasting, understanding your past and letting go of traumas, reading books, listening to teachers, introspection and humility. And, arguably even more importantly, knowing when to get up and leave, and go outside, and contend with life.

Eat healthy foods to receive constant nutrients for optimal brain function, body function, and mental and emotional stability and peace. Ensure you are receiving proteins, vitamin d, probiotics, omega 3's, fruits and vegetables. Animal organs, grass fed meats, pasture raised eggs. Focus on real foods for human beings. Each and every individual is different. Find what works best for you.

Exercise is clearly beneficial. But how you exercise, whether it is walking, running, martial arts, weightlifting, yoga or swimming, is all up to you. How often you do it, is up to you. Invest in yourself. Commit yourself. Put yourself in the right headspace to be the next version of yourself, and you're able to normalize it. Get what you practically need. Join a gym that inspires you. Join classes to have structure and be inspired by others. Go run or bike around the areas that interest you and makes you think and feel at a higher level. Get a skateboard, bike, or ball to do the sports you like. Be part of a community or team so you have camaraderie and fun with others. Put yourself in the position to actually succeed. The lack of these simple steps forward, ensures you stay in place.

...

Habits serve as the bedrock for the rest of your life. They ARE your life. They are intimately your life and simultaneously serve as the foundation for the greater aspects of your life.

To eat healthy meals, to exercise, to meditate, to fast, and to limit your time with your vices, for the sake of it being the "right thing to do", is not the greatest motivator for an individual to consistently engage in them, day in and day out.

But when you understand that this will create for you the exact quality of life that you crave, these habits begin to make more sense.

When you understand that the peace of mind, the bliss, the health, the stamina and vitality, the confidence and comfort within your own body, the focus, that you desire, is achievable, then you understand that the choices that you make, are everything.

When you understand that you can make yourself a more effective creator, you begin to see it is your duty to take care of yourself. Where waking up with energy and vitality is your default. Where focusing on what matters and creating through the day, is more effortless. Where you have the ability to be expansive in your creativity, and follow lines of thought and have the mental stamina to continue down ideas and connect them.

When you understand that adhering to certain habits within your own life, will allow you to live the life you actually want to live, you begin to see the power of self care.

...

You have control of what you are.

Meditation. Time and space for yourself. What you eat. What you drink. You exercising. You going out into nature. Fasting. Your ecosystem. The music you listen to. The videos you watch. The conversations you engage in. Going on walks. Your limitation of vices. Your limitation of social media and the internet. The work into your craft. The presence of specific daily habits.

This is your way of mastering your energy while you are here on this earth.

Know what affects YOU. Go through your own trial and error. Learn through your own experiences. Do your own research. The codes to a better life for all of us are being revealed. Through the internet, through the wisdom of focused creators, through scientific research, through evolving subcultures that support the individual and their health and success. The common individual has access to their own best self if they listen closely and pay it their attention.

Go through the years of, aside from the learning of sciences, trades, arts or whichever fields of your focus, the learning of yourself.

You learning about yourself, and taking care of yourself, serves as one of the fundamental pieces to the richness of your life, your relationships, your personality, your effectiveness with your purpose, and the overall time you have here on this Earth.

...

There are many different versions of you.

You must know who you want to be.
You must decide.

There's a you that goes on runs in the morning.
A you that has coffee first thing in the morning.
A you that makes time to read books.
A you that barely reads and furiously creates.
A you that socializes.
You can't do everything. You can't do it all.
You must choose.
You must choose who you will be.
Pay attention to how you respond to certain things.
Pay attention to how you are designed.
You see different levels of confidence.
You see different areas of creativity within yourself.

Create boundaries for yourself. But not for disciplinary sake. Not as a punishment. This isn't retaliation aimed at yourself, for constantly messing up.

You must understand the power and the beauty of boundaries. This is you knowing yourself.

This is knowing how you are designed, and adhering to this. This is you taking care of yourself.

This is you doing your job, and ensuring you are protecting your energy, protecting your mind, protecting your body, protecting your health, and aligning yourself with a precious experience of time here on earth.

...

You living right now is a miracle beyond your control. It's not forever. It's not up to you whether you will wake up and get another day. If you are lucky, tomorrow you will wake up, open your eyes, and realize you are still here on Earth. You have been given another day.

You do not rise above this process. You do not live by this process, until you finally are above it.

Rather, you live by this process, and remain living by this process. You remain humble. Living with the intimate under-standing of your humanness. Your flawed nature. You do your best, living on this earth, to be a good human, while you are here. You do your best to keep your self tended to. Respect-ing yourself. Keeping yourself maintained. Keeping yourself flourishing.

Forever meditating. Forever fasting. Forever going for walks. Forever being introspective. Forever humbling yourself. For-ever listening. Forever realizing your limited nature as a human, but doing your best to see how far you can go... See what wisdom you can attain. See what territories you can explore. See what work you can create. See what you can do in this current time in history.

You are not above the process.

You are the process. You are the doing. You are the being. You are moving. You are a living human being. You are consciousness within a temporary physical being. You are a piece of the universe expressing itself through human form.

At our peak, at our highest form of ourselves... we are explorers. We are creators. We are thinkers. We work together. We create. We design. We share ideas. We dance. We play. We help each other. We ride this limited experience.

So take care of yourself. Allow yourself to be the most effective experiencer and receiver of life you possibly can be, while you are here. Be filled with energy and vitality. Be filled with creativity and genius. Be filled with joy and happiness. Live the adventure. See how far you can go. See what you can do. Enjoy your time here.

28

Chapter 28: Context and Perspective

Look into the stars. Look far across the vast ocean.

This will put everything into the greatest perspective.

This will help you realize daily, that a lot of what you think matters, doesn't actually matter.

What matters is this great adventure on Earth.

…

You must give what is challenging on your journey, context.

Otherwise, it doesn't make sense to do what is challenging. It doesn't make sense to do that which causes discomfort and pain.

You won't be as invested. You won't be as committed. You won't have the fortitude and focus to stick in it when it gets tough. Because, in your mind, there is no reason to.

You must give the discomfort and pain, when it inevitably comes, context.

You must have a reason for why you are continuing forward. You must remember why you are doing this.

…

Your energy cannot have conditions. We must not wait for specific external conditions. We must not wait for things to be perfect. The right living situation, the right job, the right environment, the right mood, no physical ailments.

Waiting for everything external to be right for us to feel good and focused.

Your energy is unstable and frantic. Going with the environment and reacting to how the day is going.

Although it is definitely more enjoyable when the external conditions are ones that you prefer, they should not dictate the quality of your energy and your focus.

Although your aim is to improve your life, do not wait for your life to be improved to master your energy.

Master your energy now. Focus your energy now. Get in tune with yourself now.

You must be able to temporarily forget the present circumstances and put your mind to where you want to go, who you want to become, and what you want to create. Submerge your mind into your own creativity.

...

Live how you want to live now. Feel it now. Embody this now. Accept where you are. Know where you want to go.

This is what allows you to truly connect with your work. This is what allows you to see your future so clearly.

...

Remember your family. Remember your community. Remember your country. Remember your ancestors. Remember the youth.

Remember what matters.

29

Chapter 29: Relationship with your mind

In developing yourself, what arguably matters most is the tending to your own consciousness.

Everything else is often noise.
Attacking symptoms instead of the origin.

With the giving of your energy to the clearing of mental and spiritual debris, the healing of your pain, the expansion of your self awareness, and the rising of your own consciousness, much of everything else will fall into place. Healthier communication, healthier habits, healthier mind and thoughts, and intuitively eating what is healthier for you, intuitively moving away from toxic relationships and creating healthier relationships, intuitively spending less time on what drains you and spending more time on what is good for you. And more focused energy towards your purpose, family, community, and humanity.

Educating yourself in different fields of self development is helpful. Educational. They give you the tools to operate and navigate the world. But what will always be the most important way of developing self, is focusing your attention on your consciousness itself.

It's all about your energy.
It's all about your self awareness.
It's all about your consciousness.

The thing that controls the lever of gratitude.
The thing that changes the textures.
The thing that shows you different perspectives than what you are usually accustomed to.

You wake up and go about your day.
Complaining. Having a bad attitude. Being reactive. Thinking about judgements and letting this control you. Thinking about negative scenarios. You begin searching for stimulation. Scrolling and clicking. Talking and thinking. Arguing with others. Eating and drinking. Trying to outthink your negative thoughts. You are still stuck in mind. Trying to fight fire with fire. Getting pushed into a river of anxiety, swirling and getting carried away in the momentum of your thoughts.

Your consciousness, the very thing that experiences life on earth, and changes the quality of life in earth, and interprets life on earth, remains untouched.

Unexamined.
Unexplored.
Unharnessed.

...

Silence and space must be created.

The last few decades, meditation has become more and more commonplace. What was previously seen as too spiritual, religious, or "weird", is now being seen as a healthy practice for humans to engage in with their own minds and consciousness.

Allow more space. Allow more silence. Not distracting yourself and placing your attention on the numerous things around you, but instead, placing your attention to the present moment and life itself.

Slow down. Listen and feel.

...

Meditation is the way of reclaiming your mind and it's power. It's up to you to liberate yourself.

You begin to see aspects of your life that you must take responsibility for. Things that you were blinded to, as you were so focused on other people and what they were doing.

A lack of meditation, and the accurate reflection meditation leads you to, will have you thinking your problems and stresses in your life come from other people. Meditation will quickly show yourself that the problem, very often, lies within you.

Your own unkempt, undisciplined mind has been manipulating you and influencing your personality, thoughts and actions in life.

The beginning of you meditating, is the beginning of you seeing all of this.

The more you meditate, the more you cannot not see.

Your own negative thought loops.
Selfish thoughts.
Self obsessed thoughts.
Judgements.

And as you see it through meditation, and you go about your day, you see your mind going down these paths. And you'll be able to catch yourself and go down these paths less and less.

You'll let these thoughts, slide by you.

This is the beginning of the discarding of negative thoughts, and the releasing of the power behind them. Letting go of negative thought and thought loops. And when they inevitably occasionally come to visit, they have little to no power.

Negative thoughts begin to have context. You understand the reasoning behind them. You use them as messages, and continue on your path in life. You are empowered.

The more you meditate, the more you'll be able to catch yourself engaging in toxic behaviors and go down those paths less and less. You'll catch your own stubbornness and ignorance more. You'll catch yourself being led into anxiety and fear by your thoughts, and be able to detach from them.

You are exploring your mind, finding and identifying negative programming, releasing them, and increasing the quality of your thinking.

And the better quality of your thinking, the better quality of your life. You are discovering the internal noise that distracts you from living the life you want to live, and letting it go.

You are, moment to moment, able to live in the energy you want to live in.

You'll find yourself thinking more intentionally. And less distracting thoughts. And when those distracting thoughts do come, they come and go. You're not as metaphysically intertwined with them. There's an ease to your thinking.

You've identified their annoyance. You've identified their distracting nature. You've identified their true pointlessness. And so they float on by.

Anxious thoughts, fearful thoughts, OCD thoughts, paranoid thoughts.

Thoughts of potential fights and arguments.

Thoughts of what can go wrong.

Thoughts of complaining, what is wrong right now and general lack of gratitude.

Thoughts of hate. Thoughts of anger. Thoughts of envy. Thoughts of insecurity.

None of these serve you.

When they come, like a car passing you on the highway, you wave, and continue on your own way.

You are alive. You are more you. You are more present.

When you meditate, you're having more intimate play with your own energy. You feel it. You develop more awareness of it. And you begin to be able to tap into yourself differently, feel yourself differently, and carry yourself differently.

You're able to let go of the heaviness.

And live in the energy that you truly want.

A lot of people are unaware that there's something blocking themselves from a richer experience of life. It's up to you to identify the noise within yourself. To feel it's attachments. To see it's foolishness. And to let it go.

Allow the textures of your vision start to change.

Allow the textures of your thoughts and emotions start to change.

Allow your mind to shed layers.

Go deeper into the embodiment of who you truly are.

Allowing silence into your life, will allow you to more effortlessly be aligned with everything that truly matters to you in life. You will be aligned with your self, but something simultaneously greater than your self.

Meditate to access the feelings and wisdom that you yearn for. Meditate to access the quality of experience of life, that you know is possible. The high level of thinking, being and living.

Words often ruin moments.
Be quiet. Silent moments with yourself.

Sit in your energy.

Silence. Stillness.
Allow this to shine through.

This is where the real you awaits.

Rekindle your connection with consciousness.

…

For many, the beginning of meditation is the first step of self awareness.

If you zoom out, and look at your life, you may notice that the era of your life where you began meditating, was the beginning of your self awareness.

You understanding your life more.
You understanding why you are always in a bad mood.
You seeing how much you complain.
You seeing how much you judge others.
How repetitive and boring your thoughts are. How intrusive thoughts come, and you just blindly listen to them.

You notice it was the beginning of many things.
The beginning of real wisdom.
The beginning of seeing life through others' perspectives.
The beginning of real empathy.
The beginning of real love.

You begin to reshape your mental experience.

Unbearable experiences become more bearable. Your attitude changes. You enjoy life more.

You begin to become more intelligent.
More creative.

You enjoying life more. Listening to music at deeper levels. Richer conversations with people. Heartier laughs. Loving time with yourself. Seeing the good in people. Wanting good for people.

The entire way you interface with life on earth.

...

Discipline yourself over your mind.

Developing a better relationship with your mind, through hard work. Through facing the uncomfortable, feeling your mind squirm and wiggle and be scared. And doing it anyway.

Letting the anxious thoughts, in practice, not have any control over you. You breakthrough.

Letting fearful thoughts, in practice, not have any control over you. You breakthrough.

Letting desiring staying comfortable thoughts, in practice, not have any control over you. You breakthrough.

Hot saunas and steam rooms.
Cold shower and ice baths.
Long distance runs.
Weight lifting.
Consistent gym workouts.
Physical sports and crafts and the consistent study of them.

They are all mediums in which you can learn to discipline yourself. To master your mind.

Build lean muscle. Lose excess body fat. Expose yourself to heat. Expose yourself to cold. Go on long runs. Sculpture your body.

Build this momentum. Live in this momentum. This is your lifestyle.

Developing a different relationship with discomfort.
One where you are not afraid of it.
But rather face it, endure it, and conquer it.

And not just once. But routinely.
You develop a new relationship with your mind.

Your fear is not something that you listen to.
It's something you consistently conquer.
Emotionally, internally conquer.
You physically doing the actions.

It's hard to live a life you find worth living, if you are held a coward within your own mind and body.

You develop a new relationship with the thoughts that typically confine individuals. The fearful thoughts. The anxious thoughts. The desiring comfort thoughts.

You do the hard things. The difficult. The things that scare you. The things that are outside your comfort zone.

And you routinely conquer them.

You become more free. You think at a higher level. You feel at a higher level.

You do not fear, fear. You do not listen to anxious thoughts. You do not allow desiring comfort thoughts to lull you back into your comfort.

You enter what is uncomfortable. Routinely enter what is uncomfortable. And free yourself.

You are no longer stuck. You refuse to be stuck.
You move forward in your life.

...

Meditation is not the one solution to your entire life.

You are still living this human experience. You must do. You must act. You must create. You must live your life. You must still work on your craft. You must still get experience. You must still look at your relationships and learn. You must still move into the unknown.

Exercise, touches your life in ways that meditation simply can't.

You must still go outside and socialize. This helps you feel good and makes your life better, in ways that meditation simply can't.

And you working, creating, solving problems, moves you forward in life. Use spending time with yourself, as a tool. To live your human experience more fruitfully. Do not try to meditate your problems away. Meditation will reshape your mental experience, and help you be able to face life with more ease.

But then, face life.

...

You meditating, and spending more time than others learning to be silent and observing, doesn't make you better than others.

There may be others who are engaging with life, and are more self aware, mature, wiser, than you, but don't meditate.

This is a personal journey.

This is for YOU developing a better relationship with YOUR mind.

...

Some individuals may require less meditation than others. Out of billions of individuals on earth, it only makes sense that some individuals have a better relationship with their mind than others. They are able to wake up and ride the momentum of their life. They have good friends around them, they are in a good neighborhood, they have things in life they are excited for, and they are focused on their purpose. It comes naturally. Theres a lightness to their life.

They may also have periods of meditative like moments throughout their day or week, that allows them to gather many of the benefits they would receive from purely sitting and meditating. Whether they wake up and stay lying in bed, before they engage with the day. Or maybe they wake up and ride the momentum of their ideas and energy and immediately engage with life. Maybe, later on that day, it's the moment before they sleep, in which they lay down, take a moment, and reflect. Or maybe they do some fort of breath work in the day. Or have a leisurely bike ride. Or a jog. Or sit in their porch and ponder. Or even in the moments of them working on their craft, they are able to be at ease and breathe.

In any case, it's these meditative moments that bring peace into their life. It's these meditative moments that reshapes their internal experience.

...

Maybe, arguably, almost everyone would benefit from sitting down and purely meditating. No activities. Just sitting down. And meditating. It may be an aspect of this human experience, that when done on its own, is so powerful, that every single individual would benefit. Maybe individuals that already live fruitful lives, would be able to access a space that, although their current way of being is incredible, would be even more fruitful.

In any case, explore YOUR self.

...

As you wake up, your mind begins going.
You have no choice in the matter. You are alive.
And this is what your mind will do.

But you can change the quality of your thoughts.
You can change the relationship with your mind.
You can change how you interface with life.
You can change the quality of your time here.

As you discipline your mind through hard work. As you meditate and identify thoughts that your mind will derail to. You'll find your mind in a place so precious and fruitful, that words cannot do it justice. It's something beyond human comprehension. It's something that we cannot fully articulate. We can explain through science, we can paint the details through flowery descriptions through literature, we can elude to it through art. But we only see portions. It can be spoken of. It can be talked about. It can be described. But we only get glimpses and pieces. Ultimately, all of this fails to fully capture and embody what happens within. It's something beyond our language. It's something you have to experience yourself. It's a metaphysical place you must discover, and explore, yourself. It's something, within you. The beautiful consciousness within man.

30

Chapter 30: Vulnerability and kindness

Individuals are walking around, tightened up, taking themselves so seriously. When nobody even really cares.

Wearing cool clothes, knowing the cool spots to go, listening to cool music, or knowing how to create cool photos, doesn't make you cool. It means you are good at identifying what will give you the highest status in the minds of others, and following the trends.

A lot of people spend a lot of their time and energy being cool. This is their focus. But once this is accomplished, what exactly have you accomplished? What good have you done on this earth? What influence have you left in the hearts and minds of people? What exactly has your life been about? Are you even any happier? What exactly was the point?

The chase for mystique and separation through superiority, whilst, by definition, sacrificing unity and togetherness, is more transparent than ever before. And its transparency and obvious selfishness nature will only grow. As we move deeper into the 21st century, the smoke is clearing. Its low aim is becoming more clear. Culture is shifting.

...

Do not waste precious time and energy on this planet, chasing what is cool. There is no need to photograph everything. There is no need to film and share what you are eating, the places you are going, and the clothes you are buying. Put your phone down. Live in your life.

Micromanagimg your image and how other people may perceive you. It makes your life cartoonish. A caricature of what you are supposed to be. A layer removed from the deeper meaning of life.

This is time and energy that can go into a deeper, more meaningful, experience of you.

In your seeking of fame and popularity, you remain a child. In your wanting of others to think you are cool, you remain a child. You live as a small portion of your actual potential. A version of yourself that still needs further evolution.

...

Being cool is overrated. It's time is over. As we move into the future, more and more individuals will begin to realize this.

The people who care so much about this, ultimately deep down you don't care to impress to begin with.

The people whose opinions do matter to you, those whom you do admire, don't care of your coolness, nor will they fall for it if you put all your energy into a good presentation. They care about your energy. Your ideas. Your work. Your kindness. You getting out of your own way and being a fun person to spend time with. You caring about other people. You operating in life with higher values. You having higher boundaries within your mind. You having a good soul. You focusing on real things.

Not a version of yourself that is filled with self importance.

...

Do not chase the validation of small minded people. You will live your life on earth, as if you are in the corner, poking at a rock.
An endless, fruitless, behavior.

Neither should you chase the validation of people you admire. Although it may be something you deep down desire, this is an immature endeavor. And ultimately an overly-self involved one.
This creates a limited version of you.

There's better ways to spend your time.
Focus on being the best version of your own self. Focus on creating a quality life. Focus on creating quality work.

Let your work, let your energy, speak for itself.

As soon as you come to terms with the fact that you have no other choice than aim for your highest high, and you make that spiritual agreement, much of the day to day suffering of life is alleviated. Whether you have insecurities or not, is unimportant to you. Whether you get validation or not, is none of your concern. Whether people think you are cool or not, is not up to you, nor do you care to go into others' minds and manage it. Famous or not, you are an artist, that remains true. Rich or poor, you are an artist, that remains true.

The time you have here on earth, is focused.

...

We're not going to get to a better future by being cool. You being cooler than others doesn't do anything for anybody. We're getting to a better future by us ourselves, individually, living in a state of vulnerability and humility.

Your kindness, your positive attitude of life, your creativity, your humor, your lightness, your energy, is what makes you a "cool" human being. This is what matters.

Your energy on this earth is a piece of art in and of itself.

This is what matters most...

Your energy.
Who you are.
Who you decide to be.
How you feel within, and you sharing this.
How you treat people.
How you live your life.
Your craft.
What you can do with your mind.
Helping others.

...

Show your humanness. Do not hide it. Your humanness, and the acceptance of your humanness, is your salvation.

Micromanaging your image and how people see you, is keeping you from being who you truly are. Exposing your own vulnerabilities and insecurities, not in going out of your way to show them, but in deciding not to hide them, and to own them, will raise you to the clarity of creativity, peace of mind, and confidence, that you seek.

Being you, being yourself, being honest, being vulnerable, builds your confidence, love and trust in yourself. It is when you hide who you are, and pretend to be something you are not, is when you feel worse.

Be you. Do not hide yourself.
Be yourself. Be completely transparent.

There's a connecting energy within vulnerability.

People feel you within themselves.

And something about this, is naturally healing. It's nourishing to the soul. You feel recognized. You feel appreciated. YOU.

You feel loved without "I love you" ever being said.

If you buy clothes, it's because you genuinely love it.
If you take photos, it's because you want people to get a glimpse of things you are really passionate for and excited to share.
If you have a hobby, it's because you are genuinely obsessed with it, and you can't help but be attracted to it.
The people you hang out with, you genuinely resonate with.
The music you listen to, genuinely moves you.

Like what you do. Like who you are. Like what you are into. Like your life. This is real confidence. This is real coolness.

31

Chapter 31: Open mindedness, open discussion, and humility

When you backwards engineer where society is today (chaotic, divisive, fearful, depressed, anxious, suffering, outraged, addictions), you begin to see where it all stems from.

The birthplace of this chaos, is in the individual.

The chaos in the individual, when scaled, becomes the chaos of the society. Fearful individuals, when multiplied, create a fearful society. Individuals who think and communicate divisively, when scaled, create a divided society.

We must claim personal responsibility for the state of divisiveness we are living in. We must look within ourselves and see how we ourselves operate in our own day to day lives.

...

Close-mindedness is more common than we think. We label others as having a tendency to be close-minded, but never seem to see it within ourselves. You ask any individual if they are open-minded, they will most likely say yes. If someone were to ask you, you would probably say yes. But we would not be living in our current state, if most of us were open-minded. We are here, because many of us are more close-minded than we think.

We have our own limitations. We have our own emotional reactions to conflicting information. We have our own tendencies to contort information around us to fit our own narrative of how we see the world. We have our own tendencies to only interact with those that share our views of the world. And when we do interact with those that have opposing views, we have our own tendencies of trying to correct them, instead of listening to their experiences and possibly see knowledge that we may not know.

...

In this age of the birth of the internet, with all of this information available, its very easy to wander around and find yourself in an echo chamber. A place where your reality is the only one that makes sense. Your beliefs are the only ones that make sense.

Because of your own experiences, insecurities, traumas, you are led to a certain place. This is just how humans and the human experience works. We follow what interests us. We follow what relates to us. We follow our traumas and seek to find the answers to them. We are led to find confirming information of what we believe. And often what we would like to believe.

Everyone has been hurt. We are all frustrated with the sorrows around us. Everyone is trying to find answers. Feminists seeing the world through the lens of patriarchy. Conservatives seeing the world through liberals being radical. Liberals seeing conservatives as being hard headed and destroying the country. Seeing through race.

You are living a life that is specific to you. With your own perspective, own experiences, and in your own period in time on this planet. You become who you become, because it is inevitable. But make sure that you don't become the first thing you grow into and cling to it. Do not become an imitation of the true you. Do not cling to the first beliefs and perspectives you find, and fall into an echo chamber.

...

We accuse others of being so sensitive, yet we ourselves have become so sensitive, unable to be open minded and see the glimmer of truth in someone else's perspective. We have become so enraged by the information we take in, our own stance is further reinforced, and we are unable to be open to see any legitimacy behind the reasoning of any opposing viewpoints.

Echo chambers lead to their own rewriting of history. They have their own narrative of how and why events happened. This leads to the fortification of their beliefs and a further crystalizing of their stance. Crystalized ignorance. Echo chambers lead to the stagnation of your soul's progression. Lacking more information. Lacking conversations. Lacking any pressure on your own beliefs so you can challenge them and evolve.

When beliefs are held encapsulated within the mind of a human being, and defended as if their lives depends on it, no real growth occurs. You are less like a mature critical-thinking individual and more like a rebellious child, bucking back against any encroaching entity that is different than you. In this state of mind, there is no interest in you to find the truth. The only interest, if you really look within yourself, is to be right, and prove the "other" wrong, and attempt to correct the "other". So you are unable to change your mind to begin with.

When somebody's temperament is that of outrage, whatever points they defend and whatever beliefs they hold, will never meet with the proper critical scrutiny and analysis for an individual to mature and evolve their beliefs. Instead of advancing through beliefs and perspectives and widening their perspective on the world and maturing through higher levels, like a video game they become stuck at level 5. Instead of zooming further and further out and seeing the world for all of its moving parts, intricacies and nuances, they maintain their own perspective and never see beyond their own views or the views of the group they like to identify with.

The modern day individual has reached astronomical levels of sensitivity, where anything that doesn't agree with them, is not only unwanted and unsettling, but threatening. If you live your life, having visceral emotional reactions to every external sentence, opinion and belief, you will live a fruitless life. You will be living in circles; no new epiphanies being had, no realizations being had, no higher way of living being learned. Stuck.

This is an age of everyone, already knowing everything.
There is nothing new to learn.

…

There's a particular type of ignorance that has emerged in the last 10 years that is unique to the modern day individual. Both young and old generations, living in the world of the internet, thinking they know and understand the world. That they have the answer. But little to no grounding in reality. Becoming professionals and experts in fields that they have not studied. Little to no understanding of the intricacies of systems and the nuance. Little to no understanding of others' experiences of life on this Earth. Living in enclosed spaces with limited experiences and knowledge available. Living on the internet. Living in echo chambers.

Scrolling. Scrolling. Scrolling. Scrolling.
Clicking. Clicking. Clicking.
Driving yourself insane.

Arguing, commenting, complaining.

All alone. No real connection with others. No socializing.

Replacing real life conversations with neighbors, friends and strangers, with comments, videos, and articles on the internet. Listening to very specific people on the internet

Seeing the extremes on the internet and interpreting them as accurate representations of large groups of people, leading to much more fear and distortion of their own reality.

A lot of people hate the world, because they don't talk to the world. They alienate themselves, and in their self isolation, they begin to have enemies in their own minds.

Don't listen to the divisiveness.

Go out and talk to people, socialize. Connect with other human beings. The act of you talking to people, immediately dissipates many of the enemies you have formed in your head. You begin to realize people are much nicer than you think. You begin to realize just how similar people are to you. You begin to realize just how much you truly have in common with your countrymen. Our fellow countrymen. Our neighbors. Our family. Our friends.

Get out of your self imposed solitary confinement and breath real air!

...

In this modern day age where victimizing yourself has become normalized, even encouraged in certain fields, you have individuals that walk around in their day-to-day life, like heat-seeking missiles, looking out for cruel acts.

People of color, looking out for cruel acts by whites, to reinforce that a racist world exists.

Whites, looking out for cruel acts by people of color, to reinforce they are ignorant and criminal.

Feminists, looking out for cruel acts by men, to reinforce that the patriarchy exists.

Incels, looking out for cruel acts by women, to reinforce that women "are all like that".

Rich. poor. Conservative. Liberal. Friends. Family. The list goes on.

With a lack of self-awareness, you will become a copy of the many other individuals similar to you, that find themselves falling into the many echo chambers that exist today. And with the internet, combined with your lack of self-awareness, you will only fall more deeply into your echo chamber and cement the beliefs you have.

...

Both the young and the old can be ignorant, In their own unique ways. The old may not accept new ways of doing things, and the young may not know of the importance of the values held so dearly by the old. Both men and women can be completely oblivious to the others subjective experience of life and the hardships that come with it. All races can be ignorant in their own unique way, only really seeing through their own lens, and not fully grasping, nor taking the time to grasp, the experience of other races. The poor may not understand the fundamentals of sacrifice, hard work, ingenuity, seeking knowledge, and patience of those in higher socioeconomic classes. The rich may not understand the vicious cycles of poverty that keep many poor from ever reaching past a certain point of wealth.

Each and every individual from each and every demographic, can have ignorance about so many aspects of the individual's human experience, different fields of knowledge, and of the world.

...

Have you ever listened to someone from the opposite side, with viewpoints different than yours, for more than an hour? And with the aim to understand, not the aim to get outraged and dismiss?

Have you listened to a full length conversation of the individuals in which you vilify and have casted away as ignorant or bad?

Ignorance is an inescapable frequency you are left in, as individuals that practice humility, open mindedness, and self awareness, rise to higher levels and live a more enjoyable experience on the same earth the ignorant live on, but simultaneously, a different earth.

The ignorant are banished to continuously experience problems and suffering. Stuck being a portion of their capabilities. Stuck serving and creating at a limited level. Stuck solving problems at their level of understanding, only nibbling at the real grander issues.

The open minded are gifted more richer experiences, and being with richer individuals that live within the same frequency, and richer internal feelings of being alive. Happier. Lovelier. More intelligent.

...

You are born where you are. Experience what you experience. Know what you know. And this is you.

We are all a victim of ignorance. There's a lot that we don't know. There's a lot that we haven't experienced. Perspectives a complete mystery to us.

Until you make the effort to learn and connect with minds and their perspectives, you will walk the earth and its lands as a walking embodiment of ignorance.

Ignorance is a battle that most be fought within oneself. You may share knowledge and fight it in society. This is a worthy endeavor. This book is a form of that. But inevitably, this information must be taken in by the individual receiving it. The same way you read these words and do with it what you will. The individual must be vulnerable. The individual must lay his being out on the operating table and look at himself. Ignorance is a personal battle.

...

You don't know everything. You don't have it all figured out.

Trial and error is an important component for your life's progress. Because it is inevitable. Ignorance is part of the human experience. You must embrace its inevitability. The quicker you embrace your ignorance and your inevitability of making mistakes and having limited perspectives, the quicker you can learn from them and continue to advance.

Your journey will be riddled with mistakes and accidents. Having only a small perspective of much grander perspectives, and thinking you're right. Misunderstandings. Immature ways of communicating. Immature ways of interpreting relationships. Immature ways of interpreting reality. Immature ways of living your life. Inexperienced ways of approaching your craft and your field.

If you think a certain way, it's very hard to use your own imagination and think of alternate perspectives. Of bigger perspectives. It's up to the meeting of your mind with minds that think differently than yours, where you will continue to grow and evolve. Conversations with individuals from different backgrounds, with different experiences than you, that think differently, combined with your open mind, is what allows you to assimilate information, shine light on blindspots of your own perspectives, and see even higher perspectives.

You will unlock wisdom. You will see higher ideas that combine the wisdom of multiple individual's perspectives. You will see higher level paradigms.

Open-mindedness unlocks. Patience and humility unlocks. Communication unlocks.

This is learning. This is personal evolution. This is a life well lived.

...

Your own humility, and curiosity will take you far. Start to look around.

Wisdom is a quality of mind. Of course, its experience and knowledge, but more than anything, it is a quality of mind. What kind of environment is your mind living in? A mind of wisdom is humble and knows that there is always more to learn. A mind of wisdom seeks to understand. A mind of wisdom is not quick to judge, and if they do judge, they are quick to notice that they are falling into the trap of judging and have compassion for themselves for doing so, and try to re-understand.

A mind of wisdom knows it is human. It knows it is not infallible. It does not pretend to know everything.

It does not pretend to not have an ego. It is aware of having an ego, and practices putting it aside, to listen, and learn.

A mind of wisdom is aware of other individuals living fruitful lives. And seeks to understand.

You have limitations to your foresight. You have limitations to your intelligence. You have limitations to your knowledge of other fields.

Have more conversations. Become more self aware. Become more of a nuanced thinker. Chew on more ideas and understand complexities. Develop yourself as a person.

...

People are more intelligent than meets the eye. People are more intelligent than what can be expressed within the small time frame given with which you judge them in. And it's hard to receive their beliefs, their nuanced thoughts, and their subjective experience of life and any wisdom that may have come along with it, through the layers and layers of our own ignorance. We judge. We project. We assume. We categorize in multiple different labels. We judge appearance. We judge race. We judge sex. We judge class. We judge hair color, eye color. We judge accent. We judge the vocabulary. We judge it all.

There's wisdom and knowledge in individuals. There's subjective experiences in individuals. And our own ignorance blinds us from seeing it.

Our need to conserve and protect our own realities keeps us from seeing it.

And us protecting our reality through a shield of ignorance, keeps our inner world intact. It gives us stability. We don't need to question our own beliefs. Our own values. How we've been living. The direction we are heading in our lives. Everything remains...stable.

But the ignorance that keeps our inner world stable, is the same ignorance that contributes to the instability in the outer world.

Our own ignorance that keeps us from true progression in our inner world, is the very same ignorance that contributes to the lack of progression in the outer world.

...

On your journey of life, there are moments in which you must shed your paradigms. Breaking down mental structures and re-crafting them into something with more wisdom and integrity. But in order for that to occur, there is a transition period where the structure in which you currently live in is deconstructed. Torn down.

What you thought was right, is wrong. What you thought is the way to see something, you have found is limited in its perspective. There's more to understand. You must go through transition periods in which you may question yourself, question your life, question the world, question everything. Your confidence will drop. Less willing to speak your mind, because your beliefs are in complete shambles. You may become depressed. More anxious. Your reality is disheveled. You have no idea if you're right or not. You feel...lost. You begin to question and be unsure about a lot of things. You begin to question other aspects of your life. You begin to question how you have been living on Earth. How you have treated others. Whether you have been a good person or not. You begin to question your own intelligence.

This is a good thing. You are living an examined life. You are alive. You are awake.

And this is the very thing that the modern day individual is terrified to do. They refuse to do it. Everyone is right, and everyone "else" is wrong. The "other" is wrong. And so the individual's growth is gridlocked. Thus, society's growth is gridlocked.

An examined life is the key for growth. Humility is the catalyst for examination. A lack of humility and some self-doubt means you have BLIND confidence. You remain unexamined. You remain in a direct tunnel of your current beliefs that give you confidence, and you are blind to all the information outside of it. Although confidence is good, and is empowering, BLIND confidence also feels good and empowering, but is LIMITED in its nature. You do not know that you do not see.

You have reached a ceiling and you will go no further until you humble yourself.

...

Humility, open-mindedness, and self-doubt, are the keys to unlocking higher power and wisdom within oneself. These are qualities of strength. Not weakness. Why are you so sure of your beliefs?

Be open minded, try to understand others, and have rationality and critical thinking as a processor. You must want to know the truth and what is wise, whether it comes from you, from people like you, or from the "other".

It's also important to understand that this message is not just for the "other" that you think needs to hear this. This is the exact blockage that is keeping you yourself ignorant. It's not just the other that needs to hear this. YOU need to hear this.

The individual must keep an open mind and communicate with other individuals to broaden their understanding of life and not just the understanding of their own identity's life.

...

Humility is having a student mind. Holding a mental air of naivety to have your mind be open to see things from different angles. Humility is a constant practice. It's a way of living your life that you commit to, and if your ego arises, a path that you can always recommit to.

It's a way you choose to live your life.

Humility opens you up to a composure and peace of thinking and acting, that without it, you would find incredibly difficult to access.

...

Be who you would want to meet. Don't wait for others to show it first. BE it first. Be the lighthouse.

Don't wait for the actions and behaviors of others to give you permission. Don't wait for individuals that share the group you identify with. Don't wait for the "other". To make you feel comfortable to now do the same.

Be brave. Be your own individual.

You wish people were more kind and empathetic and listened to others more? Be more kind, empathetic, and listen to others.

You wish people were more willing to express their real thoughts and opinions in the face of judgement? Speak your thoughts and opinions yourself.

You wish people were more open minded and wanted to listen and learn? Lead the way.

...

We ourselves must open. YOU must open.

Use your mind.
See the nuanced realities of others.

Increase your intelligence.
Increase your wisdom.

Increase your effectiveness with your craft.

Increase your creative contribution to your community.

Increase the quality of your time here in Earth.

Build self awareness. Build this space. Cultivate this distance. It takes patience. It takes openness. It takes refusing to be emotional reactive, and if you are being emotional reactive, to try your best to catch yourself. And if you catch yourself in the middle of it (which is difficult to do, you have so much emotional momentum), then good. But if you don't, but you catch yourself after the episode, then thats also good. Because you are still building awareness. You are identifying the bullshit that your character engages in.

Build this space. Cultivate this distance. Meditate. Practice openness. Practice seeing other people's sides of the argument. Practice trying to understand what other people are saying and why they make the decisions they make. Be empathetic. Listen to others. Truly listen. Speak less. Listen more.

...

We must re-open dialogue. Real dialogue. Respectful discourse. Real listening. Real speaking.

Discourse and the freedom to speak honestly, has been suppressed by the wide demand to be comfortable. And with this demand, and it is a demand; this means to enforce others to speak in a way that keeps you comfortable.

This is an abysmally low aim for a culture to aim for. This weakens our ability for real discussion and understanding. This blocks our ability to think and rethink and rethink our belief systems and shed light on our own shortcomings and ignorance. It soon becomes a nuisance to society, to think for yourself. And if thinking for yourself is a nuisance, then developing yourself as a human being becomes akin to a fish trying to swim upstream. A task for more difficult then it needs to be.

An individual thinking for themselves, trying to understand the world, trying to learn, trying to think outside the box, trying to develop their own ideas, trying to articulate themselves and what they currently know, trying to be a better version of themselves, although others may think this is okay, in reality, every step they are taking to actually do this, is looked down upon.

Those that are opponents to freedom of speech are opponents of freedom of thought. And those that are against freedom of thought, are against freedom of the individual and the very spirit of humanity. The very heartbeat of mankind.

...

We must believe in our freedom to speak, our freedom to think, our freedom to have conversations, and our freedom to evolve. This is the human spirit.

Be brave. Have conversations. Be free in thought. Allow yourself to think for yourself. Allow yourself to entertain and chew on ideas. Allow yourself to speak your thoughts. Allow yourself to try to understand.

Use your mind, see different sides, have real life conversations, meditate to let go of your own attachment to identifying with particular groups, and continue to do real research and have real dialogue. Have your ideas met with real criticism and refinement. Be open minded. Be an individual of deep thought, humility, and introspection.

Be an intelligent human being.
Be brilliant.
Think for yourself.

We don't have a lot of time here!

32

Chapter 32: Peace of mind

Peace is not some far off reality that you cannot attain.
Peace is a space you live in that you must curate for your self.

It's a space that you create within your mind. An atmosphere you curate within your mind.

…

If peace is not something you are accustomed to, sometimes you must force peace into your life. You must pierce through the clutter of your life, and establish a foothold of peace. Force the habits that will bring you more peace of mind, the habits that you continuously avoid, into your life. If you do not make time for them, and begin a more peaceful life for yourself by disciplining your chaotic self and doing these habits, it will be difficult to ever really transition to that peaceful life. You will always find reasons to never do the very things that will begin to introduce into your life more peace, calm and groundedness.

Do the things that will begin to introduce to you, the existence of calmer states of mind. Meditation. Walks in nature. Walks in your neighborhood. Yoga or stretching. Breath work. Exercise. Being without a phone for the beginning of your morning. Hobbies. Eating less.

You must truly desire peace, and be wanting and ready for peace, to truly let go of that which disrupts your peace. You must be truly tired of the frenetic energy that the activities you participate in, are delivering to you. You must let go of the little bits of good that you receive, for the frenetic energy that comes attached with these bits of good, brings you more unhappiness than the bits of good give happiness.

The indulging in pointless conversations. Not checking the news as often. The lessening of junk entertainment, social media and porn.

...

Peace is also a space around you that your physical body lives in. It is not only an atmosphere you curate within your mind, but it is an atmosphere you curate for your physical body to operate in. Your ecosystem.

Communicate with those who have been interrupting your peace, or distance yourself from them.

Live in the neighborhood that resonates deeply with you. Cleanly kept. Neighbors who are happy in their own lives. Beautifully gardened.

Curate the space you live in. Curate a home that you find peaceful. The design. The atmosphere.

...

The rest of the world can be in chaos. But this does not mean that your peace can, or should, be interrupted. Maintain your peace. This is not negligence. You are not pretending to be ignorant as if nothing wrong is going on, and the world is perfect. Rather, you are witnessing what is going on around you, and maintaining a level of spiritual and emotional maturity.

There is no need for yet another person to be flooded with stress, worry, fears and anxieties. You being grounded, allows you to be of even greater service to those around you. You staying in love and happiness does more for those around you. You carry with you, a sense of peace, that touches others, and allows them to begin to relax and feel peace within themselves. You allow others around you to get the chance to feel that, everything might actually be okay.

You, keeping peace within yourself, keeps the energy of peace alive.

...

Don't stay hypnotized by the pain. For the rest of history, there will always be some forms of suffering. This is the human condition. This is life on earth. For as long as there is a history we are able to record, there will be some forms of suffering.

Don't stress about things you cannot change.
Don't stress about things that you have no control over.

Like everyone that came before you, and everyone alive now, you will pass. You are human. Your time here is temporary. Even at the very height of power and influence, there's only so much you can affect, before you too are washed away by history.

Do not stress.

Live in this present moment. Right here. Right now.

...

Create. Work. Contend with life. Be excited. Travel. Explore. Discover new wines and cheese. A traditional American cheeseburger with a strawberry milkshake at your local diner. A drive down the coast with the windows down. Sitting around the campfire. A morning cup of coffee with your fellow countrymen in the cafe. Sitting and chewing on ideas. Listen to good music. Read literature. Watch creative films. Enjoy the company of friends. Spend time at the local park. Spend time by the water. Spend time eating a good meal with those you love.

A simple existence.

A human experience.

33

Chapter 33: Present Moment

The past is residual. Like the ash from a bonfire. It only exists as thoughts that are had in the present moment.

And the future is the future. It is not here yet. It may not come. But it may. You may not be blessed with more time and more present moments. But you may. So have a vision. Plan to live more life. Know what you want to do. Where you want to go. What you want to see.

But know that the present moment is all there is.

And while you are here on this planet, getting to experience what you are currently experiencing, appreciate it for all that it is.

…

You are alive today. But are you living in today?

WAKE UP.

All of life is lived in todays.
TODAY is all that exists.
Tomorrow is a mental construct. It's an IDEA. It doesn't exist.
Because tomorrow, is going to be another TODAY.
When you wake up "tomorrow", you're going to wake up to another TODAY.

So how you feel about TODAY, and how you see TODAY, and how you treat TODAY, is most likely how you're going to see tomorrow and live tomorrow. As when tomorrow comes, you experience it as today.

Every day should feel like a Friday. You are free. You are alive. Live your life.

Have a sense of urgency. Live!! "Tomorrow" is never going to come. More todays will come. And you will experience todays, everyday, for the rest of your life.

The concept of tomorrow has had the byproduct of instilling a sense of limbo in the human being. It has put the individual in the perfect trance, where comfort is embraced, procrastination is rationalized, and all of the important matters in your life are things that you "truly care about", but will just do some other time...

The present moment, is where your entire life is lived.

...

Of course more "tomorrows" will come. The social construct of a yesterday, today and tomorrow, still exists. We need these terms and language to communicate.

Of course tomorrow will come.
But it's going to feel, more or less, like today.

All you have is the present moment.

The day you marry, will feel like the present.
The day your first child is born, will feel like the present.
The day you try to finally go workout, will feel like the present.
The day you leave this life experience, will feel like the present.
What you do WITHIN TODAY, within this present moment, IS UP TO YOU.

...

Don't be scared. Fear may be your initial reaction. Death feels so close.
But don't be scared. Be joyful. This is where life is truly lived.

You are blessed. You are lucky to be alive.

This awareness is a gift. Without it, you will remain asleep. Living as a drone. Not seeing life's true gifts. Not seeing the preciousness of your life and the lives of others. Not chasing your dreams.

Realize that death and life are intimately intertwined.

…

It's why when you have near death experiences, you become terrified, but equally, exhilarated. You clutch to life. You don't want to go yet. You're not ready. You haven't truly "lived" and you want more time.

Deaths of loved ones.
Health scares.
Turbulence on a plane.
A car crash.
Being on top of high heights.
Earthquakes, storms, and other natural disasters.
Realizing your body isn't as nimble and youthful, and you're getting older.

These moments are gifts. It's the universe saying, "Wake up. This isn't going to last forever".

Do not push on "living" any longer. Upon the moments you leaving, you may realize in those sudden passing moments, that this was all one big experience. You could've done anything you wanted. There were no limits.

There were so many missed opportunities...

Respect life. Respect your time here. For you never know when this experience ends.

34

Chapter 34: Mortality and momentum of existence

Death. The finiteness of life. Your temporary physical existence in the universe. The inevitable, unavoidable, ending of your life. The big picture. The biggest of pictures. This is the most important piece of context to your life. Because this changes everything. It makes you reflect on the meaning of your time here. It makes you face yourself. It changes how you conduct yourself. It changes how you think. Of what's most important to you. Of what you want to do with your time. And this fundamentally changes your story.

What you truly value deep down, what you value most, will rise into your awareness. And when you finally see what ultimately matters to you, you more easily live by these values.

Instead, we live our lives, suppressing what matters to us down, and what is left as "important" is what is perpetuated by your environment. Our job, school, the news, consumerist behaviors, what our family and friends say, social media. THIS becomes the context in which you live your life. This is how most people live their life. And this is why most people are not only unhappy, but don't create what they want to create and don't become who they want to become.

The true depth of life goes undetected.

Their true deep inner values goes ignored.

They never realize just how precious their existence is and instead of living a life that is true to them, they passively flow with the current of their environment.

Real life is so breathtaking and jaw dropping that we choose to ignore it. We choose to be numb to it. It's in front of us but we do not take it in. And we do this because it would be so overwhelming, that our whole life and all of our actions, would come into question. We would be forced to evaluate our entire existence. It's so overwhelming. The truth of everything. The fragility of everything.

How delicate the ecosystem and our environment is.

How we are floating on this planet and we have very little idea where we came from and no idea where we're going.

How our human species and every other living creature on this planet, including yourself, has a mortality rate of 100%.

How amazing to think that amidst all that goes on in daily life, everyone ultimately dies. Nobody makes it out alive.

We are continuously being born and dying.

Millions of us born and living our time in life. And getting old. And new individuals being born as we get old. We won't see the era they will see. But they won't see what we saw. And we communicate to the best of our abilities, history, knowledge, customs, traditions and wisdom. And them, fueled with excitement and naïveté, move forth into the future. Experiencing more life on this Earth themselves, gathering their own wisdom, creating their own work, getting old themselves, teaching the new young, and continuing the process. Like a long term existential relay race, passing the baton to the next inhabitants of earth.

Everything that surrounds you most likely originated from the idea of someone that is now dead. The inventions you use, the traditions you are a part of, your fields of study, the language you speak. Our modern day individuals, with our newly created music, art, films, philosophy, literature, scientific discoveries, customs, traditions, morals, ethics, and events, stack on top of what past individuals in their own current time developed. And they stacked on top of what individuals before them in their own current time developed. And the individuals before them. Each generation experiencing life.

Eventually, you must understand that the life that you currently have, and the individuals around you, had no voluntary choice in experiencing. You are here. This generation is here. And you must understand that the life that you currently have, like those before you, is moving in one direction. Its eventual ending.

Life is short. Blink of an eye and you are at the age you are now. Another blink of an eye and you are old. Your experience as a human on this planet, will end. Everyone dies one day.

Eventually, you must face the very realness, of life and death. You have no choice.

...

Many of us do not understand how death arrives in a person's life. The abruptness. People don't like to think about it. They see it everywhere around them. They see it in the news. They see it in current events in earthquakes, floods and hurricanes. They see strangers in the obituaries. They hear about someone famous, that they grew up listening or watching, passing away in social media. They hear about old friends in their hometown from other old friends. They hear about distant family members from their parents. People see the ending of life everywhere, but numb themselves to the fact that this, one day, will happen to themselves. Disconnected from this fact of life. Numbed. And this disconnection, has led people, en masse, to live their lives with no understanding of its significance and preciousness.

Many people that died, that experience has came at a moment in their lives in which they were making plans for their future. It came abruptly. It came when they did NOT expect it. Living just another day.

Life is mysterious. And death is mysterious.
You're born, you're here, and then you're gone.

In the same way you enter a dream, you entered this world. Unknown of its beginnings. Placed in a new land. Looking around your surroundings and experiencing what there is to experience. And when you pay attention to the details of your experience, you can't help but feel its surreality. Everything. It's just. So surreal. The sky you see above. The oceans. All the strange creatures that walk these lands. The inventions created like the airplane or the car. You look at the fire of a lit candle and see this glowing heat move, sway, and dance. What is this place? It's so mysterious... And in the same way a dream ends, you will depart from this world.

Death awaits everyone.

You have no idea how long you will be here. None of us do.
But we know we are all going to die one day. We will all experience death.

It's part of the human experience.

But this fragility of life, this preciousness, is forever ignored. We distract ourselves from it. Arguably, we structure our very daily lives to distract ourselves from it.

We distract ourselves from the finiteness of our own life. The finiteness of our loved ones. The finiteness of mankind and the planet itself. How we will all die someday. Mortality.

And with the avoidance of death, comes the avoidance of life.

This is why most individuals are physically alive, but are not truly living. They have not grasped the temporary nature of their lives and everything that goes on around them. There is no sense of urgency. There are no higher values to live up to. There is no reason to be courageous and leave your comfortable lifestyle. There is no real appreciation for Earth and it's wonders. There is no real gratitude for all of the good things in your life. There is still an entertainment of petty and forgettable negative emotions. Concerned about gossip. Chasing cooler symbols of status. Getting likes on social media. Getting frustrated over arbitrary daily events.

And in our unconscious day-to-day living, in our ignoring of our own truth, we crave light.

We become lost in our own fantasies and day dreams of how we ourselves could be heroic in a war, confident with our crush, defend someone in a fight and be victorious, or be on a stage performing in front of thousands.

We become obsessed with heroes in movies, television shows and books. They are alive, living their truth, with courage and honor. The superhero, the detective, the warrior, the average joe turned hero. Our eyes widen, we tense our bodies, and fixate with excitement when their stories reach their peak and the outcome hangs in the balance.

We become obsessed with the "celebrity". Actors, musicians, artists, directors. We stand in lines. Wait in queues. Waiting for the moment to see them in person. We scroll through their videos. We hang onto their every word. We are fixated. We can't help but stare. They embody the characteristics we want within ourselves. They abandoned their lives of mediocrity and followed their calling to something greater than themselves. They are alive. You see it in their glow. What may be interpreted as physical beauty, is in reality, internal beauty. You see the honoring of their soul, in their eyes. You feel their aura of confidence, from them creating a life true to themselves. You hear an acceptance of life and mortality, in their spoken words. They are actually alive. They chose to live their actual LIFE. Not repetitive emotions. Not repetitive beliefs. Not repetitive attachments. Not repetitive use of their time. Not a job they hate. Not a city they are bored with. Not friend groups that judge them. They chose life. They grew. They listened to their intuition, abandoned the mediocre life that surrounded them, and went after what is true to themselves.

We crave light.
But we numb ourselves.

A visceral sense of urgency, a sense of not wanting to wait any longer, is essential to creating and reaching your potential. And the finiteness of your life, delivers you your sense of urgency. Death waits for you as it once did for all of your ancestors. Understand that.

...

The greatest gift you can ask for in life is simultaneously the most terrifying thing imaginable. But it is the very fact that it is terrifying, that makes it a gift. The knowing of your own mortality. An individual's greatness and their understanding of the finiteness of life, go hand in hand.

A life well-lived intimately knows death. It knows that life and death is one in the same, and that ignorance of one is ignorance of the other.

When death comes close to you, by taking a loved one or by almost taking you, when you meet the fragility of life face to face, you discover a wisdom so profound that it alters the way you carry the remaining time of your life. Death, and the possibility of it. Death, and the inevitability of it. It alters your perspective, how you treat others around you, how you spend your time, your goals in life, your personality, your temperament, everything.

You can no longer pretend it does not exist. You get a brutal awakening to the reality of your own limited time here on this planet. You did not expect it. But when death arrives, nobody ever does.

You either carry the trauma with you and continue to live your life more or less like you did before, but now with more anxiety, more stress, and panic attacks in fear of your own time to come...growing fears of public spaces, strangers, vehicles, traveling, food, natural disasters and other uncontrollable aspects of life...and more powerful distractions, whether it be drugs, alcohol, social media, video games, relationships, sex, porn, gambling, or obsessions with health and diets in an attempt to prolong your life and run from death.

Or you process it, understand it, heal from it, and install a new lens for your life. And live with more of a sense of what truly matters. Your eyes open. You become awakened to your impact on others, whether a simple thank you or hello or smile, or creating something powerful that you believe in that you want to share with the world. You love your friends and family more. You love your fellow man and woman more. You crave peace amongst mankind and just want everyone to be happy, nourished, safe, and free to live their own lives with their own loved ones. You focus on your true passions and your true purpose. You live in harmony and understanding with the reality of your existence. You appreciate life while it is here. And live life better than ever before.

Death, in its irony, gives you life. The greatest paradox in existence. Death and life are intimately intertwined. Yin and yang. To get the honor of truly knowing life, to have deep gratitude for life, to live your life with awareness and fullness, you have to know the other side of it.

Death.

The relationship you have with it. The intimate awareness of it.

It's the key.

To live a life worth living.

To follow your dreams.

To ACTUALLY follow your dreams.

To stop tolerating nonsense within yourself.

It dissipates the pointless mind chatter.

It dissipates so many irrelevant, pointless fears.

It dissipates the relevancy you placed on your insecurities.

It dissipates the significance you placed on your day to day "problems".

It dissipates the value you placed on a purposeless job and begins to lift you out of the the trance of trading precious time in your life for money.

It dissipates the excuses you've attached yourself to for not chasing your dreams.

It dissipates the illusion of thinking that you can say and do what's important to you, "tomorrow".

It dissipates the illusion of "tomorrow" even being a thing that exists.

The awareness of your mortality blesses you with focus. Many aspects of your life will be revealed for their true triviality. With this awareness, false paths, dead-ends, and wastes of time are revealed for the illusions that they are. You will realize life's expediency and a deeper sense of urgency and maturation will be instilled. This is your growing wisdom.

Death puts everything into perspective. The ultimate perspective.

Your truest deepest values will rise to the surface. And you will begin to live by them. Your days are numbered. And you will begin to live as such. And it seems that this is a common theme, if not the common theme, amongst the greatest creators of Earth. You don't live with any urgency towards your dreams because you still think you have something to lose. Let go of the mirage. You will not be here forever. Let go of what's keeping you in place in toxic environments that don't make you happy. Let go of the toxic habits and behaviors that you attach yourself to. You will begin to live a full life. When you have chosen your purpose over the comfortable life you've held onto, you now move in God's favor. The universe and source is behind you, fueling you. You have become something greater than yourself.

...

And even as you read about all of this death and mortality, many won't feel it. The people that have experienced death, whether death of someone close to them, or a near-death experience themselves, have the best chance of grasping the true depth of these words. But for most, they won't feel it. Death close to you, is an experience that brings effects that can not be replicated. They are sheltered in their own world, naive to death. They will only be able to grasp the surface layer of these words, and think that they understand, but they do not yet truly understand. The surface layer interpretation of these words are a completely different language to the true depth of these words. Life experience and awareness is the key to learning the deeper language. Life experience and awareness is key to understanding death and transforming your life.

So, get close to death. Expose yourself to the destination of all that came before you, all that surround you now, and eventually you yourself.

Talk to combat veterans.

Go to nursing homes. Go to graveyards. Go to terminal hospitals.

Watch documentaries of war.

Speak to the elderly. They know more than you know.

Marines huddling around priests on ships before storming beaches in World War 2, making their amends with God.

Dying soldiers told the Last Rites, as consciousness all of a sudden becomes uncoupled from their being, and feels as though it is now slipping through their fingers.

Nearer My God To Thee playing as the Titanic sank and humans faced their deaths.

The Lord's Prayer spoken in the last moments of tragedies. The lack of ability to comprehend what's going on as the final moments of their life is so unexpectedly upon them.

Old men and old women, on their deathbed, realizing that their time is up. The ride is over.

Watch interviews with people who have been through war, and what it was like to be in the battlefield where life and death intertwined so viciously. Watch documentaries of the greatest individuals of mankind and see that, as great as they are, still share with the common man, the experience of death. Great battles that ended the lives of thousands. Great wars that ended the lives of millions. Individuals that died from disease, famine and suicide. Old age and the millions of elders in nursing homes, with their children, or alone in their homes, waiting for their inevitable exit.

Read memoirs. Read autobiographies.

Read the experiences of those that came before you.

Read the stories of men who had to use their one life and fight at war. Read autographies and see the suffering.

This is life. We will all departure from Earth, possibly returning to the unknown from which we all arose…or entering some new unknown. But our inevitable departure nonetheless.

Become more aware of the fact that every single one of your family members and friends will die one day, and this is inevitable. More aware that one day you'll die, and you'll never know precisely the moment you depart. More aware of the gradual degradation of human bodies and minds as they reach older and older age. And how, no matter how healthy you are, that this is your fate too. Watch documentaries of space and the universe. Go outside. Look at the stars. Look at the ocean. Look at the people around you. Observe the world around you. We are going through the human experience.

...

Reality must be consciously processed. There's realizations within you that are emerging. And with this, comes stress and anxiety. There's a lot to process. Everything you know is finite and constantly changing and ending. Jobs, relationships, places, friends, families, people, environments, cultures, countries, ways of living. There's traumatic experiences in every human's life. Being a human itself is traumatic. Every human has their own experience of life, but the traumatic foundation is there. Death is a part of life and each human has their own relationship with death and the ending of what surrounds them.

Go outside. Go for many walks. Go for many runs. Sit in stillness and meditate. Do yoga and stretches. Bioenergetics and chanting and moving your body. Fast. Don't numb the experience and keep everything in by drinking alcohol, doing drugs or distracting yourself with entertainment. You will only hold onto the pain and not understand why you are in pain. You are holding onto unprocessed suffering.

If you've had the death of someone close, take it in. Accept all the emotions that you have trapped within. Allow yourself to feel them fully, and let them pass. It is euphoric and healing.

You carry so much pain and emotions, you must stop pretending they do not exist. Sit down, face yourself, no computer or phone, in silence, in privacy, and be with yourself. Let emotions rise and feel through it. Do not trap them. Let them pass. Do not withhold. Release what you have held for so long. Releasing this suffering is the most powerful thing for your evolution.

Start to let it go. Cry. Breathe deeply. Do not distract yourself. Feel everything. You need to feel everything.

Zoom out and look at your life from a bird's eye view. Look at your life in its totality, from beginning to end. This is a phase in your life of realization and awakening. Processing and understanding. These days, weeks, months, even years. Do not fret. Just keep going. Your life is constant change. You must become more comfortable with change. If you're not comfortable with change, you're not comfortable with life itself. If you resist change, you resist life itself. If you attach yourself, It's only going to get harder.

...

Let go of controlling your life. You do not own your life. It is not yours. It is the Universe's. Your life is an expression of God. Of the universe. A shooting star that as quickly as it appears, it fades away.

Every heart eventually has its last beat. Every mind eventually has its last thought. Every body eventually has its last touch.

Fathom your temporary stay here on this earth. Look up at the stars. Look at the people that came before you and went. Look at the continuum-like nature of history. Take it all in.

You may fear death at first. But eventually, let go of your fear. Respect death. But do not fear it. Like all of your ancestors before you, you must eventually go as well. Live your life with honor. Pass on with honor.

Live as if this is yet another round of life, and it's only temporary, but while you are here you are going to experience as much as you can, help as much as you can, and love as much as you can. No grudges. No needless suffering. Less arguments, less hate. Less wasting time. More appreciation. More courage. More belief in yourself. Your eyes are wide open. You courageously act and move through the world. You have new senses to you.

Turn your fear of death, into your love for life, knowing that this experience will one day end, but you are here right now. Love life, and truly live it, more than you ever have before.

Let your new love for life, and your new relationship with life, transform every aspect of your life. Let yourself get accustomed to this new way of being. Let go of obsessively controlling. Do not panic over the inevitable ending of your life. It will come eventually. Don't spend your life tip toeing, trying to avoid the unavoidable. Don't spend your life, waiting for what will inevitably happen, to happen. You will go when it's your time. Moment to moment, choose to be engaged with how you truly want to live this temporary experience. Be so engaged, so in love with life, that when it comes, whether few days, few years or few decades from now, you leave life honorably. Enjoy you being lucid inside the dream that is your life. Don't think about death too much. It defeats the purpose of life. Live your life.

It's not up to the designed to completely understand the design. We can reflect. Look around and study. Look within and introspect. And try to understand what is going on to the best of our abilities. But there will always be an element of mystery that separates us from fully understanding life. Every day alive in this planet is the greatest psychedelic ride there is.

Live as though this is your second chance at life. We're on a one-way ride in life. Never going backwards, only forward. This is the human body you will eventually experience death with. In the same ethereal way you fall asleep at night and drift off, you will leave your human existence. Live knowing that your bloodline, your ancestors, for thousands of years, were born on this planet, lived on this planet, and left this planet. And you are in the next generation of man up. One day, you will leave here, and go to the other side…

Honor your ride.

35

Chapter 35: Higher personal responsibility

In the past, the philosophies formed and the ways of living that were chosen, have been beneficial to the individual and its group, and helped the individual and its group specifically, survive. Historically, humans have lived in a state of scarcity. Scarce resources, just trying to survive.

Philosophies, and chosen ways of living in the past, did not take the lives of others outside their own group into account. And they did not take their own environment, and the environment at large, into account. There's been pockets of actual harmonious living and mutual respect, but because of the survivalist nature of history, these pockets tend to be taken advantage of, enslaved, or wiped out.

The caring of other individual's groups, and the environment at large, has not been a primary aim. Unless it directly affected the individual and their own group's survival, it did not matter.

...

In this current time that we live in, we are still in the remnants of this mentality. This is a mentality that must be transcended. We must move forward, and embody a new harmonious way of living, that's both beneficial for the individual and for who and what surrounds the individual. It must be supportive for the individual, and the environment in which we all live in.

...

It's human nature to want to wait until circumstances are too sufferable, to then finally change. Not to voluntarily and pro-actively change, but rather, change in reaction to an undeniable shift in lifestyle. Rarely do humans exercise forethought and willpower necessary to change the course of the future before this shift.

Only until their status quo is gone, and too much damage has already been done, do they wake up at the steering wheel of a car that they now see has been sliding, inch by inch, down a muddy hill. The comfortable lifestyle that they have gotten so accustomed to, has changed for the worse. And its trajectory is to keep changing for the worse. They have to take action now. Their hand is forced.

If we hope to have our future children and grandchildren live amongst the same natural beauty as we do, with access to water and food, we must wake up NOW. Before this moment. We must begin to adopt a lifestyle that will be uncomfortable and not as "luxurious", but exchange this for sustainability and promise for the future. And if the change is made now, this will ultimately be a lifestyle that will be eons ahead, in terms of living standards and stability, of the disastrous lifestyle we will be left with if we do nothing.

We have two choices. A little discomfort now. Or, terrible discomfort when we are older and even worse discomfort for our descendants.

There are no other alternative choices. We cannot continue living with our eyes closed.

Only until the alcoholic has wrecked their car, do they realize their terrible addiction to drinking.

Only until the gluttonous man has a heart attack, do they realize their unhealthy relationship with food.

Only until the drug addict overdoses, do they realize that this path will eventually kill them.

Only until an individual hits rock bottom, do they realize that if they were to go any further down, that they are now choosing death over life. And the realization of this trajectory, has now finally hit home. They see it.

But it is hard to wake up a generation that has only seen pain and suffering through entertainment mediums, and not first-hand. It's hard to wake up a generation that only can know of suffering and terrible living conditions, through a stretch of their imagination.

And now, we sit here. In the present day. Awaiting to see which future will unravel.

Not taking any action within our own lives and within our own communities, but robotically continuing our day to day existence, as if we are not living in a state of crisis.

It doesn't affect us DIRECTLY.
Not YET.
Sure, the summer gets hotter, but it is what it is. It's just hot.
There are wildfires that burn thousands of acres and kill living beings. It's unfortunate, but my house is fine.
The ice caps are collapsing. There's plastic everywhere in the waters. The fish are dying. Sure, that's tragic, but what am I to do?
The rainforests are being decimated and cleared out. But I'm hungry, and there's a fast food restaurant right there.

We are sweeping the deck as the Titanic sinks. Pretending as if the future is not cataclysmic.

...

The state of the country and the state of the world, is the state of the individual. The state of the world is a macrocosm of the state of the individual.

And we are a bunch of dysfunctional individuals demanding other dysfunctional individuals to bring a balanced country. We are a bunch of dysfunctional individuals getting angry at other dysfunctional individuals for being dysfunctional individuals.

It's very easy to have an opinion and voice your suffering. It's much more difficult to observe the problem, look at it from different perspectives, formulate possible ideas and solutions, and voice those. And not only just voice them, but doing your part and taking deliberate action towards making those solutions a reality.

In our current day and age, many individuals have mastered the first half, but are novices in the second. This creates an imbalance of aggressive, victimized dialogue, with very little progress. Just a space filled with...outrage.

Performance and speaking. Arguing. Posting online.

Speaking about problems. Sharing posts about problems. Complaining about problems. Making witty one-liners, analogies and zingers about problems.

The easiest and least effortful way to respond to problems.

We have a generation yelling into a void. Refusing to be diligent, intelligent, and focus on real work to change things. But instead, collectively yelling into a void. Expecting others to do the hard work and actually act, and go through the arduous process of working, collaborating, creating, going back to the drawing board, creating more, action, and action.

...

The common individual WANTS to do good, and wants to help, and when given direction often do. To sign a petition, to raise funds for someone's business on the verge of failing, to rally for a cause and protest.

But given the nature of what our generation faces, the problems are so grand and seem so insurmountable, that we all stand still. We are filled with the energy for change, but have no direction to point it towards. We just don't know what to do. And so we go about our daily lives, wanting things to change, but not knowing how we ourselves could possibly make any noticeable impact.

...

People complain about the state of the world. But they indulge and feed the very things that are causing its current state. People are comfortable in their own lifestyles, hopeless for the future, and coping every day with the fact that we sit on a mound of upsetting facts about the current state of the world. The amount of plastic and trash everywhere across the globe. The overfished oceans. The depleting rainforests. Irresponsible business practices. Division. Poverty.

We complain that we are powerless, and that if we did have more power, we would make positive changes in society.

But the power that we do have, we label it as "ineffective" and "insignificant" in the grand scheme of things.

This relenting of our power, leads us to neglecting ourselves. It leads to us not caring about our own effect on the world. It leads to us giving up.

And our own day to day choices, under this disguise of our power being "ineffective" and "insignificant", is the very thing that perpetuates the deterioration of our society.

No one raindrop believes they caused the flood.

It's the individual's daily belief of this, that creates our current state.

We are the energy. We are how this whole thing moves. It's the people. We are the energy. None of these pieces move on their own volition. They are powered by us. Powered by our money, our attention, our time, our energy.

It's us that are ruining the country. It's us that are ruining the world. It's us that are ruining the mental health of our countrymen. It's us that is destroying the livelihood and wellbeing of our countrymen.

It's us and our own choices.

It's us and what we choose to do with our power. With our time, our energy, our attention and our money.

We spend money on excess clothing, make up, plastic, gadgets, and junk. We feed the consumerist materialistic culture. We are distracted from our purpose, not contributing to the Earth. We have given up and work jobs we don't like, being a quiet cog in all of this. We spend money on fast food, keeping these unhealthy places that are destroying the ecosystem and our health on the corner of every neighborhood. We buy things without any thought of where the trash will end up, contributing to all of the trash in the landfills and oceans. We spend our time fixated on our own self image on social media, keeping culture's focus on how we look and how cool our lives are. We click on negative news and give it our attention and ad revenue. We listen to music that speaks of destructive lifestyles and give it a higher status, so it's played more, and replicated more by others. We go outside and judge others that don't look like us or share our beliefs. We scroll on social media and respond to comments angrily. We scroll through our feeds, watching more and more things that agitate us, and walk around uptight, scared and serious. We wake up everyday and take part in the deterioration of our own society.

We never look at ourselves and how WE operate in the very community that we complain about, that we are also a part of.

We play a role in this too.

Each human being is a piece in the overall grand picture of the world.

...

Change in this world starts with you in your own world. You in your life, you have streams from you going to all corners of the earth, with your energy.

You interact with an individual, and they interact with ten more throughout the day. Your smiles, your kindness, matters. You have the power to change minds. To make others feel loved. To inspire others.

Take care of your energy. You play a role. You matter.

The conversations you have with the individuals around you. How you spend your money. How you use your attention. Your relationship with your purpose.
Streams of energy going from you, to the world.

This is a new era of hope. Led by the human spirit.
Transform your typical sense of despair and helplessness.
Wake up everyday with a sense of hope, focus and excitement.
In order to make the real changes necessary for growth in the 21st century, we must be light.

Be what you want to see in your community!

...

Like the survivor of a major disaster, wreckage on top of their body, reaching their hand out between a crack of debris, needing help, mankind does the same.

This generation has the power to save it.

...

Understand that you have a huge impact on life here on earth, through your day-to-day, way of being, interacting and living.

This is not to say that there are some entities in power that don't have our best interests at heart. There are. But we are in zero position to complain if we are doing little to nothing to improve the circumstances of the world, our community, our families, and ourselves.

We need to STOP, and begin to look inward.
And start holding ourselves accountable.

We cannot lean on government and corporations to do the right thing, when there is so much more room for our own actions.

We must strive to reach maximum capacity of our OWN actions. The individual must take responsibility for themselves. What can WE do? And are we doing it to its fullest?

It's the people who control the reins. The greed of a few on top doesn't have to be the reason for the planet's destruction, if the common individual refuses to participate and feed into the greed.

We do not have to follow the government and corporations off the cliff. And it is entirely our fault if we knowingly do so.

We must not WAIT for the government.

We CAN'T wait.

...

Taking personal responsibility is what will lead to your own power.

Your own power will lead your own conscious revolution.

Your conscious revolution is what will lead the collective conscious revolution.

And the collective's conscious revolution will lead the change in our own respective countries, that we so desperately seek.

No waiting for a politician. No waiting for a movement. No waiting for others to move first.

We move first.

You move first.

I move first.

There is great power in our numbers. It is THE power.

But all of this begins with you acknowledging that you matter. You truly matter. You are far more powerful than you can possibly imagine. You have far more influence than you can possibly imagine.

Your small actions aren't so small. *They're everything.*

…

Those that are older than us, are getting older. They will soon pass.

We are getting older. If individuals were to bring in change, just who exactly would that be?

If not us, then who?

We are becoming those in the position for change. It's on us. We are the leaders and creators. We are the visionaries and changers. It's on us to bring in the change that mankind starves for.

People have been hopeless for too long. Now is the time to be hopeful. Birth of a new culture. Birth of new standards for ourselves. The beginnings of a future where we thrive, begins now.

Wake up and start being the change.

Be the change you want to see in the world.

Embody the person you would want to meet.

Embody the ways of living that you want individuals on Earth to have.

…

The individual needs actionable steps.
Steps that do not need to be political.

Steps that we can all agree on as humans of this Earth, that are steps in the right direction for our own health, our own happiness, our community's success, our country's success, and the world's longevity.

Be greater than your race, your sex, and your political party. Be human.

Allow this to be where we begin to unite and work together.

...

The people need to know WHAT TO DO. We need understanding, consensus, mass mobilization, and action.

Our focus should be on action, understanding, conversations, and improving.

Purchase less plastic, and recycle when you do. Aim to abandon plastic completely in different aspects of your life, and don't use recycling plastic as the reasoning for your continued purchase of it, as this rationalizes it's continued use and lends to its continued high production. Use reusable grocery bags made from cotton, hemp, or paper. Glass, aluminum or ceramic bottles, containers and coffee cups. Reusable, biodegradable or compostable containers.

Less small single-use plastic water bottles. Instead buy biggest jugs possible, or use reuseable containers and refill them. Or purchase aluminum cans if needed, and recycle. Limit your use of unnecessary paper, cardboard, or other recyclable materials, but if you do use them, ensure you recycle them. Lessen your use of packaged goods, to the point where at the end of the day, when you look at your garbage, there is drastically less waste.

We can no longer buy and consume and throw all of the trash in the garbage with no thought of where it ends up. Continuing our lives, continuing to consume, continuing to throw trash in the garbage and forgetting about it, letting the garbage get picked up and forgetting about it, as we can continue the process.

Strive to be next to invisible in terms of the waste you have at the end of the day. And the waste that is leftover after what you have purchased and used, is recyclable containers and packaging.

As our demand of these sustainable choices increases, the desire to supply more increases, and its everyday norm increases. Real change. Created by you and your own actions. Not waiting for corporations to have an all of a sudden change in their consciousness and want to help Earth, rather us raising in our own consciousness, choosing the best options for Earth, and allowing our demand of these better options to move corporation's actions to.

The sustainable option, for businesses, what once was an uncomfortable choice due to the awkward and costly transition, is now the most profitable option. And now we have corporations that will help Earth as a byproduct of their behavior.

...

Less fast fashion. Buy clothes from companies that have sustainable production practices and more mindful business practices.

If make up bothers you, then limit your make up usage and exit the competition. Claim your natural beauty and your peace of mind.

Less unnecessary self indulgence with clothing. Image distracts us all. "Look at me" behavior is killing the world. Do not feed materialism and keep this idea alive through your own participation. You can do your part and live by a greater focus.

...

Shop local, shop at farmer's stands, markets and fairs. What you think sounds out of your reach, is actually more simple and attainable than you think. Find the farmer's produce around you, and re-establish new routines and begin spending your income in these places that reinvest in sustainable business practices. Supporting local individuals. Supporting your neighbors.

Participate less in the fast food restaurants that derive their meat from the inhumane practice of factory farming animals.

No more supporting factory farming and the food companies and restaurants that supply them. We must be the generation to phase these practices out and leave them in our past. Little to no meat from inhumane practices.

Cared for animals, fed their proper diet. Grass fed cows. Good cuts, ground beef, organ meats, butter and milk. Pasture raised chickens and eggs. Organic fruits and organic vegetables. Sustainably sourced honey. Less seafood, and when eaten, only from wild caught sources.

Know what you put in your body. Eat consciously. Whole food diet, with little to no processed and refined foods. Of course, you will not be perfect, but you can strive to have less of these unhealthier foods, and more real whole foods.

...

Exit the chase of buying things, things, things, so blindly.

Enter the space of having gratitude for what you have, getting only what you really need, getting some of what you desire, not overindulging, and focusing your efforts on the richer textures and richer qualities of life.

Your purpose. Your craft. Travel. Nature. Family. Friends. Your beloved ways of spending your time, whether it's soccer, or film. Reading of certain eras of history, or skateboarding.

Exploring different songs and genres, whether classical or house music.

A quieter, more subtle, day-to-day energy. But where real happiness and fulfillment awaits you.

...

Have a birdhouse, bird feeders, bird baths. Have a bee home. Plant trees on the land you have. Plant gardens in your front yard, in your backyard, on your small balconies. Plant fruit trees and allow you and your neighbors to enjoy your fruits. Have chickens, and share the eggs.

If possible, walk or bike to your destination and enjoy exercise and being outdoors. Spend more time being active. Change your lifestyle. Use shared public transportation when possible. If purchasing a new car, consider purchasing electric, or a vehicle that gets good gas mileage.

If possible, utilize solar power for your home.

Be wise and conscious of your use of water and light in your home. Use it when you actually want to use it, and no more.

Your actions directly take part in healing earth and uplifting mankind. Your actions directly take part in fixing the problems that surround us. You are playing a part in our generation's history.

...

This is a revolution for the individual. A revolution of consciousness.

Respectful revolution.
Love for each other.
No fear.
Appreciation for civilization, and the work done before us.
Appreciation for civilization, and what we currently have.
Appreciation for civilization, and striving to do real work and contribute.

Love for our neighbors. Love for our brothers and sisters. Love for religions. Love for races. Love for our differences.

Realizing we have far more in common.
And working together.
Believing in the good of man.
And living in this energy.

A noble life.

Choosing to live with courage.
Choosing to be what you admire.

We will not follow big business and governments off the cliff. We will not be contained. We will not be shackled.

Each individual is developing a more harmonious relationship with the planet. On our own accord. *We* are developing a more harmonious relationship with the planet, and with each other.

For each other. For our children.

For the first time in history, mankind is uniting with our Earth.

You play a role. You matter. You are part of mankind.

The people are uniting.

...

We should not accept legislation that attempts to ride the coat tails of our own maturing lifestyles and take advantage of our good nature, and tries to restrict, limit, control or moderate the individual's life.

We do not need legislation that tells us how much water we can use, and fine us if go above that. We do not need legislation that tells us the temperature that our thermostat should be, and fine us if we go above that. Taking farmland. Taking homes. Taking small businesses. Taking private property. Taking gas powered cars. Taking our arms and our way to protect our families, our homes, and defend the spirit of our nation against tyranny. Taking ownership away from citizens. Depleting the spirit of man.

We should not look for nor should we accept unnecessary legislation that restricts and limits the individual, their lifestyle and their livelihood. We must not accept these restrictions, that may be used in the name of "climate change", "global warming", "humanity", "crisis" or any other terms and phrases they may use to convince the public to relinquish freedoms. Impoverished individuals already find it difficult to survive. Many individuals already find it difficult to get by. And regardless, this is a slippery slope that we as countrymen, must not entertain.

There's ways for politicians to truly serve communities, the country, and humanity. Restricting, creating punishments, and making it more difficult for the individual to prosper, is not one of them.

Freedom is everything. Freedom is the spirit of humanity.

...

These changes are personal. They're in-house, and nothing to do with anyone in charge. They're for ourselves. They're for our neighbors. They're made with love. They're made with love for our fellow brothers and sisters.

The changes necessary should not be seen as restrictions of our freedoms and our pleasurable and pleasant way of life, rather as the claiming of our rightful place as a human being on this planet and taking responsibility for our own individual footprint. The maturing of ourselves. The maturing of our species.

The choices we are now making, will not move away from an enjoyable existence. It moves away from a collapsing paradigm, and enters a new one. We are not moving away from an enjoyable existence. We are ensuring one. We are moving with the times.

...

We should not fall into any movement or ideologies that claim to have the answers. Ones that create enemies of the other political side that have a different viewpoint than them. Ones that see themselves as the savior.

They are good intentioned but horribly destructive...

Trying to police everyone else's thoughts, everyone elses's behaviors, instead of working on themselves, becoming a better human themselves, becoming more competent, learning more, LEARNING MORE, and contributing something of real value and merit.

Do not be a fool.
Do not be a fool and complain about the world.

Countries are complex. Civilization is complex. This is extremely difficult to build and we are more than lucky to enjoy its existence. Do not try to reinvent the very society that millions took millennia to get to. You do not have it all figured out.

Even these recommendations above, only come from one individual's limited perspective and knowledge. This is not doctrine.

Like a teenager in their bedroom, fists clenched, mad at their parents. Angry and frustrated. But a child, with little understanding of why the parents say what they say, do what they do, and why the household is ran the way it is run.

Do not sit and complain and pout, and wish to drastically change and uproot everything built. With little understanding. With little real life experience. With little to actually give the world. Grow up. Become an adult yourself. Develop yourself. Learn your niche. Refine your craft. Aim to make a real contribution to society.

The world is a beautiful place.
Get your act together, and you'll see the same thing.

...

You can't be in the frontlines of every change. Figure out the 1-2 positive changes that mean the most to you. Focus your energy here.

And, if you feel called, play small supportive roles in others.

Ocean clean ups, repairing infrastructure, deforestation, pollution, plastics, new innovation for sustainable energy, homelessness, mental health, clean water. Although you may not be on the tip of the spear of these groups, your role is still important. Even in the smallest of ways, you can play a vital role in the strength and effectiveness of these separate movements, and play an irreplaceable role for those leading them.

Contribute to what you want to see in the world. Be a member of local museums and libraries. Donate to the causes you believe in. Donate to the arts. Donate to your schools. Make real contributions. Add to what you want to see in the world. Help with what you want to see in this world.

Make your life worthwhile.

The buildings that we respect so much today, and see as important pieces of history. That we appreciate so deeply. Creating them ourselves. Continuing this essence. Continuing the human experience. Continuing to build. Continuing to add to history.

Building our own organizations.
Building our own museums.
Creating our own beautiful art works.
Publishing.
Creating spaces for other individuals.
Co-founding organizations.

Donating money or certain materials. Volunteering. Joining organizations and following the lead of those that have devoted their life to figuring out and implementing the solutions. Spending your money on their newly designed products. Sharing and spreading their creations through your social media.

Support young individuals with new innovative ideas.
Support businesses with sustainable business practices.
Support individuals around you that are trying to improve your communities.
Support those who are trying to change culture for the better.
Support those who are trying to help Earth.
Through our actions, we shape the world.

…

Everyone wants to be gossipers of politics, consumers of constant news and problems, and be filled with negative emotion from mild annoyance to vehement frustration, but nobody wants to have the education, dedication, and service, and become somebody.

Individuals who feel called to become public officials and statesmen, who have a vision, who feel called to make innovative and creative changes through legislation and governmental leadership, must move forward in their life. Mayors, governors, councilmen and congressmen.

Selfish politicians have been the bottleneck for change. Politicians have not been the conduits of positive change and serving the people. Their real purpose. Instead, they have been the gatekeepers of change. Holding change back. We cannot stay stuck any longer.

We need younger people moving into positions in office. Individuals who are passionate about the success of the future, for they too are moving into it. They are part of the newer generations and they think differently. They understand the landscape of the current world. They think more harmoniously with the future and want it to be a thriving place. They are more innovative. Their minds are more in the future, than that of older generations in those positions.

Youthful individuals full of innovation and ideas, with an understanding of our technologically advancing society, rooted in morality, rooted in understanding the importance of our structures and traditions, but with the vision to create, the vision to not deconstruct but to build upon, must move into the political positions to make that change. And we must support them when they need that support.

We must vote for individuals who care about the people, regardless of their political party. It's about electing individuals with good in their heart, and the people's livelihood as their purpose in life. Will our political leaders have different ways of solving problems? Yes. But this is to be expected. We must have real dialogue. We must make real compromises. We must enact solutions. And we must keep moving forward.

We must have individuals in positions of legislative leadership to put into action the ideas of the innovators, as time progresses. We must be able to have ideas supported and funded, to receive the resources and space, to organize, create, innovate, and establish the new futuristic way of living.

We should not feel we must constantly keep our eyes on those that are meant to actually help us, and ensure they are still helping us. We must truly pay attention to the character of those we have elected, and what they choose to do in office. We ourselves must pay attention to who is currently elected, and how they are voting, and ensure that they can be trusted. And if they are not truly serving the people, we must vote for someone else that will.

Instead of constantly trying to convince the individuals in politics to take the right actions that serve the people, we must support and vote in the individuals that have the intelligence, morality, and interest of the common people, who do not need any convincing. Individuals dedicated to their work. Learning the nuances. Educating themselves. Intelligent processors of information. Humble. Wise. Principled men and women. Equipped to lead our nation.

We must have a more efficient and more effective government with politicians that serve the people, come to a consensus of what will be done for the people, and move and act to support and serve the people.

Improving public schools.
Improving prisons.
Improving our police, their training and their standards.
Improving our borders and immigration.
Cleaning up our cities.
Protecting the environment.
Cleaning up oceans.
Protecting wildlife.
Protecting land.
Helping the homeless.
More affordable healthcare.
Protecting the freedom of the individual.

Making donating food easier and more practical.
Making recycling easier and more practical.
Decriminalizing drugs.
Look into what other countries are doing as a model.
Studying issues and making real contributions.

Revitalizing healthy patriotism and love for one's own country.

Healing the country, a shared vision, a shared spirit, a shared community.

...

What do YOU do? What is your chosen craft?

Live aligned with the future.

We are all moving into the future together. You are not left behind. You are not too old, you are not too young. You are right where you need to be. Learn. Create.

Help the world and do what you love. Align these two.

What do YOU do? Use your own gifts, use your own focus, and help.

Invent, create, teach, share, lead, support.

Tech, artificial intelligence, earth sciences, agriculture, space travel, philosophy, music, literature, arts.

Construct. Create.

Aimed creators working on their work.

Reimagining society and giving it direction into utopia.

Futuristic craftsmanship into everything. Beauty. Family. Human spirit. Earth. God. Creativity. Innovation. Sustainable. Genius.

New structures. New inventions. New practices. New works of art.

...

It's time to focus our minds and take humanity to the next level. It is in our hands.

High quality farming and sourcing. High quality food and dishes. Regenerative farming. Supporting local farmers.

Supporting your fellow countrymen. Healthy, nourishing foods must be invested in more and more readily available. Gas stations with healthy alternatives. Healthy fast food restaurants with sustainable packaging. Healthy quick choices at affordable prices.

Create biodegradable products and packaging. Coffee cups, water bottles, fast food packaging. Making this more and more common, and eventually a staple of modern day living. Creating more composting facilities for neighborhoods and communities.

Ways to protect bees and wildlife of regions. Ways to protect fish. Ways to protect forests and oceans.

Getting clean water to more parts of the country, and more parts of the world. Making clean water more accessible to more people. Making it a foundational and reliable staple for all people.

Redesign buses and trains, have a more enhanced restructured public transportation system throughout cities and countries, redirect more funding for their cleaning and maintenance to have clean buses and trains. Improve public transportation to where the average citizen of every city would be happy to use it as an option, and many would begin using it as an option.

Improve and repairing our infrastructure. Designing new bridges, fixing our roads, creating better cities.

Fashion and clothing. Sustainable clothing that is high quality, beautiful to wear, beautiful to look at, and affordable for the common individual.

Create sustainable versions of everyday products. Make it more available for the common man and woman. Make it more accessible for the common family in the country.

Grocery shopping. Offering more foods in bulk, in refillable containers. Getting rid of unnecessary small packaging.

Improving the lives of the homeless. Creating real care. Improving state of homeless shelters, creating homes, medical care, mental health care.

Fighting the opiate crisis.

Redesigning and improving homes and neighborhoods. Neighborhoods like in the Hollywood hills are the optimal neighborhood, but the optimal neighborhood is currently exclusive to the wealthy. Clean streets, safe, quiet, nice lighting, different architecture amongst homes, different landscaping, unique and comfortable homes. Making this more and more common for the average individual.

City cleaners organized and paid, cleaning block by block in cities. Cleaning streets, beaches, parks, highways. Beautification and sanitation.

Designing ways to clean our oceans, shores and lands of micro plastics.

Remedying and solving the problems of our country. Helping each other, brothers and sisters, in their human experience on this Earth.

...

Geniuses solve crimes. Geniuses create and lead solutions to humanitarian issues. Geniuses create music that inspire and fuel the individual. Geniuses create art works that get individuals to think from different perspectives. Geniuses solve logistical problems. Geniuses make sense of philosophical nuances and contradictions. Geniuses solve humanity's problems and invent. Geniuses lead nations, construct and adapt through hardship, and help maintain civilization. Geniuses envision better versions of current solutions and innovate.

Don't wait for others to create what you yourself want created in the world.

Don't wait and expect others to have met their creative ideas with their immature afraid selves, but face the work and evolve and go through the process and create what you want to have been created. Yet you yourself, not going through that process. You yourself not facing your own ideas. You yourself not being challenged to humble yourself, learn, and work towards your vision, and create. You yourself not exiting your comfort zone and following your dreams.

You want a film to exist in culture? Create it.
You want a book to exist in culture? Write it.
You want a club with a certain vibe, curate it.

Work on the business that you want to see. That you're passionate for. With a business model that you want to see implemented in the world. With a product that you know will help people.

With a positive and encouraging company culture. Supplying benefits and livable wages for employees to thrive on. A powerful structure within society. Your own art piece.

You want there to be a place where like-minded individuals can inspire each other but cannot find it? Create it.

If you want areas of neighborhoods cleaned, organize the groups and lead it.

Add your own contribution to your places of business and homes. It's the artwork and graffiti on walls of individual businesses, and the fruit trees and gardens of individual homes, that create the atmosphere of a city.

You want more opportunity and resources for people similar to you? Build it.

It's the individual and their vision, that creates something from its birth as an idea in their mind, to its complete form unto Earth. Masterpieces do not fall unto Earth. They are crafted. By the individual that faces themselves, and creates.

And if you don't have a vision like this, but are passionate for the idea, then be a part of someone else's vision for whom you can play a supportive role. Lending your creative ideas, helping the daily functions, and being part of a team that helps this vision exist. These supportive roles are equally important for earth.

Problems need solving. Mysteries still unexplored. Humans need help. Our towns, our communities, our countries. Culture is always needing new works for new times. It is up to the individual to use their own gifts and expertise and go into the fields they feel called to and begin their work.

...

Learn about your city.

Travel through the neighborhoods. See the wealthy neighborhoods and how they live their day to day lives. The cars they drive, their grocery stores, their parks. See the average, and see the most troubled neighborhoods.

Begin with where you are at and what you know best. Learn about the problems your city faces. Learn about the beauty and the culture.

What can be solved and implemented in a city, can often be extrapolated and implemented in many cities.

But it's figured out and acted on a city level.

Think of more than yourself.

Think of your family. How you can become a source of inspiration.

Think of your community. How you can impact the lives of other individuals just like you, with similar conditions.

Think of your city. And the change you can create.

Use your mind. Understand your distractions and focus on something bigger than yourself. Live a life full with the energy you want the most. Your time spent with your craft, surrounded by your favorite creative works, doing what you can do, to contribute to the world. Do what makes you happy in this life. Do what makes you contend with life with excitement, enthusiasm and splendor. Do what makes you wake out of bed and want to live this life.

Wake up early and explore the world!

...

The speed in which we enter a future where the livelihood of the common man and common woman is respected and restored, and the fears of the demise of our environment and our civilized society is a distant memory of a past era, is predicated on the individual's ability to raise their circle of concerns, and begin to focus on what's bigger than themselves.

And the changes necessary for the individual to make to live more harmoniously with the world, can be enjoyable. There is no reason innovation, reformation, and proactive action, has to be sufferable. Becoming more conscious of your own footprint, and making the adaptations necessary in your own lifestyle to align with more sustainable living, can be an exciting venture. This is the greatest mission of our lifetime. Be filled with a sense of purpose and meaning.

There's no reason why we have to stop doing many of the current activities that we enjoy. There's no reason to stop enjoying life.

Go deep into your work, but be equally excited and enjoy your life. Your work is not the only way to contribute to Earth. This is also doing your part. You are tending to your own energy. Your happiness and peace of mind, matters.

Watch good movies. Eat delicious foods. Dance. Listen to music. Look at funny memes. Date. Travel. Explore. Have fun. Go outside. Love. Go into nature. Laugh. Run. Play. Dance. Travel. Experience different cultures, foods, dances, festivals. Enjoy the creations made on this planet by human beings. Films, books, art, music. Enjoy your own particular hobbies and crafts. Enjoy the planet.

Enjoy your period in time. This era is beautiful. This era will be looked at for centuries as the great mixing of cultures, of the common people, new profound artistic discovery, and a long spiritual metamorphosis. Films, video games and other worlds being created that we can enjoy. New emerging music never before heard. Jazz, rock and roll, soul music, hip hop, electronic music. Internet and world wide communication. The sharing of cultural practices, foods, fashions, and traditions. The experiencing of all the corners of the earth. The deepening of our understanding of existence here.

But live righteously.

Elevate your thinking into one of love of yourself, love of your fellow human being, love of your fellow living beings, and love of your planet. Live in harmony with the planet. Live in harmony with the individuals around you. Be your true self. Communicate with those around you with patience and understanding. Uplift others. Make lifestyle changes towards what's sustainable. Be smart with your consumption. Follow your purpose and make the impact you are meant to make. Be aware of your power as an individual and use it. This is the responsibility of the everyday individual.

…

We can't expect every individual to be equally enthusiastic about change and so willing to make drastic changes to their lifestyles. We can't expect every individual to uproot what they enjoy, and the lives they have made, to now sacrifice many aspects of it in pure service to a better future. To pay attention to every news headline, attend every protest and rally, be focused on every social cause, and have the only conversations you ever have be of the change needed.

Be human. Remember your humanness. The future we envision that is so bright, the heart of its soul is humanness. Enjoy your life.

Simply begin to be an individual of forward movement. Someone who cares. Begin to see the responsibility on your shoulders as a human on this earth.

...

We don't have the right to give up on mankind now. To call it quits. To succumb to our depression about the state of the world. To run away into the caves of society, and hide in our video games, streaming services, social media, porn and drugs, in our attempt to forget about the world. To run away with whatever amount of success we have and focus on our self image, acquiring more accolades, and living our own glamorous lifestyle, and forget about the world.

In so many periods of our past, in the terror and the suffering that they experienced, they had the opportunity to quit and watch the world burn. They didn't. They endured. They pushed. They moved mankind forward. And because of that, we must do the same. If our great, great, great grandparents could see us and what our generation faces, they would tell us to raise our head up. And keep going. Let their sacrifices not be in vain. If not for them, for the future inhabitants of this earth. Our children.

It's not up to us to decide when our circumstances have gotten too dire to continue on.

Carry the baton of our ancestors, forward.

36

Chapter 36: Direction of the Earth 2

The Renaissance was a period of great change. An era that bridged that gap between the old and the new. The emerging of new philosophies, new discoveries in science, new expressions of art, and new ways of thinking and seeing life.

An elevation of life on Earth.

Today, we are the experiencers of the emerging of the internet, new tools with technology, the new ability to communicate with one another across the globe, the mixing of cultures and ideas, and the awakening of the individual and their potential.

We are in the midst of a new renaissance.

Genius is a plane of thought, capable for every human being, given the dedicated curation to their own human existence. The understanding of your nature and proclivities. The harnessing of your energy, thought power, and intuition through diet, meditative practices, intelligent conversations, time with your craft, the elimination of toxic relationships, and the letting go of distractions. The exploring of your gifts, and the feeding of your time on earth, to your chosen purpose. Letting go of what derails you from richer thinking streams, and committing to the richer thinking streams within your mind. Waking up every day and focusing on your highest vision. Understanding your finite time here on Earth.

The greats of our past are our ancestors. There is nothing special about the greats we look up to, other than the relationship they had with life and the relationship they had with their crafts.
We stare at the greats before us that lived in previous generations like they are cut from a different cloth. Like they are part of something that we are not.

We admire their creativity. We admire the innovation they made. We admire the pieces of work they created.

And we look at ourselves and in our period of time, and think so little of it.

We must see that our relationship with life is everything. This is the magic. And this is never-ending. We too are capable of something special. We too can create and innovate. And so too the generations after us.

The place that the greats before us accessed and lived in, is a place within the mind that is always available.

Our focus on our crafts.
Our protecting of our energy.
Our caring of our time on this planet.
Our focus on contributing to our culture.

The submerging of our mind into history. Understanding traditions, the individuals before us, how they approached their craft, how they lived life. Real values.

The submerging of our mind into culture. Understanding where we are now. Our art. Our music. Our films. How we currently think. How we move.

The submerging of our mind into future visions. What we see. How we can contribute. Our desire to see a better future. Our desire to create better generations.

The embodiment of true character. Humility, respect, and appreciation for life, honesty, a letting go of ego and the image of self, love, a sense of personal responsibility, and honoring your limited time on earth... and bravery in the face of it.

...

No longer will amazing creations belong heavily exclusive to the individuals on this earth that have received the fortune of being born in inspiring cities, having supportive families, going to well-funded and well-equipped schools, and feeding their genius since youth.

Individuals will be able to craft and design themselves. This is the moment we've been waiting for. The floodgates are opened. The walls are broken down. The internet. The knowledge. The communication. The resources. The collaborations. The ability to learn from other geniuses. The ability to learn our craft deeply. The ability to learn how to navigate our own mental landscape. We all have access to genius within ourselves. The poorest of us have access. The most depressed of us have access. The individuals stuck in jobs they hate, have access. The curious have access. The individuals with ideas have access. The individuals with no ideas, but a desire to learn and grow, have access.

Geniuses, and the creation of them, will no longer occur by happenstance.

This generation is the Lewis and Clark of the combination of limitless information, world wide networking and collaboration, deepening into our own consciousness, budding self-awareness, self-design, and new heightened abilities for our own purpose. And from here, we are the Lewis and Clark of technology, of sustainability, of space travel, of solving our communities problems, of solving humanities problems, and of so much more.

As a species, we are learning. We will know the territory as intimately as we know the surface of Earth.

...

Go deep into your craft. Be of service to humanity.

The focused minds of earth are the deepest divers of humanity's consciousness.

When you reach deep into your own creative bag, you are reaching into the bag we all reach into. It is the universal human experience. The human spirit. It is what ties and binds us all together. It's the deepest home we have. It's where we all come from and from whence we will all return.

The deepest energy.

Listen to the universe. Listen to your genius. Chart new territory. Invent. Innovate. Create. The artists, writers, musicians, inventors, designers, scientists, directors, actors, engineers, architects. Everything that you do, everything that you are, everything that you create, is the leading edge of this human experience on earth. You moving into new directions, is mankind moving into new directions.

Humans are in and out of the planet, every day.
And now it is your turn here.

We all have the potential for creation. We all have the potential for genius. We all have mastery of crafts within us waiting to be harnessed. This is a new era. We are connecting to something within ourselves. We are realizing the power in our fingertips and minds. Keep going.

You must go deep into your craft. Study the great moments of history. Study the great movements of history. Study the great pieces of work. Study the great thinkers and doers, before us. Those that lived here, had their time here, and have passed. Study the landscape of our modern world. Study the great thinkers and doers living right now as you read this. Those that you share your time on Earth with.

And become a great thinker. Become a great doer.
Begin to take the torch of innovation, and carry it through the modern day.

...

We've never been here before, in this specific time in history. Everyone on this planet today is experiencing the world together.

Day by day, we enter uncharted territory. This has been the experience for those before us. And this is the experience for us today.

To live on the edge of the unknown… and to create in the face of this. The human experience. This is what it means to be human.

Focus your mind. We need you.
Let us not sit in the stands. Instead, become designers of our time here.

…

Most individuals are terrified, and stick to what is comfortable. At least in this stage of mankind. To go within, to live by your own purpose, at this point in mankind's life, is considered a revolutionary act.

The highest level creators alive today may support you and speak of how people should follow their dreams. But for the common individual, alone in their own pocket on Earth, they are surrounded by judgement from friends and family. They are ridiculed by coworkers. They are looked at as wannabes, fakes, and frauds. As they do not have their completed work to show and prove what is within their mind, they are looked at as fools. As they don't have the validation of society, they are looked at as fools. As they don't have riches, fame, and accolades, they are looked at as fools.

To your friends, you are known. To your family, you are known.
But to Earth, you are unknown. A blank slate.

You can be what you want to see in the world. You can be what resonates truest to you.

Allow this to inspire the curation of your time here.

...

We are moving into a stage of mankind where people will become more and more frequently reborn in their adult life. 20's, 30's, 40's and beyond. Inner geniuses will become nurtured and birthed into our world.

And not reborn on a specific birthday. But reborn over a time frame of years in their life, in which they begin to introspect, grow, evolve, study, learn, follow their own purpose, study their craft, create, mature, become more kind, become more loving, become more understanding of their limited time here, and live as close to god as they can while they are here.

...

Everything's being written.

Everything has already been written.

Every second you walk towards your fate.

In some far off distant future, your life is already complete. Like a package. The full story, already done. And future inhabitants of this earth, can pick up your life story like a book, and read it. Hear about it. Talk about it. Watch it. Wonder about it.

Whilst you sit here, reading these words, you are living within your unfinished life. Experiencing it moment by moment. Living within this unfinished work of art. Painting with your brush what you feel pulled to paint. Not knowing what will ultimately be the finished work that is your life. The life that others know. But one that you will never really know.

It's not up to you to know. This knowing is not for you. It's on you to paint.

Do not be afraid to move forward and live your life. Your decisions are destined. Every photo taken has a small melancholic feel, as you know these are permanent captured moments that will remain after you leave the earth. Some of the moments that you experience today, will be stored within your mind and remembered on your transition out of this earth. Some of the events you attend and conversations you have, will be the last time some people will see you before you leave Earth.

This life is a temporary home. A temporary experience. A drop in the bucket of eternity.

...

Realize you have a purpose.

Realize you have a footprint on this earth.

You cannot be perfect. You are human.
But honor that footprint.

Use your attention wisely. Use your time wisely. Use your energy wisely. The individual living with this wisdom and focus, multiplied throughout the world, is our salvation.

Live with humility, integrity, and love. The individual living in this open space, multiplied throughout the world, is our salvation.

Live with the focus of a good state of Earth. The individual living with this vision in their mind and felt within their heart and soul, multiplied throughout the world, is our salvation.

Live with your purpose as the North Star for your personal life and help your community and culture to the best of your own abilities. The individual living with their true purpose guiding them, multiplied throughout the world, is our salvation.

...

You are not promised creating the perfect pieces of work you wish to create. You are promised a more meaningful path. A deeper relationship with life. Being a helpful energy on this earth.

You have no idea how long you will be here. None of us do.

But we know we are all going to die one day. We will all experience death. It's part of the human experience.

One day, you will leave here, and go to the other side.

While you are here, honor your ride.

…

The eyes of history are upon us. The eyes of Mankind are upon us. The eyes of our ancestors are upon us. The eyes of our children are upon us.

Wake up!

The power is in our hands.

This is the birth of a new Renaissance.